CW00428431

STEAM TO SILVER

STEAM TO SILVER

A history of London Transport Surface Rolling Stock

J Graeme Bruce
OBE, BSc (Eng), FIEE, FIMechE, FCIT

Capital Transport

First published 1970
by London Transport

Fully revised edition 1983

ISBN 0 904711 45 5

Published by Capital Transport Publishing
38 Long Elmes, Harrow Weald, Middlesex

Printed by SP Company (Westminster Press)
89 North Road, Brighton

Bound by The Garden City Press
Pixmore Avenue, Letchworth, Herts.

PHOTOGRAPHIC CREDITS

Ian Allan Library District Railway loco No. 34, G class loco No. 95, Met electric motor car in original state, Met 1904 electric stock train, Aveling & Porter loco Manning Wardle loco at Quainton Road, Met steam loco No. 3, Met electric loco No. 10 (W.E. Gladstone), British Westinghouse loco No. 10.
J.H. Aston Circle stock train at Moorgate.
J. Graeme Bruce collection District A stock at South Harrow.
Capital Transport D stock train at Putney Bridge, COP stock train at Earl's Court, A stock train at Shadwell, C69 stock train.
Harry Clarke/LURS F stock, P stock and A stock at Neasden.
C.R.L. Coles Met loco No. 14 with T stock at Rickmansworth, F stock train at Eastcote, P stock train at Rayners Lane.
Piers Connor collection 1900 electric train with staff, B stock train at Ealing Broadway, Handworked door stock on East London Line, Met steam loco No. 23 1910 motor car and Q stock at East Putney, T stock at Northwood, BTH 'standard' stock at Ealing.
Iris Doyle collection Met steam loco No. 59.
R.J. Greenaway Q stock, C69 stock and COP stock at Hammersmith, C77 stock train, D stock train at Olympia, D stock motor car No. 7537.
R.J. Greenaway collection South Acton shuttle car.
H. Household District A stock train at Acton Town, B stock train at South Kensington.
Alan A. Jackson East Ham sheds.
Len's of Sutton Southend saloon stock train, GN&C steel-bodied motor car at Drayton Park, BTH loco No. 11 at Willesden Green.
Locomotive Club of Great Britain District Railway loco No. 44, C class loco No. 30, K class loco with goods train.
Metro-Cammell Dreadnought Third Class Coach.
J.C. Parkin R stock train at Gunnersbury.
Photomatic MW stock train at Willesden Green.
S.L. Poole GN&C wooden-bodied train at Finsbury Park, Q stock train at East Ham.
G.F. Walker A60 stock train at Harrow.

Photographs not otherwise credited are © London Transport Executive

The cover painting is by Peter Green, GRA

Contents

8 The Beginnings of the Underground
12 The Original Underground Trains
16 District Steam Stock
20 The Metropolitan Extends to the Country
22 Bogie Stock and the Chesham Shuttle
24 The Metropolitan & Great Central Joint Committee
27 Electrification Experiments
30 The District A Stock
33 The District B Stock
37 Metropolitan Early Electric Stock
40 Electrification of the Circle Lines
42 The Hammersmith & City Line
44 The East London Line
46 The Whitechapel & Bow Line
48 The Great Northern & City Line
52 The Brill Branch
54 Expansion North West
56 Main Line Electrification
58 Metropolitan Electric Locomotives
62 The Rothschild Saloons and the Pullmans
64 The 1913 Metropolitan Stock
66 The Metropolitan Shuttles
67 The 1910/13 District Stock
70 Metropolitan Post-War Electric Stock
72 The MW Stock, Later Known as T Stock
76 Renovation of the Circle Stock
78 The F Class (1920 Stock)
82 The G Class (1923 Stock)
85 The 1927/31/35 Stocks
90 The O & P Stocks and the Metadyne
96 The Q Stock
98 The R Stock
104 Met Electrification Experimental Stock
110 A for Amersham Stock
114 C for Circle Stock
118 D for District Stock
123 Note on Carbuilders and Principal Equipment Contractors
124 Note on Electric Braking

Introduction

Railway rolling stock has a history of development arising for two main reasons: advancement of technique which enables existing and known requirements to be met more adequately and reliably as knowledge of materials is improved and new types of equipment are devised; and—what often seems to progress even faster—changing requirements on the part of operators and passengers which constantly keep the rolling stock engineers on the search for solutions to new or altered problems.

The requirements of an urban underground railway system are severe: in function, the rolling stock must perform its duty with the utmost efficiency, carrying large numbers of passengers securely and at brief intervals enabling them to get in and out with great speed; in performance, good acceleration and braking are paramount; in reliability maintenance must be easily carried out, and as little of it as possible must be necessary; financially, it must be economical in first cost, in maintenance and in power consumption.

Mr Bruce has set down here, with as much clarity as the nature of the subject allows, the story of the development of the rolling stock constructed for the 'surface' (or sub-surface) lines of London's Underground railway system. Starting from the original steam-hauled carriages of the Metropolitan and Metropolitan District Railways (which, it must be confessed, were not very enterprising in their activity in this field) through the early, exciting, and experimental days of their electrification in the first decade of the twentieth century to the complex sequence of construction and shuffling which followed the amalgamation of the two railways under the London Passenger Transport Board in 1933, and so to the present time. If any one feature more than another stands out from this account, it is the necessity, so skilfully met by successive generations of engineers, to compromise what they would like to do with the imperious demands of the operators—themselves attempting to cope with surges of passenger traffic, restricted stations, and rigid patterns of operation imposed by tunnel conditions and track layouts. That will remain the rolling stock engineer's most taxing task.

Mr Bruce enables his readers to judge how far the conditions of effective and efficient operation have been met, by setting down this tale of successes—in a few cases, the less than complete successes—that the engineers have achieved.

R.M. ROBBINS

Author's Note

The history of the surface rolling stock of London Transport is more complicated and much less of a continuous story than that of the deep level Tube rolling stock. The Metropolitan Railway and the District Railway had differing rolling stock policies which, after the formation of London Transport, had to be consolidated—but the traditions of the two railways died hard.

Each chapter deals as far as possible with a particular subject from beginning to end and so covers a wide span of years. There is some overlapping and a small amount of repetition of information in order to make each section a complete story. Car numbers have been used sparingly, being given only where their inclusion adds directly to the understanding of the text. Where two sets of numbers are given those shown in brackets provide the number allocated by London Transport after 1933. The term 'coach' is used to describe any compartment type vehicle with swing doors; all other vehicles of the open saloon type are called 'cars' in accordance with the practice adopted by London Transport and, to some extent, by the Metropolitan Railway previously. Where closure dates are mentioned, the date quoted is the last day of service.

The information contained in these pages spans 120 years of development and has in some cases been difficult to collect. I am grateful to a great many of my colleagues, both serving and retired, who are too numerous to mention by name, for the information they have wittingly or unwittingly provided for this book. However, I must specially mention K.R. Benest, John Day, Charles E. Lee and B.J. Prigmore as well as the late Harry Clarke who helped in the preparation of the historical information for the first edition. The technical details for the more modern rolling stock were originally provided by permission of the reigning Chief Mechanical Engineers, A.W. Manser for the A Stock, G.S. Bingham for the C Stock and S.F. Smith for the D Stock. Mr D.K. Ware, now the Development Engineer (Railways), was helpful regarding the provision of the technical details of the D Stock, which first entered service after my retirement.

Individuals who have been particularly helpful during the preparation of the Second Edition are Gordon Hafter, who followed me as Rolling Stock Engineer and is now Director of Mechanical Engineering (Railways), and Ken King who as Traffic Superintendent bore the brunt of my questions but never failed to provide an answer. Messrs G. Jasieniecki and M.A.C. Horne read through the final draft and made many useful comments, and Piers Connor, Bob Greenaway, Brian Hardy and Peter Wilson provided help with the photographs.

Harrow, April 1983

J. GRAEME BRUCE

The Beginnings of the Underground

Broad gauge Great Western train at Praed Street Junction. The original construction has remained unchanged since the junction was opened in 1868 and the arched roof can still be seen today.

The Circle Line, still known by some as the Inner Circle, is the oldest of London's Underground lines. It was always known as the Inner Circle until the 1940s because for many years there were also a Middle Circle and an Outer Circle. Most of the traces of these, however, have now been lost.

It all began over a hundred years ago when the first section of the Metropolitan Railway was opened from Bishop's Road (Paddington) to Farringdon Street on 10th January 1863. Construction of the line started in 1860 with the financial support of the Great Western Railway and the Corporation of the City of London, inspired by its Solicitor, Charles Pearson, who was the driving force during the planning stages. The scheme was also backed by the Great Northern Railway, which wanted to use the new line to gain access to the City.

The choice of Farringdon Street as the terminus of the new railway was dictated by the availability of the space previously occupied by the City Cattle Market, which was transferred to a new site in Islington and subsequently became famous as the Caledonian Market. Passenger traffic to this point would also be generated by the decision of the City of London to open a central meat market at nearby Smithfield, to which, incidentally, a spur line was later built, enabling GWR meat wagons to be conveyed over the newly-constructed railway.

The line was built on the 'cut and cover' principle just below street level and, as it was intended in the original project to use smokeless locomotives (see Chapter 2) no ventilation was provided. Later, gratings and openings in the roadway were installed to help clear the tunnels of fumes created by the steam locomotives subsequently used. The tracks were laid with dual gauge using three rails so that trains of both standard gauge (4ft 8½in) and Great Western broad gauge (7ft0¼in) could use the tunnels. The Metropolitan Railway made an end-on junction at Bishop's Road with the Great Western Railway.

The Circle Line since then has seen, on some sections of the track at least, all the surface rolling stock developed by London Transport and its predecessors, the Metropolitan Railway and the Metropolitan District Railway (known and referred to subsequently as the District Railway) as well as some of the London suburban rolling stock of several main line railways.

Following the opening of the first section of the Metropolitan, an eastward extension to Moorgate was brought into service on 23rd December 1865. This remained the eastern terminus of the line until Bishopsgate (now Liverpool Street) was reached some ten years later. This point was reached in two stages. Initially tracks were laid into the Liverpool Street terminus of the Great Eastern Railway and a service was operated there beginning on 1st February 1875. From 18th November 1876 a shuttle service ran to Aldgate. Subsequently, from 4th December 1876, through trains ran from Aldgate to Hammersmith and the spur into the Great Eastern Liverpool Street station was then only used on special occasions. The Metropolitan station which was called Bishopsgate until 1st November 1909 (when it was renamed Liverpool Street) was not ready until 12th July 1875.

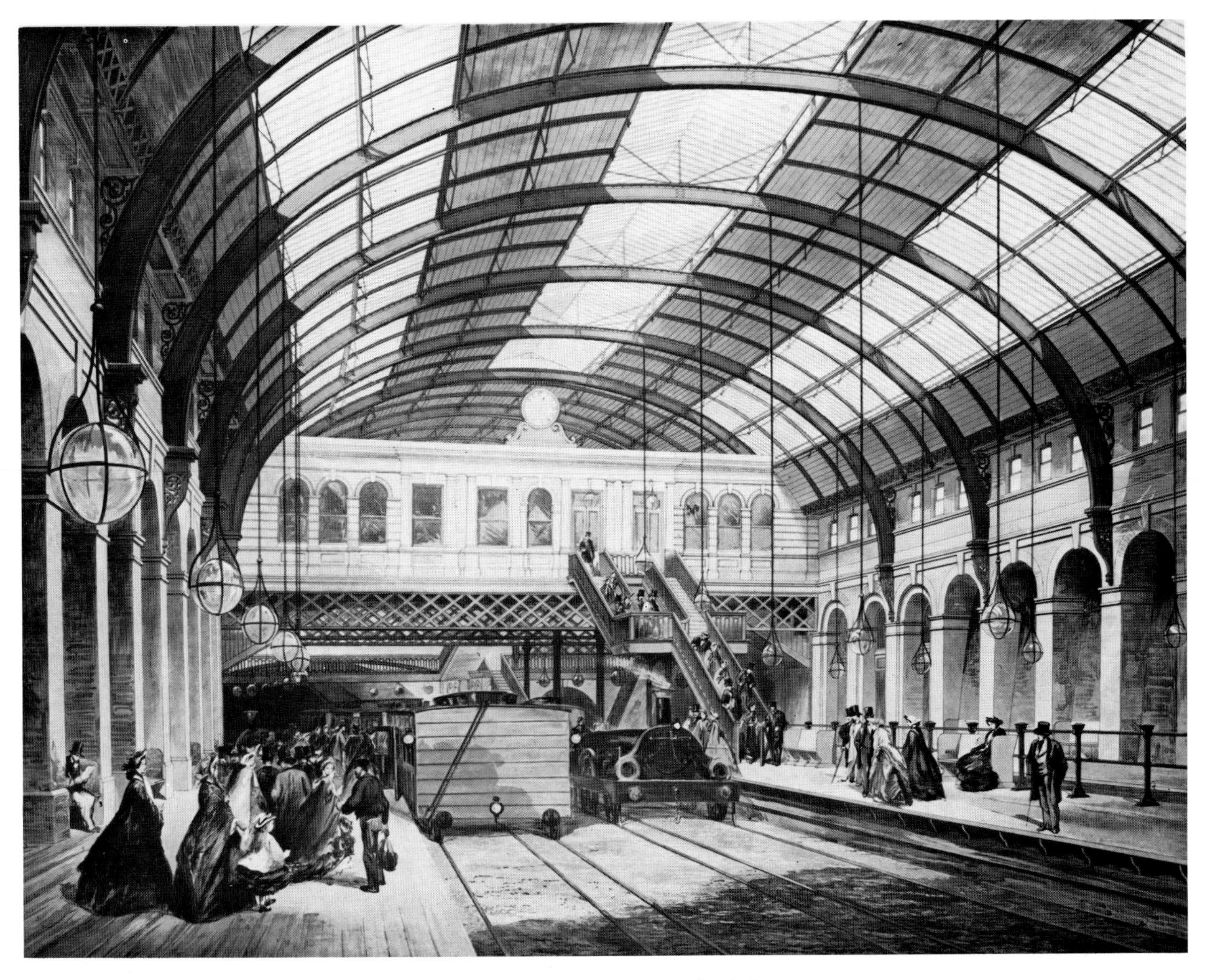

King's Cross station on the Metropolitan Railway in 1863. The Great Western Railway provided the locomotives and rolling stock for the first seven months of the line's operation and two GWR trains are illustrated.

A connection was opened with the Great Northern Railway at King's Cross in October 1863. Soon after the completion of the line to Moorgate it was decided to quadruple the tracks between King's Cross and Moorgate. These additional tracks known as the 'City Widened Lines' are still in use today but form part of the suburban network of British Railways and the connection with the Underground has been severed.

The section of the Widened Lines between Farringdon and Aldersgate was brought into use on 1st March 1866, that between Aldersgate and Moorgate on 1st July 1866, and both were joined up with the main line tracks near King's Cross and St Pancras on 17th February 1868. This enabled the Midland Railway to open a service to Moorgate Street on 13th July 1868, some months before its own terminus at St Pancras was brought into use.

On 1st January 1866 a junction with the London Chatham and Dover Railway was completed following the construction of a bridge over the River Thames at Blackfriars and this enabled a through passenger service with the Great Northern Railway to be introduced on 20th February 1866. This service between north and south London continued until 30th June 1908. From 1871 passenger trains from the south were worked into Moorgate Station by means of an additional connection. This service was discontinued on 1st April 1916.

While all this was going on at the eastern end of the new line, a separate company built a branch railway at the western end to Hammersmith. This was opened on 13th June 1864, and is now the western terminus of the Hammersmith & City Line of London Transport. A branch to Kensington (Addison Road) left the Hammersmith line near Latimer Road station and connected with the West London Railway, providing a valuable link with the railways of South London. This spur (now removed) was, however, important in the story because it provided eventually the means of running a Middle Circle service.

The Metropolitan Railway was also extending its line to the west by branching off after Edgware Road station to South Kensington. This line was opened to Gloucester Road on 1st October 1868, and to South Kensington 12 weeks later, to make a junction with a new railway — the District Railway — which was opened from South Kensington to Westminster Bridge station on 24th December 1868, and then to Blackfriars on 30th May 1870.

Profiting by the experience of building the Metropolitan Railway, the line was constructed by cut and cover methods, but as many stations as possible were left in open cuttings. Where this was not possible ventilation openings were provided. South Kensington and Sloane Square were in the open although well below street level. In addition, there were at least eight clear openings between South Kensington and St James's Park.

Most of the section beyond Westminster was constructed as part of the Victoria Embankment for which the District Railway had to make a financial contribution. The Victoria Embankment was opened to road traffic on 13th July 1870 by the Prince of Wales (later to become King Edward VII).

Met loco 49 and an Inner Circle train approaching Aldgate, about 1900.
The lines to Aldgate East can be seen diverging to the right of the photograph.

West Brompton station in May 1876 with District Railway loco No. 10, built in 1871 by Beyer, Peacock. The station was a terminus at this time.

Met loco 55 at Aldgate running bunker first on a Hammersmith train.

The District constructed its own tracks from South Kensington to Gloucester Road on the south side of the Metropolitan tracks and then branched away to West Brompton. A shuttle service from Gloucester Road to West Brompton was operated by the Metropolitan on behalf of the District from 12th April 1869. In addition, at about the same time, the District constructed a line in the shape of a U-bend from the High Street Kensington junction with the Metropolitan, through Earl's Court, to the West London Railway at Kensington (Addison Road), in this way joining the West Brompton line for a short distance. The first regular service between High Street Kensington and Cromwell Road junction began on 3rd July 1871; and from Earl's Court to Kensington (Addison Road) on 1st February 1872. This connection to Addison Road provided the means of working both the Middle and the Outer Circle services. Through trains from Blackfriars to West Brompton began on 1st August 1870, worked by the Metropolitan Railway until 3rd July 1871 when the District acquired its own rolling stock. The District was extended one more station eastwards on 3rd July 1871 to Mansion House, which was originally constructed as a terminal station with three roads and two platforms. Locomotive spurs were provided for coal stages and water cranes. This arrangement continued until 6th October 1884 when the Metropolitan and the District Joint Line was built joining Mansion House with Aldgate and Whitechapel. The Metropolitan reached the Aldgate terminus on 18th November 1876, and extended its line to Tower of London station on 25th September 1882, but the triangular junction with the District was not completed until 1884 when through running to the East London Railway became possible. The station called Tower of London (on the site of the present Tower Hill) was closed on 13th October 1884, being replaced by the new joint Metropolitan and District station at Mark Lane. A complete reconstruction of Mansion House then provided four roads, of which three were terminal, a layout which remained until 1910.

The Inner Circle, the Circle as we know it today, began working on 6th October 1884, as a joint service of both the Metropolitan and District Railways. The trains which ran in a clockwise direction—that is on the outer rail of the circle—were provided by the Metropolitan, while those on the inner rail, working anti-clockwise round the circle, were provided by the District. From time to time some Metropolitan trains had to work on the anti-clockwise service, to equate the mileage, as by far the greater proportion of the trackage of the circle was owned by the Metropolitan. Before the completion of the Circle, however, the train service from Moorgate, and later Aldgate, to Mansion House was known as the Inner Circle. On 1st February 1872 the London & North Western Railway began working a train service from Broad Street by way of the North London line and the West London Railway to Earl's Court and Mansion House. This was, in fact, a variant of a service which had worked into Victoria LBSC station by much of the same route. This service, worked throughout at this time with LNWR locomotives and rolling stock, was known as the Outer Circle, although this too was horseshoe-shaped, and not a complete circle. On 1st August of the same year the Great Western Railway began working standard gauge trains between Moorgate on the Metropolitan by way of the Hammersmith & City Line to Addison Road and through to the District Railway to reach Mansion House. This service, also a horseshoe in form, was known as the Middle Circle. The Outer Circle survived until 1st January 1909 when the service ceased to work east of Earl's Court. The Middle Circle service on the other hand was cut back to Earl's Court on 30th June 1900, ceasing altogether on 31st January 1905. A remnant of this service survived under electrification as a shuttle connection from H & C stations to Addison Road, but this last operated in October 1940. Only the Inner Circle remains, so that today the service is known simply as the Circle Line.

A short-lived Midland Railway service between St Pancras and Earl's Court by way of Cricklewood, Acton, and Hammersmith, a kind of 'Outer' Outer Circle, was operated from 1st May 1878 to 30th September 1880 after the District train service had been extended to Richmond.

The Original Underground Trains

One of the original A class locomotives rebuilt in 1887,
probably photographed at Neasden works immediately after its rebuild.

When the service on the Underground first began, the rolling stock was provided by the Great Western Railway which owned a shareholding in the company. The timetable provided for the operation betwen 8am and 8pm of a train every 15 minutes. The time taken to work from Bishop's Road to Farringdon, a distance of $3\frac{1}{4}$ miles, was 18 minutes stopping at all stations.

The stations were Edgware Road (sometimes spelt at the time as Edgeware Road), Baker Street, Portland Road (which became Great Portland Street on 1st March 1917), Gower Street (which became Euston Square on 1st November 1909) and King's Cross.

The locomotives and carriages were of broad gauge and had been designed by Daniel Gooch, the Locomotive Superintendent of the Great Western Railway. A number of 2-4-0 tank engines built by Vulcan Foundry and Kitson's of Leeds were provided to haul trains composed of eight-wheeled non-bogie stock known as 'Long Charleys'. By July 1863, relations between the Great Western Railway and the Metropolitan had deteriorated to such an extent that the Great Western decided to withdraw its rolling stock and gave notice of termination of contract as from 30th September. Subsequently the Great Western advanced the date to 10th August, virtually giving only seven days' notice, and also making it clear at the same time that they would not sell the locomotives and rolling stock. One of the causes of disagreement had been the Metropolitan Railway's wish to increase the service to a greater frequency than four per hour.

The Great Northern Railway then provided both the locomotives and many of the carriages until the Metropolitan Railway could obtain rolling stock of its own.

Originally Sir John Fowler, the Chief Engineer of The Metropolitan Railway, proposed to use 'Smokeless' steam locomotives in which the boiler was provided with a small firebox heated by white hot firebricks which would be transferred from lineside furnaces at appropriate points. In addition, the steam would not be blown to waste after passing through the driving cylinders but condensed in the feed water tanks thereby raising the initial temperature. One such engine was built but did not proceed beyond the experimental stage and earned the soubriquet 'Fowler's Ghost'.

In anticipation of the projection of Great Northern trains into Farringdon Street from King's Cross, Archibald Sturrock, the Locomotive Superintendent of that railway, had designed some tank engines with condensing arrangements because in granting powers to operate an Underground Railway, Parliament had decreed that the 'engines must consume their own smoke'. This was subsequently watered down to the more practical requirement that 'engines must condense'. Further locomotives were hurriedly converted to provide this facility to enable the Metropolitan Railway's requirements to be met.

It was not until July 1864 that sufficient new vehicles were available for full operation by the Metropolitan on its own account. The original order for 18 steam locomotives was placed with Beyer, Peacock & Co. of Gorton, Manchester. These original locomotives were the famous A class, which was the basic design for practically all the locomotives used on the Underground operations until electrification. Forty-four of the A class were built between 1864 and 1870 followed up to 1885 by a further 22 of the improved B type. The District Railway obtained 54 similar locomotives between 1871 and 1886. This locomotive type, a 4-4-0 tank engine can therefore be considered the pioneer motive power on London's Underground.

As originally built they did not have cabs, just a spectacle plate or weather board for the protection of the driver. The District locomotives could, in later years, be distinguished from the Metropolitan by the fact that this weather board was not flat, being curved at the top over the footplate.

The original livery of both railways was similar, at least when dirty. The Metropolitan livery was described as dark green and the District's as dull green. The Metropolitan changed the livery to chocolate brown, described by some authorities as dark red, about 1885. The original 18 locomotives were named with classical names such as JUPITER, HERCULES and MEDUSA but subsequent locomotives were distinguished at first only by a brass number carried on the front of the chimney. When the colour was changed the numbers were painted on the side tanks.

All the original Metropolitan locomotives were designed for 'left hand' cab driving position, because of the need for the driver to observe thoroughly the station duties and yet make a quick start away. Most stations on the Circle had conventional platforms. Wrong side positioning for the driver, therefore, occurred only at the termini, or when running bunker first.

The engines weighed about 46½ tons in running order with 1,000 gallons of water in the side tanks. The coupled wheels were 5 feet 9 inches in diameter driven by two 17-inch cylinders, with a stroke of 24 inches inclined at 1 in 9. The original boiler pressure was 120 lbs. per sq. in. but on the later locomotives this was raised to 160 lbs. per sq. in. Despite condensing arrangements, stations such as Temple and Portland Road were always full of thick sulphurous fumes. When the Circle service was complete the Metropolitan locomotives took on coal and water at Edgware Road, the District locomotives at High Street Kensington.

The order for the original carriage stock was also placed in Manchester, with the Ashbury Railway Carriage & Iron Co. The first vehicles were similar in design to the Great Western Railway's but standard gauge instead of broad gauge. As they were narrower, they had relatively high roofs to accommodate the gas bags provided for lighting. The Great Western had, in fact, pioneered the introduction of coal gas lighting for the stock to be used on the Underground and the Metropolitan continued with this arrangement. The gas at this time was not compressed but carried in inflatable weighted bags on the carriage roofs. The 39ft 6in body, constructed mainly of teak, was built on an angle-iron frame which was about 6 inches shorter than the body. There were three different body arrangements in a standard length: First Class with six compartments, Second and Third Class with eight compartments, and composite with seven compartments containing three First Class compartments in the middle of the coach. The doors of the compartments originally had square tops. It was in 1867 that the traditional Metropolitan-type rounded-top door, reducing the liability to damage in the tunnels, was introduced. The first Metropolitan coaches were finished in varnished teak, the first class compartments being painted white above the waist rail.

A composite First and Second Class eight-wheeled coach of the original Metropolitan type rolling stock. A batch of 20 of these was delivered in 1866. Subsequent batches had doors with rounded tops instead of straight ones to avoid damage to open doors in the tunnels.

An eight-coach train of Metropolitan four-wheeled stock on its way to Rickmansworth behind one of the 1880 batch of Beyer, Peacock 4-4-0 locomotives.

The original vehicles (the 'Long Charleys') were 42 feet long over buffers and were carried on four axles grouped in pairs but not provided with bogies. Flexibility at curves was provided by a translation movement of the radial axlebox attached to the mainframes by means of links hung from the ends of the springs at angles of about 30 degrees. The outer wheels of each pair were over six feet from the ends of the coach so that the vehicle, apart from the translation movement, was virtually rigid wheelbased. This arrangement varied on the different batches of stock and was finally modified on the introduction of the automatic vacuum brake. When the vehicles were introduced the only brake fitted was Newall's handbrake in the guard's compartment which applied wooden brake blocks to four wheels of that coach.

The Wilkins and Clark chain brake which was later improved by Francis Webb, the famous Locomotive Engineer of the London & North Western Railway, was adopted in 1869. This was a form of continuous brake, in that a cord passing over the roofs of the carriage released weights which then operated the handbrake lever in the guard's compartment provided on each car. This brake, although effective, was very jerky and resulted in a number of serious injuries to passengers. In 1875 Smith's simple vacuum brake was adopted, to be converted later to the automatic vacuum. The Westinghouse air brake was not introduced on the Metropolitan until electric traction.

Lighting in an Underground train is very important and the Metropolitan coaches being gas lit were a considerable improvement in this respect over the suspended oil lamps in current railway use. The coal gas was carried in long India rubber bags enclosed in wooden boxes housed in the roof which were replenished at the Edgware Road shed as required. It was probably this arrangement and the possible fire risk that caused smoking to be prohibited in the early years of operation.

The Metropolitan and the District had been specifically exempted from the Railway Regulation Act 1868 which required all railways to provide smoking accommodation. However, to meet public demand, and because the rolling stock of main-line railways which ran over the Metropolitan made provision for smokers, both the Metropolitan and the District introduced Smoking carriages on 1st September 1874.

In 1870 the Metropolitan began acquiring from the Oldbury Carriage Co. some more carriages which were four-wheeled, coupled in pairs. Each pair was close coupled, the pair measuring 43 feet 8 inches in length—almost equivalent to the earlier eight-wheeled vehicles. Each body of the coupled pairs was 20 feet long and contained either three First Class compartments or four Second or Third Class compartments. The wheels were 42 inches in diameter, the springing being provided by 5ft long carriage-type springs mounted on top of the axleboxes. A combined central buffer and coupling provided the semi-permanent connection between the two-car sets but the outer ends were fitted with Sterne's patent buffing gear which had a pneumatic action. The width over the mouldings was 8 feet 3 inches; inside the compartments the maximum height was 7 feet 1 inch.

The First Class compartments seated four passengers aside with arm rests. The Third Class compartments with wooden bench seats were only 4 feet 10 inches between partitions. Partitions between First Class compartments were of full height but in the lower-class compartments, with fewer lamps only shoulder-heigh partitions were provided.

Coal gas lighting was provided with two lamps in the First Class compartments but only one in each compartment of the other two classes staggered across the vehicle. The lamps were fed through iron pipes from the rubber gas bags, each bag being designed to fold up as the gas was used up. They were provided with an indicator which showed E for Empty or F for Full. Gas holders were provided at certain strategic points to replenish the gas bags of the carriages, but it was not until the Julius Pintsch system was adopted that the gas was provided in containers under pressure.

Met loco 27, one of the batch originally built in 1867, in the passenger locomotive livery worn by the time of their general withdrawal in 1919.

Met loco 23 in rebuilt condition with enclosed cab and painted in London Transport livery for operation on the Brill line.

District Steam Stock

District Railway engine No. 25 as originally built by Beyer, Peacock, the first of the second batch built in 1876.

When, on 3rd July 1871, the District Railway began working the services with its own rolling stock it ran from Mansion House in the east through South Kensington, where a junction with the Metropolitan Railway was made. Between Gloucester Road and South Kensington the District provided duplicate tracks and virtually a separate station at South Kensington.

The Western extension of the District through Earl's Court to West Brompton came in 1869, although a station at Earl's Court was not opened until 31st October 1871. The initial service was provided by shuttle from Gloucester Road. The District tracks between Gloucester Road and South Kensington were available for use but no continuous service was provided while the Metropolitan Railway worked the District services.

A station at Earl's Court Road was not originally intended as most of the adjoining land was a market garden and little potential traffic was seen. Eventually a small station on the east side of the road was built of timber. This station was destroyed by fire on 30th December 1875. Temporary repairs were made and a new station building on the west side of Earl's Court Road was opened three years later.

At this time there were six trains per hour between West Brompton and Mansion House. This service then contributed to the provision of a 5-minute service between Gloucester Road and Mansion House together with six trains per hour from Moorgate Street to Mansion House. The area around Earl's Court was developed so that when the station was rebuilt it was enlarged to consist of four roads on either side of two island platforms.

The problem which was built into the provision of this station was the inclusion of two flat junctions; in the west between the Addison Road and the West Brompton lines and in the east between the line to High Street Kensington and to South Kensington. When the rebuilt Earl's Court station was opened to traffic on 1st February 1878 a flying junction enabling the trains from High Street to avoid conflicting with the eastbound Mansion House trains was also provided.

The District remained faithful to the original Beyer, Peacock locomotive class for all the passenger working until electrification. The earlier locomotives had a leading Bissell radial swivelling four-wheeled truck, but the later deliveries had Adams bogies and the earlier locomotives were converted. There were a number of differences between the earlier and later locomotives which could be easily distinguished by the expert. For example, the first 36 locomotives had brass dome covers with integral safety valves; later locomotives had safety valves over the fireboxes. Some of the earlier locomotives were modified to conform to this arrangement. The weather plate was bent back to give some protection to the crew. The back plate of the coal bunker was also raised over one foot to provide protection when running bunker first which was a regular practice, as turntables were not provided. The average coal consumption of these locomotives was 30 lbs a mile.

All 54 of the locomotives of the District Railway were still in service in 1905 when electrification took place.

The District Railway constructed a maintenance yard and depot at Lillie Bridge which was completed by the summer of 1872. Access was obtained from a spur from the Addison Road line which was used for regular passenger trains on the Outer Circle service of the London and North Western Railway from 1st February 1872. After the extension to Hammersmith was opened to traffic on 9th September 1874 another access road to Lillie Bridge depot was provided from West Kensington station.

District Railway engine No. 33 and a three-coach train of four-wheeled stock. The locomotive is in its modified condition (compare with No. 25 opposite).

The original trains on the District Railway were composed of eight four-wheeled carriages. The make-up of these trains consisted of two First Class, two Second Class, and four Third Class, the classes being distinguished by large numbers painted on the compartment doors. There were four compartments in First Class coaches and five in the others. Each compartment was designed to seat five a side, even the First Class. In addition to the extra length of each First Class compartment, the class distinction was achieved by varying the quality of the upholstery.

Although the Metropolitan Railway had successfully opposed the Parliamentary powers sought by the District Railway for a connection between High Street Kensington and Gloucester Road, the District proceeded to construct such a connecting spur on ground which they now owned. Subsequently this spur became known as Cromwell Curve.

This connection became a bone of contention between the two railways and was eventually settled in the courts with the ruling in favour of the Metropolitan that the Inner Circle mileage was to be calculated from South Kensington in favour of that railway even when trains were worked through Cromwell Curve.

The extension to Hammersmith with intermediate stations at West Kensington and Barons Court was completed on 9th September 1874. The original station at Hammersmith was small but with further extensions in mind it was rebuilt with three platforms. A pair of terminal roads with a scissors crossing were located at one side of the middle platform, while the two roads on the other side formed the lines for a short

A nine-coach rake of District Railway steam stock at Lillie Bridge. The coaches were in their natural teak colour, which was varnished.

District Third Class steam stock brake coach No. 8. This coach was used in the stores train after withdrawal from passenger service but was restored to the condition shown here for the District Railway's diamond jubilee exhibition in 1928.

connection built from Hammersmith to a point known as Studland Road junction, which enabled the District Railway to gain access to the Kensington to Richmond line of the London & South Western Railway. Running powers were given to the District Railway and the service to Richmond commenced on 1st June 1877.

The District Railway then began constructing an extension on this line from Turnham Green to Ealing Broadway, which was opened on 1st July 1879. Powers were sought for an extension to Uxbridge but these were opposed by the Great Western Railway. However, as some sort of compensation, a connection with the Great Western was constructed at Ealing Broadway so that on 1st March 1883, a through service of District trains was inaugurated to Windsor. Twenty-two through trains were worked on weekdays, but the traffic did not reach expectations and the service was withdrawn on 30th September 1885.

The Hammersmith Junction Railway had been partly financed by the Midland Railway in return for running powers to gain access to West Kensington (North End) and High Street Kensington where land had been acquired for the provision of coal depots. These depots became operational in 1878.

Interior of restored car No. 8. Gas-light fittings borrowed from the Metropolitan Railway were used in the car when it was exhibited.

At Mill Hill Park (now Acton Town) the Hounslow & Metropolitan Railway, at first a separate undertaking but worked by the District, branched southwards to Hounslow Town, the service being opened on 1st May 1883. Just over a year later, on 21st July 1884, the single line to Hounslow Barracks was opened, which eventually became the main line. Hounslow Barracks was renamed Hounslow West on 1st December 1925.

Meanwhile, on 1st March 1880, the line was extended from West Brompton to Putney Bridge, and on 3rd June 1889 by means of running powers obtained from the London & South Western Railway this service was projected to Wimbledon.

As these services built up traffic, longer trains of nine carriages were introduced, which after 1879 became standard. The additional carriage was Second Class, and thereafter purchases of rolling stock were made in multiples of nine vehicles.

The line to Putney Bridge was opened in time for the University Boat Race which produced a considerable increase in traffic. The removal of the tolls across Wandsworth and Putney Bridges on 26th June 1880 also benefited the railway by encouraging people from south of the river to reach the station. From April 1880 a 15-minute service was operated, every half hour to High Street Kensington and every half hour to Mansion House.

When the service began to Hounslow through trains were operated from Mansion House but subsequently from 4th December 1883 the Hounslow trains started at Earl's Court.

Lighting was provided from the beginning by coal gas supplied from mains established at Mansion House and Kensington High Street. The gas bags were arranged along the centre of the roof. In 1878 the Pintsch compressed oil gas was introduced, a plant being installed at Lillie Bridge to compress the gas to 90 lbs per sq. in. The gas was stored in cylinders which were taken at night to suitable locations and connected to stand pipes. Each coach had a cylindrical wrought iron gas tank which was recharged at these stand pipes during the day as necessary. Subsequently, a main was laid from Lillie Bridge to Hammersmith to avoid the transfer of the gas cylinders to this point.

The vehicles were all four-wheeled, having a length of 26 feet 6 inches over the body frames and 29 feet 2 inches over the buffers. The original vehicles were built by the Ashbury Railway Carriage Company, but the District bought its subsequent carriages from a number of builders. The original stock consisted of 152 carriages, but at the end of steam operation a total of 394 were owned.

The brakes originally fitted were of the Wilkins and Clark chain type, which were replaced first by the simple Westinghouse non-automatic brake and later by the fully-automatic Westinghouse.

In the 1890s compartments were provided with a 'next station' indicator placed in a slot in the upper part of the partition between the compartments. It was originally operated by the guard pulling a string to display the plate bearing the name of the next station, but this was converted to a mechanical trip device placed on the track which automatically brought the plate with the name of the next station into view. The station names were interposed with advertisements but the equipment was not considered reliable because it required to be properly set at each terminal station, and if this were neglected, chaos resulted.

When the service originally began,about 12 departures an hour from Mansion House were operated, alternate trains going round the Inner Circle to Moorgate and to West Brompton. The Inner Circle service was shared with the Metropolitan. The Outer Circle service from Broad Street and Addison Road, operated by the London & North Western Railway, and the Great Western's Middle Circle service from Moorgate by way of Addison Road began in 1872. These services increased the number of trains to 16 an hour. When the District Line extensions were introduced the frequency went up to 19 an hour, which was the most that could be worked with steam traction.

The trains provided by the District for these services remained unchanged as to rolling stock types until electrification. At the end of steam operation the District fleet of 395 vehicles comprised 215 Third Class, 92 Second Class, one Composite and 87 First Class coaches, including three nine-coach trains representing their half-interest in the Whitechapel & Bow Joint Stock.

District Railway locomotives awaiting scrapping at Ealing Common after the electrification.

The Metropolitan Extends to the Country

C class locomotive No. 30 approaches Harrow-on-the-Hill station about 1900, before the lines to Harrow were four-tracked. The train's 50-mile journey from Baker Street will terminate at the end of the Brill Branch.

The Metropolitan & St John's Wood Railway, promoted in 1864, which had the Metropolitan Railway as a substantial shareholder, opened its line from Baker Street to Swiss Cottage on 13th April 1868. This line was only single-tracked with passing places at stations. There were a number of short sections of steep gradients, especially the hump over the Regent's Canal, and to negotiate these difficulties five powerful 0-6-0 tank locomotives built by the Worcester Engine Co. were purchased. However, these locomotives proved to be over-powered for the duty and when the Metropolitan had locomotives to spare because it had ceased, in 1871, to provide the motive power for the District Railway, they were sold, and the Beyer, Peacock 4-4-0 type took up the duty. The Taff Vale Railway bought four of the 0-6-0s (two each in 1873 and 1875) and the Sirhowy Railway bought the fifth (in 1873).

At first a through service was provided from Swiss Cottage to Moorgate but in March 1869 this was discontinued. A through service to the City was not reinstated until after electrification.

The St John's Wood Line reached West Hampstead on 30th June 1879, with an intermediate station at Finchley Road. The Metropolitan Extension Line service as it became called began operating to Willesden Green on 24th November 1879 with a station at Kilburn & Brondesbury. The extension work continued until Harrow-on-the-Hill was reached on 2nd August 1880 with a station at Neasden & Kingsbury. By this time it became clear that the single track between Swiss Cottage and Baker Street was totally inadequate. The single line had originally used human tokens to ensure line clear for passing trains. Later a wooden staff was issued to the train guard before he started his train. Two tracks over this section were completed by 10th July 1882, and shortly afterwards the St John's Wood Railway ceased to exist as a separate corporate body, being absorbed by the Metropolitan Railway.

By 25th May 1885 the Metropolitan had extended to Pinner, Rickmansworth being reached on 1st September 1887. The line was pushed on towards Aylesbury which was connected to Baker Street by 1st September 1892. Meanwhile, the main line had reached Chalfont Road (since 1915 named Chalfont & Latimer) and this, together with a single line branch from Chalfont Road to Chesham, came into use on 8th July 1880.

The Metropolitan continued to push out into the country by taking over the Aylesbury & Buckingham Railway (opened in 1868) so that by 1894 Verney Junction (just over 50 miles from Baker Street) in the depths of Buckinghamshire had been reached. Through trains to this point from Baker Street began working on 1st January 1897, but local trains of the Metropolitan had run to Verney Junction from April 1894.

These extensions brought the need for more locomotives and between 1891 and 1901 the C, D, E and F classes appeared. The C class were 0-4-4 tanks and four were built by Neilson & Co, similar to some contemporary engines constructed for the South Eastern Railway. The D class which appeared in 1894 consisted of six engines by Sharp Stewart and were 2-4-0T type, similar to although not identical with a design used by the Barry Railway. The E class were actually designed for the Metropolitan

Metropolitan Railway First Class 'Jubilee' stock coach No. 346 dating from 1892. The first coaches of this type were built in 1887, the year of Queen Victoria's Golden Jubilee.

Railway, and out of the seven locomotives in the class three were built at Neasden, while the remainder were constructed by Hawthorn Leslie. The F class built by the Yorkshire Engine Company were 0-6-2T, and apart from the wheel arrangement were similar to the E class which were 0-4-4T type. Not all of these engines were fitted with condensing apparatus, which was a statutory requirement for tunnel operation south of Finchley Road.

The terminal track provided at Baker Street when the St John's Wood line was originally built was single, with a platform on both sides, and provided a running connection to the Circle Line. When these extensions called for a greater terminal capacity a track was provided on either side of the existing two platforms. In order to provide an easy interchange connection with the Circle Line without having to climb a stairway, a movable gangway was installed across the middle road which was only drawn back for empty rolling stock transfers to and from Edgware Road where the original Metropolitan locomotive shed and works were situated.

Public demand caused the reintroduction of the through service after electrification, when the connection with the Circle Line was doubled and the gangway replaced by a drawbridge. The present track layout was introduced at the same time, on 4th November 1912. The station in its present form and the premises known as Chiltern Court were not completed until 1929.

As a result of some minor derailments with the original rolling stock a new four-wheeled design was produced in 1887. Three complete trains of nine vehicles were initially built by Cravens Brothers of Sheffield. The bodies were 27 feet 6 inches long, and had a wheelbase of 14 feet. There were two Second Class and two First Class coaches in the nine-vehicle rake and all were fitted with Smith's simple vacuum brake. The First Class coaches had four compartments while both the lower classes had five.

Each train was made up with two brake coaches, a Third Class at one end which had three compartments and a luggage compartment used at busy times to carry eleven passengers on wooden benches alongside the guard. At the other end of the rake a Second Class brake coach had the normal five compartments, one of which was occupied by the guard and could accommodate five passengers as well.

These trains were not originally fitted with steam heating coils but this amenity was added later. However, the Pintsch high-pressure gas lighting system was installed when built. As the introduction of these vehicles coincided with the celebration of Queen Victoria's Jubilee they became known throughout their life as 'Jubilee Stock'.

To provide a service to Aylesbury a further four trains of this stock were purchased in 1892 from the same builders. They were delivered in eight-coach sets made up into two four-coach portions allowing the trains to be divided at Chalfont Road so that one portion could proceed to Chesham while the other went on to Aylesbury.

These sets had long buffers and screw couplings at the outer ends of the four-coach portions. This uncoupling arrangement did not last long and the inner brake coaches were converted to standard types, but the formations remained at eight-coach length.

There were 59 of these coaches and at the time of electrification some were rescued from the scrap heap and converted at Neasden Works to run with electric motive power over the electrified tracks to augment the service at peak periods. They were finally withdrawn in 1912.

Locomotive No. 77, an 0-4-4 E class built in 1896 at Neasden Works, photographed in charge of a rake of eight-wheeled bogie coaches with round-topped doors.

Bogie Stock and the Chesham Shuttle

Bogie stock train after conversion to electric working. Two three-car sets of these vehicles were retained for steam operation on the Chesham shuttle and remained in service until 1960.

It became obvious that the four-wheeled and the rigid-wheelbase stock was unsatisfactory for the Extension services—the name given to the through workings to Rickmansworth, Chesham, Amersham and beyond.

Between 1898 and 1900, 54 vehicles were built which were variously known as 'Ashbury' Stock or 'Bogie' Stock. The Ashbury Railway Carriage & Iron Company of Manchester received the first order for four six-coach trains equipped with bogies, the first on the Metropolitan. These trains went into service in 1898.

The bodies of the vehicles were 39ft 6ins long but the overall length over buffers was 42ft 4¾ins. The width of the body frame was 8ft 3ins, but to clear the outside grab rails another five inches were needed. The total height of the body above rail level was 11ft 7ins, a further six inches being required to clear the top of the 'torpedo' type ventilators.

Three classes of accommodation were provided with ten seats in each compartment irrespective of class. The rule in each compartment was five a side, and there were retractable armrests in the First Class compartments. The Second and Third Class coaches had seven compartments but brake coaches were provided with five compartments in addition to a luggage compartment. The First Class coaches had six compartments giving more leg room for the passengers. The moquette upholstery was trimmed with lace and cord, but all the compartments had upholstery of some kind, although the Third Class was austere. The floors were deadened to reduce running noise by incorporating some felt as a lining above the steel floor plating. Spring blinds were fitted to the sidelights of all compartments and steam heating was supplied throughout.

For the first time on the Metropolitan this stock was equipped with electric lighting providing two lamps of eight-candle power in each compartment. A battery, connected to an axle-driven dynamo working on Stone's system, provided the power for this illumination. When the vehicle entered service, no passenger alarm was incorporated and this safety device was not installed until some time later, although the trains were fitted with the automatic vacuum brake system. The vehicles were fitted with pressed steel bogies at 25ft centres, each bogie having a 7ft wheelbase. Each wheel had two cast iron brake shoes, coupled by rigging to the vacuum brake cylinder.

The normal formation of these trains was: B2T-2T-1T-1/3T-3T-B3T which formed a rake 252 feet in length. The First/Third composite coach had only six compartments and both the First and Third compartments were roomier than their counterparts all of one class.

As soon as the original sets were in service it was felt that some further trains of this type were required. The Metropolitan Railway intended to build some of them in its own workshops at Neasden, but pressure of work necessitated most of the order being placed with outside carbuilders. Five additional train sets were ordered. One set was built by the Metropolitan Railway itself, two sets were constructed by Cravens of Sheffield, and two further sets were built by Ashbury, the original carbuilders. The first of these additional sets went into service in 1900.

Until electrification, this stock maintained the through services to Chesham, Aylesbury, and Verney Junction from Baker Street.

The fleet of 'Bogie' stock later increased from 54 to 58—one in 1903, two in 1908 which had originally been used in electrification trials at Wembley Park in 1899, and a fourth in 1910, originally used in the Earl's Court electrification experiment.

When the electric train services on the Metropolitan Railway, south of Harrow, began in 1905, the need for steam passenger trains decreased. This not only rendered all the older rigid wheelbase stock redundant, but it also made some of the 'Bogie' stock surplus to daily requirements. Arrangements were then made for some of these vehicles to be converted for electric working, and between 1906 and 1924 all the 'Bogie' stock was converted to electric working. Initially some thought was given to providing trains of this kind for dual working, changing the motive power at the outskirts of the electrified area, but this proposal was abandoned and the 'Bogie' stock became part of the electric fleet which will be considered as such in due course. Apart from the provision of an equipment chamber and a driving cab the appearance of the vehicle was altered very little in the conversion. These trains continued to provide yeoman service within the electrified area, principally on the Uxbridge line, and subsequently to Stanmore after this line was opened on 10th December 1932. They were withdrawn on 20th November 1939, when the Bakerloo Line took over the Stanmore service.

The Metropolitan Railway was extended to Chesham on 8th July 1889, and for three years Chesham was the northern terminus. After 1892 Chesham became the terminal of a branch which left the main line at Chalfont Road.

The need to provide a push-and-pull type shuttle train for the Chesham branch from Chalfont in 1941 caused the life of six of the cars to be prolonged. Three dated from 1898, two from 1900, and one from 1899. These coaches were made up into two three-car sets and each set was modified to provide a push-and-pull unit to work with a steam locomotive at one end. To make them suitable for this duty the motor bogies were replaced by trailer bogies. The equipment was removed from the compartment, which reverted to a guard's van allowing the passenger accommodation to become four compartments. As originally built these coaches had two full-length stepboards, the lower one being at axle box level and the upper at the lower side of the solebar. These boards were removed when the stock was converted to electric working and only one replaced at the top side of the solebar. There was no need for double footboards after conversion to electric working as the trains then stopped at full-length high-level platforms. On the country services they previously worked it was sometimes necessary for passengers to board or alight from a train ahead of or behind the shorter platforms. The steam locomotives for the push-and-pull operations were always supplied by the main line, at first the London & North Eastern Railway and afterwards British Railways. The engine pulled the train in the Chalfont direction, and pushed towards Chesham when the driver used the compartment in the leading coach modified to take the remote controls for the engine at the rear. The fireman always remained with the engine to attend to the fire and the boiler.

Originally, it was intended to have three push-and-pull sets for this service, as it was suggested that reversal should be arranged at Rickmansworth so that connection could be made with the electric train service terminating there rather than with the Aylesbury steam train at Chalfont & Latimer. To do this two trains in steam with one spare would have been required. As this proposal was not implemented only one shuttle in steam was necessary, with a second train as a spare. Each set spent a week in service, being normally changed over on Sunday, to allow maintenance to be carried out at Neasden Depot.

The final steam working on the Chesham branch was the last train on Sunday/Monday, 11th/12th September 1960. This steam shuttle was replaced initially by a three-car formation of T stock and later P stock and finally, when sufficient new stock was available, by a four-car set of new A stock.

The steam shuttle cars, however, obtained a further lease of life as four of the vehicles were acquired by the Bluebell Railway and one by British Railways for preservation and eventual exhibition.

The Chalfont-Chesham 'push and pull' shuttle in the 1950s with an LMS class 2MT 2-6-2 tank locomotive and Bogie stock coaches.

The Met & Great Central Joint Committee

An H class locomotive with a six-coach train of Dreadnought stock climbing Chorley Wood bank.

On 1st July 1891 the Metropolitan Railway acquired the Aylesbury & Buckingham Railway, with which at that time it had no physical connection, as the main line did not reach Aylesbury until the following year. The Aylesbury & Buckingham line, which ran between Aylesbury and Verney Junction, was reconstructed and the tracks were doubled. This work was completed by New Year's Day 1879 and a through service of Metropolitan Railway trains from Baker Street to Verney Junction was introduced.

The Manchester, Sheffield & Lincolnshire Railway obtained powers in 1893 for an extension to London, which eventually joined the Aylesbury & Buckingham Railway about half a mile north of Quainton Road in 1898. Since 1st August 1897 this railway had, in fact, been known as the Great Central Railway, providing the last main line terminal to be built in London, at Marylebone. In order to reach this terminal the Great Central was granted running powers over the Metropolitan from Quainton Road to Canfield Place (adjacent to Finchley Road station). The section of the Metropolitan Railway from Quainton Road to Verney Junction became virtually a branch line, although this point remained the out-of-town terminus for Metropolitan trains until 4th July 1936, when the passenger service beyond Quainton Road was withdrawn.

From Harrow, the Metropolitan constructed two additional tracks alongside its own, without any provision for station platforms, as far as Canfield Place and these tracks were leased to the Great Central. From Canfield Place into Marylebone, however, the Great Central constructed its own tracks. Great Central passenger trains ran into the new terminal at Marylebone on 15th March 1899, although the full track quadrupling south of Harrow was not completed until 1901.

The railway north of Harrow was served by two companies, and this was given legal recognition on 2nd April 1906 by the formation of the Metropolitan & Great Central Joint Committee to which the line from Harrow-on-the-Hill to Verney Junction, including Chesham and Brill, was leased. This Joint Committee then became responsible for all the Metropolitan lines outside the electrified area. The Metropolitan & Great Central Joint Committee never owned any passenger rolling stock; the service was provided either by Metropolitan or Great Central trains.

The Joint Committee was administered by each railway company on a five-year cycle and after 1933 London Transport took over the Metropolitan Railway role. However the Joint Committee ceased to exist after nationalisation in 1947 and the lines as far as Aylesbury South Junction became the direct responsibility of London Transport.

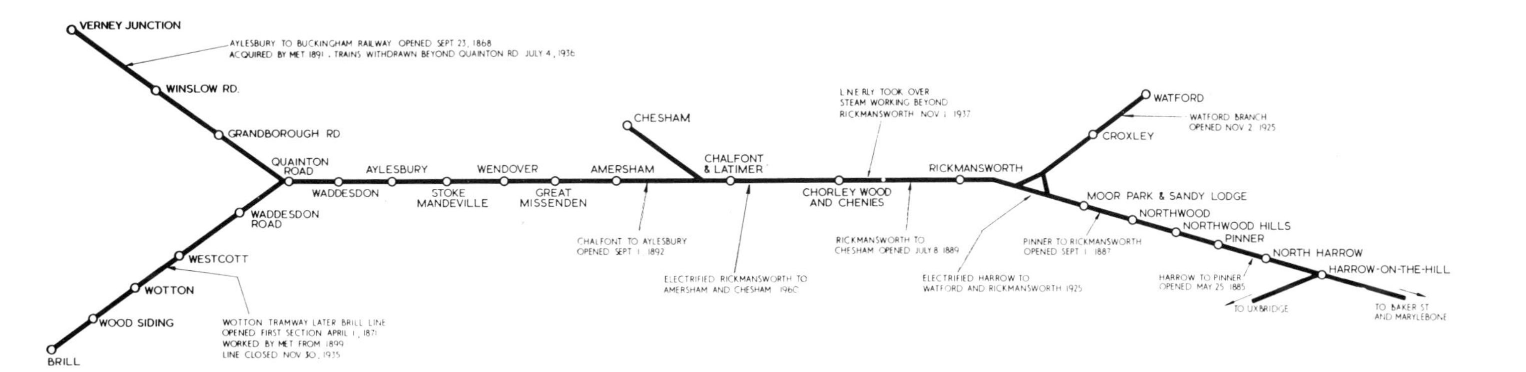

The development of the Great Central suburban services, with handsome trains of compartment stock, established a reputation for comfort and efficiency. The Metropolitan Railway, therefore, had to look to its laurels, and designed a new class of stock for the non-electrified territory which was immediately given the soubriquet 'Dreadnought'. They were both longer and higher off the ground—or to be more technical, 'from rail level'—than previous stock. They were also provided with semi-elliptical roofs. The fleet of Dreadnoughts eventually totalled 92, the last batch being built in 1923. Almost two-thirds of this total remained in service over the non-electrified lines of the Metropolitan until steam passenger service was eliminated on 9th September 1961 with the curtailment of the services of London Transport trains at Amersham.

The Dreadnoughts were 54 feet long having compartments with swing doors, provided with the familiar Metropolitan type rounded top to reduce damage if left open in the tunnels with restricted clearances. In addition the doorways were provided with fingerboards, used on the Metropolitan since the early 1870s to protect passengers' hands from injury from a hastily slammed door. These were sometimes incorrectly designated 'draught-excluders'. These vehicles were 9ft 9ins high over stepboards. One unusual feature for compartment stock was that groups of three compartments were connected by a gangway. This arrangement was introduced to spread the passenger load in the peak hours and help to reduce the station stop times at busy stations.

The first two rakes of the Dreadnought stock were provided in loose-coupled sets of five vehicles made up in the formation: B3T-3T-1T-1T-B3T and were rebuilt in 1910 from redundant First class control trailer cars built in 1905. These original vehicles were numbered from 419 to 428 in the Metropolitan number scheme, although there were four First Class coaches, four Third Class brake coaches, and two ordinary Third Class. These vehicles retained their numbers until they were withdrawn, as London Transport did not renumber the Metropolitan steam stock coaches. Twenty were built new in 1912, 42 in 1920, and a further 20 in 1923; some of these later vehicles changed subsequently to electric working.

Interior and exterior views of a Dreadnought Third Class coach built by Metropolitan Amalgamated in 1912. Groups of three compartments were linked by a central corridor.

Four locomotives of G class 0-6-4 Tanks were built by the Yorkshire Engine Company in 1915. They all were given names, No. 95 being named after the Metropolitan's general manager of the time, Robert H. Selbie.

The provision of steam coach heating and comfortable interiors made these vehicles of high standard, but they were not initially provided with electric lighting. The original trains of this stock were still equipped with Pintsch gas lighting using incandescent mantles instead of fantail burners. They were not converted to Stone's electric lighting system until 1918. The lighting control with this system retained pull-bar controls at the ends of the coaches.

More powerful steam locomotives were now required. The G class 0-6-4T type, of which four were built by the Yorkshire Engine Company, appeared in 1915, and these engines all received names as well as numbers. Three of the locomotives were named after personalities of the Metropolitan Railway of the time, Lord Aberconway, Robert H. Selbie and Charles Jones. The fourth was named Brill. Eight H class with a 4-4-4T wheel arrangement built by Kerr Stuart came in 1921. The last steam engines built for the Metropolitan Railway were six K class built in 1925 by Armstrong Whitworth, from parts originally made at Woolwich Arsenal. They were by far the largest and most powerful engines built for the Metropolitan Railway and were confined to duties north of Finchley Road, as they were out of gauge for tunnel working. The engines were 2-6-4T type and were mostly used on freight workings. The G, H, and K class locomotives were transferred to London & North Eastern Railway ownership on 1st November 1937, when this railway took over responsibility for the motive power for all goods and passenger trains north of Rickmansworth.

After the electrification extension to Rickmansworth, trains composed of 'Dreadnought' vehicles provided the steam stock trains running to Aylesbury and beyond. These trains were hauled by electric locomotives within the electrified territory and were criticised for causing delay to the service. This was partly due to the fact that the electric locomotives, with their short span for the collector shoes, became gapped at the numerous crossings when the train was travelling too slowly, particularly at Baker Street, Neasden and Wembley Park. These conditions made it necessary for the driver to shut off power to avoid snatching the couplings, and to prevent arcing. Complaints were, in fact, received during the First World War of violent flashing from these trains, infringing the black-out regulations, and experiments were then conducted providing a bus line to connect additional collector shoes farther down the train to the locomotive. The shoes were provided on the brake coaches so that one set was at the extreme end of the train.

This power bus line, which required jumper couplings between vehicles, was only provided on one side—the 'down' side (to use the Metropolitan Railway parlance), which thus made the brake coaches 'handed' so that they could only work at the 'down' or 'up' ends of the rakes. In general railway parlance the track leading to London was the 'up' track and that leading from London the 'down' track, so the 'down' side would be the left-hand side of a coach looking at it from the London end and the brake coach at the London end of the train would be at the 'up' end of the train. A small number of brake coaches were provided with bus line connections on both sides at the coupling end of the coach, so that by using the turntable provided at Neasden these coaches could be used at either end of the rakes.

From the introduction of trains of this kind, only First and Third classes of accommodation were provided, as Second Class was finally withdrawn from all Metropolitan Railway trains on 17th December 1906. This formation of five coaches provided 112 First Class and 202 Third Class seats. There were seven compartments in the First Class coaches and nine compartments in three groups of three compartments in the Third Class. The intermediate partitions in the groups of three compartments were only provided as high as the top of the quarter lights. In the brake coaches, which had seven compartments, some coaches had two groups of three compartments and one compartment with full partitions, and others possibly had a 2+3+2 arrangement. Doors were not provided in the gangway connecting the grouped compartments together.

The bogies, which were of pressed steel construction, had a wheelbase of seven feet set at 35ft centres. The wheels with full size tyres, were 36 inches in diameter.

The coaches were fitted with screw couplings and side buffers similar to those standardised in main line practice, and were equipped with automatic vacuum brakes. These trains were the first in Metropolitan Railway service to provide a passenger emergency alarm system; when the chain passing through each compartment was pulled, a valve in the vacuum brake pipe opened. This arrangement continued until the withdrawal of the vehicles.

A K Class 2-6-4 Tank, one of six powerful locomotives built by Armstrong Whitworth & Co in 1925, at the head of a Metropolitan Railway goods train before the formation of London Transport.

Electrification Experiments

The experimental electric train at Earl's Court in 1900.

The success of electric traction on the City & South London Railway encouraged both the Metropolitan and the District managements to give consideration to the improvement of travel conditions, especially on the Inner Circle. A proposal in 1896 that the Inner Circle service should be hauled by electric locomotives to eliminate the smoke nuisance was seriously considered. One of the few things that the Metropolitan and the District managements agreed about at this time was that any electrification proposals should be undertaken on a common system.

The Metropolitan Railway carried out its own electrification experiments at Wembley Park, but in 1898 joined the District in financing a joint experiment on the latter company's line from High Street Kensington to Earl's Court. A temporary generating station was built at Warwick Road, Earl's Court. Power was provided at 600 volts d.c. and supplied to two conductor rails arranged one on either side of the running rails. The position of these rails was 12½ inches from the gauge line (the gauge line being the inner edge of the nearest running rail) with the top surface for the collector shoe, contact being made at a position six inches above the top of the running rails. The provision of two conductor rails was probably arranged for two reasons. First, it was to avoid the need to improve the conductivity of the running rails through the fish plates and crossing connections and, secondly, to avoid interference with the block signalling apparatus by stray earth currents if the conductivity of the running rails was bad.

After considering the conversion of existing rolling stock for the experiment it was decided to purchase a brand new six-car train specially for the purpose. After numerous design arguments between the two railways a contract was placed with Brown, Marshalls & Company in May 1899, and it is interesting to note that the cars took only four months to construct, after which electrical equipment was installed by Siemens Brothers at the District Railway Works at Lillie Bridge.

The six-coach train consisted of two motor coaches and four trailer coaches. The trailers were not all identical; two contained six compartments and the other two had seven compartments. The motor coaches had a central gangway and a guard's compartment. The vehicles were lit by electric lamps, fed in series groups from the traction supply. Although up to this time the Metropolitan had been an advocate of the vacuum brake, the District's preference for the Westinghouse automatic brake prevailed.

The motor coaches were each equipped with four gearless motors, one on each axle, provided with four poles; 48-inch diameter wheels were fitted to enable the motor case to clear the track and this, in turn, necessitated the car underframe being raised about six inches over the bogies. The carbody floor was raised over the bogies and passenger access to this part of the vehicle was by a ramp from the centre position. Longitudinal seating was fitted over the bogies. The bogies had a wheelbase of seven feet.

Although a bus line was provided through the train, connecting all the collector shoes together on both motor coaches, no through control lines were provided, so that only the motor coach at the leading end was powered when the train was in motion. It is understood that one of the original conceptions of the proposed electrification scheme for the Inner Circle line was the provision of only one motor coach per train, fitted with a driving cab at both ends. This vehicle would then have been required to run round the train like a locomotive to reverse.

The four traction motors were controlled by a large spoked wheel which directly operated the switching contacts giving series, series-parallel and parallel combinations. Although electric braking was being incorporated into tramcar control designs at this time, braking was performed by a separate air brake control handle.

The motor coaches carried an air compressor to supply the air brake, sanding gear and the whistle with power. A voltmeter and an ammeter were also provided as part of the cab equipment, since the driver had to ensure that the current being taken did not exceed a certain maximum before selecting the next notch on the wheel controller.

The train ran for the first time on Saturday 9th December 1899, and began experimental public service on 21st May 1900. The very high fare of one shilling was charged for all classes, compared with the normal fares over this section of 2d, 3d and 4d for third, second and first class respectively. The train ran almost empty for a week, after which normal fares were charged.

The train was finally withdrawn from service on 6th November 1900 and the cars stored. Three became the property of the Metropolitan and three of the District. The District sold its vehicles to the Colne Valley & Halstead Railway while the Metropolitan placed the two trailer cars into the 'Bogie' stock fleet. The fate of the Metropolitan motor coach is not known.

The experiment appears to have been successful and both railways began plans for general electrification. The basic system of the experiment had been that of low-voltage direct current, rail-collected, at a potential of 500/600 volts which was already proving successful in America. This basic system had been adopted in London for the City & South London Railway and had just been installed on the new Central London Railway.

The joint electrification committee of the two railways was recommended to adopt two main power stations feeding opposite ends of the Inner Circle with direct current at about this voltage. The committee then issued a specification in 1900 which contained the following points:

1. A total of 220 'train miles' per hour to be operated with a seating capacity of 430 passengers per train at a speed to cover, running round the Inner Circle, a distance of 13 miles in 50 minutes making 27 stops;

2. The current conductors could be arranged either in the centre of the track with the whole network of running rails bonded together to provide the return path or by an independent pair of conductors insulated from the 'carrying ' rails;

3. Sixteen trains in service would be required to meet 220 train miles per hour, but these trains would be required to mix with other trains operated by steam from the branches.

Another view of the electric train, showing the positioning of the conductor rails.

EARL'S COURT EXPERIMENT

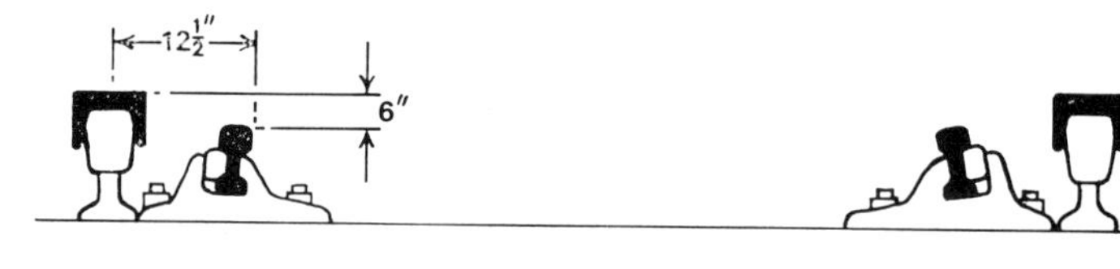

Diagram of conductor rail positions.

GREAT NORTHERN & CITY

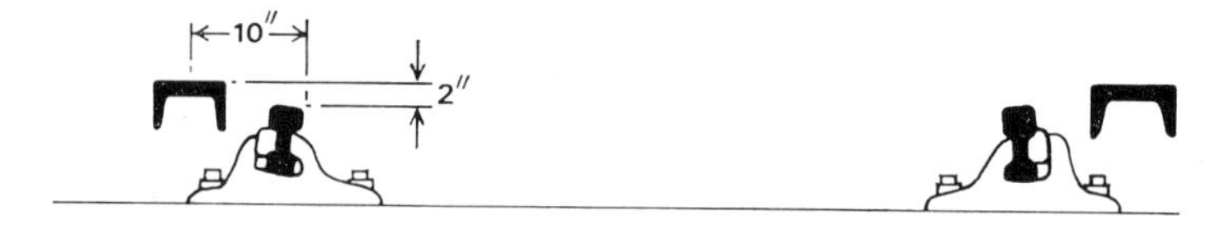

LT STANDARD

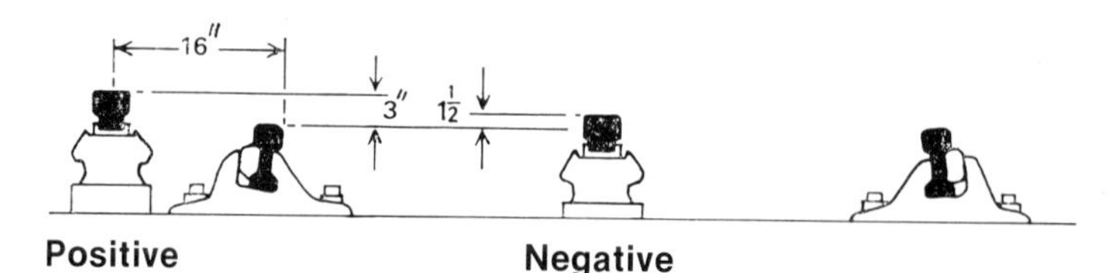

Nine different contractors submitted tenders, of which eight complied more or less with the very general specification; but that of Messrs Ganz & Co. of Budapest which was the lowest (being less than half the highest) did not. However in spite of this the electrification committee recommended the acceptance of this tender.

The Ganz tender proposed a 3,000 volt three-phase alternating current system with the power manufactured in a central power house at 12,000 volts and then transferred to five transformer substations located at South Kensington, Praed Street, King's Cross, Aldgate and Charing Cross (now Embankment) for collection by the trains from two overhead trolley wires over each track with the third phase provided by the running rails.

The main reason for the low tender was that new motor coaches only would be provided for hauling existing steam stock and the substations were simple and unmanned.

Each of the other tenders proposed different solutions.

The Electrical Construction Co. Ltd. proposed a direct current three-wire system with a voltage of 2,400 being provided across the extreme outers with four working substations at South Kensington, Edgware Road, Farringdon Street and Blackfriars to provide a potential difference of about 600 volts positive to earth and 600 volts negative to earth at the two separate conductor rails which gave 1,200 volts between the two as the power supply for traction. The actual positioning of the two conductor rails was not specifically defined but the power would be collected by electric locomotives which would haul the existing steam stock carriages.

Kummer & Co. proposed the generation of three-phase alternating current at 5,000 volts at a central power house with transmission by cable to two working substations at Gloucester Road and at Temple where conversion to 600 volts direct current would be arranged. The distribution to the trains was to have been by two-wire system with the running rails acting as the return feeder with the power feeder being a bare copper wire conveniently located, along which a trolley of some kind would run.

The British Thomson-Houston Co. Ltd. also proposed an alternating current system with a central generating station but producing three-phase current at 6,500 volts with conversion to 500 volts direct current at four substations located at the same points as those proposed by the Electrical Construction scheme.

The distribution to the trains was to be on the three-wire arrangement utilising two conductor rails in which the voltage between either and the running rails would not be greater than 500, one positive to earth and the other negative to earth, giving 1,000 volts between them for traction. The two conductor rails were to be placed one on either side of the running rails like the Earl's Court experiment.

The Brush Electrical Engineering Co. submitted an incomplete tender proposing two generating stations producing direct current at 1,500 volts on a three-wire system with no substations, with 750 volts to earth from each of the outer conductors. The system was further complicated by the fact that distribution was to be by a series of stud or contact strips placed on the sleepers which would be brushed by skates carried on the locomotives which would haul existing rolling stock.

Dick, Kerr & Co., one of the predecessors of the English Electric Co., proposed that alternating current at 5,000 volts should be generated at a central power station situated at Chelsea Creek and transferred to three substations for conversion to 500 volts direct current.

It was proposed that the transfer of the current to the trains could either be by a single conductor rail with running rail return or by two conductor rails arranged one above the other on one side of the track.

The British Westinghouse Electric and Manufacturing Co. Ltd., the predecessor of Metropolitan-Vickers Ltd., produced the most expensive tender, proposing a centralised generating station at Chelsea Creek producing three phase alternating power at 11,000 volts feeding three working substations at Baker Street, Aldgate and Westminster where conversion to 650 volts direct current would be undertaken. Transmission of power to the trains would either be achieved by a single conductor rail and running rail return or by using a second conductor rail to provide an insulated return.

In fact the method of current collection was of little consequence in the tender although subsequently this latter arrangement became the standard used in London. The Westinghouse tender also stated that existing rolling stock could be used with some saving in initial expenditure but they recommended the provision of new seven-car trains of corridor type so that passengers could move freely from end to end of the train.

Another tender was submitted by an English consortium of Mather and Platt Ltd., Siemens Brothers & Co. Ltd and the Thames Electrical Co. Ltd. This consortium also proposed a three-wire direct current system supplied by three power stations situated at Chelsea, Wapping and Praed Street, with three substations for balancing and equalising placed at High Street Kensington, King's Cross and Charing Cross. The motive power proposed by this consortium was the gearless type locomotive already operating on the Central London Railway to haul existing rolling stock.

Consulting engineers without any direct manufacturing resources J.G. White & Co. submitted a tender also proposing generation of alternating current at a central power house at 6,600 volts with three-phase distribution to three substations for conversion to direct current at 650 volts by rotary converters.

New trains would be introduced using the newly invented Sprague multiple unit control system because they did not recommend the use of locomotives even for the 'transfer of foreign trains' over the Inner Circle. They recommended that this should be achieved by coupling two of the proposed multiple unit motor cars together to form a 'locomotive'.

It is difficult, in retrospect, to understand the special attractiveness of the Ganz proposals except the price. At that time no electric railway was operating under such a system although one was under construction in Italy. Initially the scheme was accepted by the joint electrification committee of both railways, but the District subsequently withdrew its acceptance because by this time Charles Tyson Yerkes, the American traction financier, had acquired control. Yerkes' engineering advisers were not at all in favour of adopting an untried arrangement, in spite of the attractive price. The matter eventually was taken to arbitration.

The arbitration tribunal was headed by the Hon. Alfred Lyttelton, KC. The Metropolitan nominee was Thomas Parker and the District was represented by H.F. Parshall. After a hearing lasting about three weeks the award, made in December 1901, was in favour of the low-voltage direct current system.

The Metropolitan Railway had, by an Act of 1898, obtained powers to work its railway by electric traction and, as mentioned earlier, had conducted experiments at Wembley Park, quite independent of the joint experiment at Earl's Court. These experiments had been conducted under the direction of Thomas Parker, so that he was already very familiar with the general problems involved.

Several gentlemen gave evidence before the tribunal, many being in fact in favour of the high voltage AC system because it was thought that considerable difficulty would be experienced in providing an adequate supply of continuous current (as DC was then known) at a potential of only 500 volts. There was available at this time a lot of experience with 500-volt tramway systems, where it was the practice to use an overhead wire conductor for one polarity and the running rails for the other. It had been determined quite early that the troubles arising from earth leakage by such a system were minimised by making the overhead wire positive and the earth return through the running rails negative. In tramway systems the voltage drop was limited to seven volts to reduce the troubles caused by earth leakages, the electrolysis of water and gas mains, and especially telegraph systems. It was obvious that this limitation would apply to underground railways, especially the Inner Circle which was only just below street level. This factor was going to be a very onerous requirement involving the use of negative boosters to reduce the running rail voltage drop. The leakage current from an alternating current supply, especially of a three-phase system, would have caused negligible damage and this factor was one of the main points considered. The provision of two 'third' rails or the fourth rail system finally adopted avoided the necessity of meeting the seven-volt requirement in the running rails, and this system became standard for both the District and Metropolitan Railways and subsequently for London Transport.

Because of limited clearances the rail placed outside the running rails was fixed at 16 inches from the gauge line of the nearer running rail, but it was decided to place the rail of the other polarity in the centre of the track, which minimised the loss of supply at junctions and crossings. The normal arrangement is for the rail at the outside of the running rails to be at positive polarity with the surface contact three inches above the running rail level, and the centre rail at negative polarity having surface contact $1\frac{1}{2}$ inches above the running rail.

The District Railway determined to eliminate steam working altogether, while on the other hand the Metropolitan, with its country services, had a programme which limited electric traction to the more congested inner area, leaving the extension services to be worked by steam.

The District A Stock

An A stock train at South Harrow about 1903.
The driving position on these trains was unusual in being on the right-hand side.

The Ealing & South Harrow Railway had been incorporated in 1894 to build a line from South Harrow to join the District Railway at Hanger Lane. The railway was completed and fit for steam traffic in 1899, but no passenger service was operated. In 1900 this separate railway, which had not owned any rolling stock, was absorbed by the District and it was decided that the initial electrification work should be undertaken on this line.

A temporary generating station was constructed at Alperton near the Grand Union Canal, using the plant from the Earl's Court experiment, to supply power until the District Railway power house then being constructed at Lots Road, Chelsea, was opened.

The District at this time also electrified the tracks from Hanger Lane junction to Acton Town (then known as Mill Hill Park). The line, using electric traction from Mill Hill Park to Park Royal with a station at North Ealing, was brought into operation on 23rd June 1903 to provide a service for the Royal Agricultural Show which opened that day in the fields near that station. Five days later a service through to South Harrow began.

When the line opened a four-rail system was employed with the positive conductor placed outside the running rails 16 inches from the gauge line. This conductor was placed on either side of the running rails to suit convenience and safety.

Because the negative rail was not earthed it was considered that the outside positive rail could be placed closer to the running rail, at 16 inches, than had been the practice in the United States where by 1903 a considerable mileage of rail collection systems had been established. The line to South Harrow was also used to try out different equipment on the rolling stock and to train motormen for the general electrification then under way.

The A class comprised two seven-car trains built by the Brush Electrical Engineering Co. of Loughborough. The cars were 50¼ feet long and were basically of American design, bearing a striking resemblance to cars constructed about the same time for the Interborough Rapid Transit Company of New York. The choice of a seven-car train length seems to have been made because it was considered at the time that this was the maximum length of train which could be accommodated on the District Railway generally, without lengthening the station platforms.

These seven-car trains as originally constructed contained three motor cars and four trailer cars. The leading motor cars were different from those in the middle. The leading cars were provided with luggage compartments just behind the driving cabs and at the other end a platform with gates. The middle motor cars originally had gates at both ends with fold-up driving seats and a cabinet containing the master controller and brake valve, so that these cars could be driven from either end and operated as a single vehicle if necessary. The seven-car trains could be divided into smaller formations depending upon the position of the middle motor car.

The bodies were 8 feet 4 inches wide and had straight sides constructed of fireproofed wood, the roofs being lined with asbestos to reduce the fire risk. The appearance was enhanced by the provision of arched window frames. The leading motor cars had seats for 38 passengers, while the middle motor cars had 48, all in longitudinal seats, whereas the trailer cars seated 52 with some transverse seats. All the seats were finished in rattan. One trailer was upholstered in crimson velvet but the wearing properties of this material were very limited. Various external colour schemes seem to have been adopted but that best remembered by those old enough was a bright yellow picked out with maroon. No First Class accommodation was provided on these cars, but all were fitted with centrally-placed hand-operated sliding doors, in addition to the gates on the end platforms.

A special shed was built at South Harrow to look after the new electric rolling stock, and the new cars had their electrical equipment installed there.

One train was equipped with BTH type equipment and GE66 traction motors similar

The motor car of the same A stock train showing the trailer end with gates.

to the multiple unit equipments which had already begun to operate on the Central London Railway. This train, however, incorporated a 'dead man's handle' type master controller, following American General Electric practice already established on a number of railways operating in Chicago and New York.

The BTH equipment consisted of individual electromagnetic contactors controlled directly from the 600-volt traction supply without an accelerating relay so that the hand notching was under the direct control of the driver. This system was known at the time as the Sprague-Thomson-Houston System.

The Westinghouse arrangement used a low-voltage storage battery (14 volts) to provide the control, the driver's master control handle being a miniature thumb switch which provided three positions, shunting, series, and parallel, giving automatic acceleration under the control of a current limit switch.

Under the control of the low-voltage supply from the master controller, a circular contact drum underneath the car was notched by a pawl and ratchet system each time the current relay was released, accelerating the motors. Although the Westinghouse arrangements had a number of technical advantages such as low-voltage control, automatic acceleration, and a simple deadman's control, the BTH equipment proved more reliable and was adopted by the District as standard. The Westinghouse cars were subsequently converted to take BTH equipment, and at the same time all the motor cars of both trains were fitted with GE69 traction motors similar to those then operating on the Interborough Rapid Transit in New York.

Even the braking system of the two trains was different. The Westinghouse train was naturally fitted with the associated Westinghouse air brake, while the BTH train was originally equipped with the Christensen brake. These two systems were not dissimilar in their action, but the Westinghouse system proved the more reliable and was adopted as standard.

The trains were originally provided with sanding gear, probably needed from time to time to get up the Ealing Common bank. However, this apparatus was disconnected when it was found that too generous an application of sand to the rails interfered with the track circuits associated with the new automatic signalling system. This was a development of that first introduced in 1901 on the Boston Elevated Railway. Track circuit signalling was materially assisted by the use of the fourth rail traction system, which left the running rails clear of traction current so that they could be utilised exclusively for signalling requirements. The system required the running rails to be divided into insulated sections by means of block joints. A train or just a pair of wheels on any section caused the two running rails to be shorted together detecting the presence of a train. Incorporated with the track circuit was the train stop and tripcock. When a signal was at danger the train stop was raised and should the approaching train overrun, the tripcock would come in contact with the train stop, the brakes then automatically applied. This system, apart from the problems caused by sanding, was very successful and was adopted throughout the District, over the congested parts of the Metropolitan, and also on the Tube lines.

These cars later had a centrally-placed automatic coupler which was designed by an American engineer, one of the team directing the electrification. This mechanical coupler, known throughout its career as the 'Ward', has perpetuated its designer's name, because it became the standard coupling used by the Underground group of companies until the advent of completely automatic couplers. The Ward coupler only coupled the cars mechanically, as the electrical and pneumatic connections had to be completed by hand. At uncoupling it was necessary to unlatch both locking pawls by means of a shunting pole.

Subsequently some of the A class trailer cars were converted to control trailers by the provision of half a cab at one of the gate ends. The trains had a continuous bus line and originally all the bogies, even those on the trailer cars,

An A stock control trailer after rebuilding with half-cab and an improved shoebeam arrangement.

were fitted with shoegear. Subsequently the provision of shoes on control trailers enabled two- and three-car trains to be operated without the motor car becoming gapped. The collector shoes were originally suspended from the ends of wooden frames attached to the sides of the bogies. This arrangement was not satisfactory and it was replaced by a shoebeam suspended between the axle boxes.

The American influence set the pattern for the Underground group of companies. The vehicles were known as cars instead of carriages and for a time the bogies were known as trucks. The American term 'Motorman' was adopted for the driver. In addition the practice generally adopted in New York of having only one motor truck per motor car became standard on the District for a long time.

The A stock were confined throughout their life to operating at first the shuttle from Mill Hill Park to South Harrow and then, in 1905, from South Acton to Hounslow. The South Harrow shuttle trains were extended to Uxbridge over the Metropolitan Railway by the connection from South Harrow to Rayners Lane on 1st March 1910. The A stock cars were finally withdrawn in 1925.

A two-car train of A stock approaching Acton Town in May 1925 shortly before withdrawal. Two-car trains were normal on the District between South Acton and Hounslow and between Acton Town and South Harrow at this time.

The District B Stock

A Brush-built motor car of B stock at the manufacturer's works in 1905 before all of the equipment had been fitted. These cars were the first on the Underground to be fitted with air-operated doors; the operating cocks can be seen each side of the end communicating door. The system was unsuccessful and was withdrawn in 1908. As originally built, these cars were fitted with a luggage compartment; the door to this is seen at the far end of the car. The original body colour was 'engine lake' (maroon) with doors and window frames varnished to show the natural wood colour.

In August 1903, following the successful operation of the South Harrow line by electric traction, the District Railway placed orders for 420 new cars to electrify the whole system. These cars were to provide sixty seven-car trains, 12 containing four motor cars and 48 with three motor cars. The trains with four motor cars were intended to divide at Mill Hill Park into two portions, four cars to Ealing Broadway and three cars to Hounslow, each with two motor cars. However, this type of service did not materialise and the Hounslow service was maintained for many years by a shuttle working from South Acton composed of A stock. Actually, from 6th April 1906, the working of seven-car trains virtually ceased, the standard formation being a six-car train with three motor cars.

The new cars followed the basic American design with BTH traction equipment and GE69 type traction motors, arising from the experience on the South Harrow operations. Much to the chagrin of the English carbuilding industry, the order for 280 of these cars was placed with a French syndicate headed by Les Ateliers de Construction Du Nord de la France, with works at Blanc Misseron. Some of the cars (mostly the trailers) were, however, built at other works in France at Pantin, Ivry, St Denis, and Lunéville, each firm building its own bogies. The 140 cars built in England were constructed by Brush of Loughborough and the Metropolitan Amalgamated at its Ashbury and Lancaster Works.

All the cars were to be delivered by 1905 to what was originally known as the Mill Hill Park Works, which became Ealing Common Works but was later reduced to the status of a Depot after the completion of Acton Works in 1922. This depot had been constructed by the District Railway to look after the new electric rolling stock. Lillie Bridge, the original District Locomotive Works and Depot, was subsequently adapted in 1906 to look after the Piccadilly tube trains.

Both the English and Continental carbuilders were behind in deliveries. In spite of this electric services were inaugurated on 13th June 1905 between South Acton and Hounslow. A through service from Whitechapel to Ealing was operated by electric traction for the first time on 1st July 1905.

After delivery from the carbuilders the electrical equipment for the new cars was installed at Ealing Common. This was of the well-tried Sprague-Thomson-Houston electromagnetic type, one equipment on each motor car controlling two traction motors of the GE69 type placed in one motor truck; the other bogie of the motor cars was a trailer truck but carried collector shoegear.

The cars had wooden bodies 49ft 6½ins long with a width of 8ft 10½ins at the cant rail. Ventilators in the clerestory roof could be opened by means of a lever provided in the end vestibule. Rush-hour seats, of the flap type, were also installed originally in the end vestibules but these were later removed.

The cars were provided with double doors at the centre and single sliding doors at the end vestibules. These doors were originally fitted with pneumatic cylinders placed at the top of the doors to allow control by the gateman who rode on the car. Opening and closing was effected by means of a four-way cock manipulated by the conductor or gateman. There were four cocks positioned at waist level at each end of each car. Each valve controlled a separate door leaf. The gateman operated half the doors on one car and half those on the adjacent car by means of these cocks. This system did not work very well, being referred to at the time as a mechanical monstrosity. It was removed in 1908, the doors then being hand operated, with the double doors becoming a balanced pair—that is, the opening of one leaf of the pair automatically opened the other leaf. The original scheme of operation was for the end doors to be used for entrance and the middle doors for exit, but at times of heavy traffic this arrangement was impossible to control even with a conductor on every car. Communicating doors between the cars were provided over the middle buffers. These doors had windows with etched designs including the car number but once these windows were broken, or had to be replaced for any reason, plain glass was inserted.

Of the original 420 cars, 192 were motor cars and 228 were trailers. There were three types of motor car: end motor cars with a luggage compartment, end motor cars without a luggage compartment, and middle motor cars. The cars with a luggage compartment placed immediately behind the cab had a saloon seating 40 passengers. Only 20 cars were originally built in this way and these were subsequently reconstructed, converting the luggage space for passenger use.

The end motor cars without a luggage compartment had seats for 48 passengers entirely in longitudinally facing seats. There were originally 100 cars constructed in this way. Brush, Met Amalgamated and Lunéville each built 20 end motor cars while Blanc Misseron constructed 60.

The middle motor cars were provided with driving positions at both ends and two sets of companion seats in the middle of the body, which enabled these cars also to seat 48 within the passenger saloon. There were originally 72 cars of this type, 48 built by Lunéville and 12 each by Brush and Met Amalgamated. Eight of these cars were provided with partitions to segregate first and third class passengers, enabling a single car service to be operated between South Acton and Hounslow or South Harrow.

The trailer cars were similar in layout to the middle motor cars but they were built entirely of wood, while the motor cars had steel underframes on which the wooden bodies were constructed. The largest number of trailer cars, 68, were constructed at St Denis, while 42 each were built at Ivry Port and Pantin and the two English carbuilders each built 38.

Above Right A nine-car train of B stock in Ealing Common yard. *Right* A four-car train of B stock at Ealing Broadway in 1908, shortly after the original air-door equipment had been taken out of use. *Below* A Metropolitan Amalgamated B stock motor car on the traverser at Acton Works after conversion to take an A2 motor bogie. The car is seen in the new post-first world war livery of dark red body, grey doors and window frames, grey cantrail and roof, and black corner pillars and waistrails.

Three of the original motor cars were scrapped after being involved in collisions. The first one to be scrapped was in 1909 after an accident at Ealing Broadway. The train had entered service from Ealing Common Depot, running empty to Ealing Broadway to take up passenger working, and ran into the buffer stops with fatal result to a member of the crew. This accident arose from insufficient air being available to apply the brakes at a terminal station with buffer stops, and caused the introduction of one of the fundamental safety features on London's Underground, namely the control governor. The control governor then devised prevented forward movement of a train if insufficient air was available in the brake pipe to provide an efficient brake application. This equipment is now always installed as part of the safety control in all Underground trains.

In 1923 forty-two of the motor cars were converted to trailer cars when the G class cars arrived. Later, in the 1928/29 District Line modernisation programme, a further 110 motor cars were converted to trailer cars, but at this time some of the wooden trailer cars were scrapped. This conversion left only 37 of the original motor cars operating as such and at this time the original GE69 traction motors which had no interpoles were replaced with GE212 type, available when the Watford Joint Stock on the Bakerloo Line was scrapped in 1930.

Above Left The B stock, and the 1910/13 stock which followed, was originally fitted with pantograph-type protection barriers to prevent passengers falling between the cars. Chamfering of the car ends, to reduce the gap, was not employed until the 1920 F stock. *Left* Interior of a B stock end motor car with longitudinal seats divided by arm rests and with rattan upholstery. *Below Left* Interior of a B class middle motor car after retrimming with moquette seating, probably following its conversion to a trailer car. *Below* The original lifting shop at Acton Works in 1922. A GE69 motor is being lowered into an early A type motor bogie.

Of the 228 trailer cars, 32 were fitted with master controllers to enable them to act as control trailers. Twenty-one were double ended and eleven were only single ended. Eighteen of these vehicles were retained to work the local services to Hounslow, South Harrow, Uxbridge and sometimes on the Putney Bridge to Edgware Road service, surviving until the general scrapping of the B stock under the 1935/40 New Works programme. The trailer cars were scrapped in batches according to their condition, some when 1923 stock entered service, but the majority after the 1927/28 programme when most of the motor cars were converted to trailer cars. These cars, now trailers but originally motor cars, were themselves displaced in the 1935/40 New Works programme and scrapped.

As originally built, a pantograph-type barrier was provided to prevent passengers falling between the cars. These were also fitted on the 1910/13 stock. The interiors had a box-like appearance as very small windscreens were provided at the narrow centre doorways. The motorman's cab formed part of the end vestibule. The motorman was screened off by a partition. This half of the vestibule could not be used by passengers. The longitudinal seats were not originally provided with arm rests but most of the cars were subsequently fitted with these to ensure a fair distribution of the seating. The seats themselves were covered with rattan in the Third Class and plush in the First Class. The arm rests were covered with leathercloth. Carbon filament lamps provided the illumination, a very meagre form of lighting in comparison with present-day standards.

In addition to the clerestory roof ventilators, small side lights above the main lights could be pushed up by releasing a spring catch.

Power bus lines were provided so that all the collector shoes on a train were connected together. The jumper and air connecting hosepipes were below the headstocks but there was in addition a lighting jumper placed at roof level.

The original motor bogie of cast steel construction of American design, having a wheelbase of 6ft 6ins, carried the two GE69 traction motors. This bogie, designated the A type was not very satisfactory, fractures of the members being common and repairs being executed by thermit welding. Some of the 1905 motor cars were re-equipped with a plate and angle riveted type of truck which was designated the A2. This bogie became the standard for District Line motor cars for many years. These replacement bogies were constructed by the Leeds Forge Company.

The original trailer bogie suffered from the same basic defects. This bogie, designated the K type, was of equaliser bar construction and was replaced by the K2 constructed of plate and angles. This K2 bogie was one of the most successful ever designed, being practically trouble-free for its entire life, so much so that it was retained for further use on Metropolitan steam stock coaches and Circle Line trailer cars when the 1905 District cars were scrapped.

The A2 and K2 bogies were heavier than the original type and a B class motor car weight increased from 31.7 tons to 35 tons when fitted with the improved bogies. The brake power was also improved as the original trailer truck was only provided with single block rigging, whereas the K2 bogie had clasp-type double block brake rigging on all wheels.

Above View of Ealing Common depot from the Ealing end about 1921. A double-ended B stock motor car is seen in the foreground, with some new F stock further back.

B stock train at South Kensington in 1925.

Metropolitan Early Electric Stock

Six cars of the Metropolitan electric stock with gates and original livery.
The second and fifth cars are of the 1904 batch, the rest were built in 1905.
The 1904 cars were spare after the reformation of the original 10 seven-car trains
to six cars and were incorporated into the 1905 order to make up further six-car trains.
Part of the 1905 order was built with gate ends to allow operation with the 1904 cars
and the rest was built with enclosed ends, an example of which can just be seen in the background.

The Metropolitan, unlike the District, placed a number of separate orders for its rolling stock to cover the services to be electrified. There were a number of fundamental differences in the basic design of these cars compared with those ordered by the District.

The Metropolitan decided to have motor cars with two motor bogies, two sets of traction equipments, and four traction motors. The District motor cars had only one set of equipment, one motor bogie with two traction motors, and one trailer bogie. The Metropolitan vehicles, although open saloon type, were not originally provided with centre doors.

An order for 50 trailer cars was placed in 1902 with Brown Marshalls, but it was not until six months later that the Metropolitan Amalgamated Railway Carriage & Wagon Company, which had meanwhile absorbed Brown Marshalls, received an order for 20 motor cars. This delay in ordering the motor cars may have been due to the difficulty in deciding the type of electrical equipment to be installed.

In 1904 another contract was placed with the Metropolitan Amalgamated for 36 motor cars and 62 trailer cars, with an option for a further 20 motor cars and 40 trailer cars at the same price if ordered within a specified time. In the event, this option was taken up with the purchase of six additional motor cars making a total fleet of 82 motor cars, 76 First Class trailer cars, and 76 Third Class trailer cars, providing 38 six-car trains with six spare motor cars.

The original cars were 52ft 6ins long over the buffers, with a body width of 8ft 9ins. The motor cars had a full width cab at the leading end with an open platform enclosed by ironwork at the trailing end, while the trailer cars had open platforms at both ends. The gates in the ironwork at the platform side were controlled by levers operated by a gateman who could stand on the central buffer between the cars. The space between the gates on the platform side was protected by a 'lazy-tong' type barrier which was fixed to each car, adjacent barriers being fixed together when the cars were coupled.

The original 70 cars were intended to provide 10 seven-car trains, but due to inadequate platform lengths the train formation adopted was of six cars. The standard formation was then 3M-3T-1T-1T-3T-3M, all the motor cars providing Third Class accommodation. There were then 10 trailer cars surplus, and when the second batch of cars to make up 18 six-car trains was ordered, allowance was made to incorporate these 10 trailer cars from the original order.

By this time, however, a further complication had arisen. Two of the 10 trailer cars had been delivered with experimental end vestibules instead of gates. In order to match the eight trailer car with gates, a further eight motor cars and eight trailer cars were constructed with gates at the ends contiguous to the 1904 cars; that is to say, there were vestibules at the adjoining ends of the third and fourth cars only. There were then 14 six-car trains with gates.

Public service began on the Baker Street to Uxbridge line on 4th July 1904, but with steam traction. Beginning on 1st January 1905 some of the services were being operated by electric traction, and by 20th March 1905 the whole of the Uxbridge service was maintained by electric rolling stock.

By 1906 it was decided that gate ends were entirely unsuitable for service conditions involving operation in the open, and a scheme of conversion to end vestibules was undertaken. Some of the cars were converted at Neasden Works, but a contract was placed with Met Amalgamated for the modification of the bulk of the vehicles.

The cars were originally coupled in train sets by means of a plain link and pin, but the outer ends of the motor cars were provided with screw couplings. This type of block formation

One of the original Metropolitan Railway electric motor cars with gate end and no middle door, seen on the traverser pit at the carbuilders works

was considered a disadvantage, and so the cars were fitted with automatic mechanical couplings operating on similar principles to the District Ward coupling but not compatible with it. This coupling was known as the 'Buck Eye' and remained standard on Metropolitan Railway electric rolling stock.

It is understood that some difficulty arose with the Board of Trade Inspecting Officer concerning the proposal to work short trains from Harrow to Uxbridge in the off-peak, made up of three cars propelled in passenger service in one direction with the driver in the motor car in the rear. The objection was overcome by the provision of 'driving' trailer cars by equipping the first class trailer cars with a cab position and master controllers. The term 'driving trailer' was used thereafter by the Metropolitan Railway for this type of car, while the District and Tube railways used the term 'control trailer' for a vehicle performing this type of duty.

As originally built the cars were of the saloon type with end vestibules or platforms but without centre doorways, typical of American design of the period. Behind the driving cab in the motor car a luggage compartment was provided which had a sliding door into the passenger saloon. This saloon had seats for 48 passengers, which were arranged 24 longitudinally and 24 in three bays of double transverse.

The trailer cars had seats for 56 with three transverse bays in the centre and eight longitudinal seats on either side at each end. Double sliding doors were provided at the passenger gangway ends of the cars to gain access to the vestibules. Only two classes of accommodation were provided, with buffalo-hide seat covering in the Third Class and moquette in the First Class.

The lighting was arranged from the traction current supply with circuits of five lamps of 32-candle power in each series. In all, 20 lamps were fitted in pendants in the clerestory roofs, or from the cant rails—no shades were provided. About 4kw of heating from tubular resistance heaters were provided in motor cars, with a slight increase in the trailer cars.

The electrical equipment for the first batch of cars was ordered from the British Westinghouse Electric & Manufacturing Co. of Trafford Park. Each motor car was fitted with four Westinghouse type 50M traction motors providing about 150hp each. They were four-pole machines, nose suspended in the truck frames but had split motor cases. This motor drove the axle on which it was mounted by means of spur gearing with a ratio of 17/54, the motored wheels being 36 inches in diameter when new.

The traction control was the early Westinghouse electro-pneumatic type with the so-called 'turret' controller. The electro-pneumatic switches were arranged in a circle around a large coil which acted as a blow-out or arc-suppressing device for the main switch contacts. The multiple unit control of these turret controllers was arranged by means of a low-voltage circuit fed from a 14-volt lead-acid battery. This battery arrangement was replaced in 1908 by a small motor generator set, driven by the traction supply, and subsequently all Westinghouse equipped motor cars were fitted with two of these motor generator sets. Changeover switches to select either set could be operated by the driver when necessary.

A 1906 BTH motor car photographed in 1934. In common with the District stock of the same vintage, luggage compartments were a feature of this stock when built and lasted longer than those on District cars, not being taken out of use until takeover by the LPTB.

All the motor cars of the second batch were equipped with similar Westinghouse equipment, but by this time some dissatisfaction was being expressed as to its reliability and consideration was being given to adopting the BTH type of equipment favoured by the District Railway. The troubles with the Westinghouse equipments in fact resulted in the complete replacement of the turret controllers with a straight contactor bank of electro-pneumatic switches. Conversion to this type of equipment actually began in 1906.

Arising from the repair problems affecting motor cars it was evident that to keep trains in service some additional spare motor cars were required. An order for six additional motor cars was placed in September 1905, but the order for six motor car sets of Westinghouse equipment was cancelled in favour of a similar number of BTH. Westinghouse, however, would not accept the cancellation of the contract and the Metropolitan Railway had to take delivery of these equipments in addition, which were then taken into stock as spares.

Later in 1905 the optional order for a further 10 six-car trains was taken up, and this time BTH equipment was specified from the outset. The type of equipment ordered was similar to that already specified for the new Hammersmith & City Joint Stock, utilising GE76 traction motors with 150hp rating. The BTH Company at this time found that it could not meet the delivery requirements for this specification, and offered 56 traction motors of GE69 type with 200hp rating similar to those already provided for the District working. Including the six spare cars there were 26 double-equipped motor cars to be fitted, and this offer enabled 14 of the cars to be fitted out in this way, leaving 12 to have the equipment originally specified. The offer was made in the form that the GE69 equipments would be rented with the option to purchase, or be replaced by GE76 equipments, after the completion of the Hammersmith & City contract. In the event, the Metropolitan purchased the GE69 equipments. The first BTH-equipped train ran in service in April 1906.

The provision of two basically different equipments then provided an operating problem. The BTH equipments differed materially from the Westinghouse or BWE equipments as they were known, because the BTH used electro-magnetic contactors directly energised by control wire utilising the 600-volt supply, while the BWE used low-voltage electro-pneumatic contactors. The BWE system required nine control wires while the BTH system used ten. The two types of motor car could not, therefore, be connected in multiple. In addition, the two types of BTH equipment, although compatible in operation using the same system of control, were not normally matched in the same train because of the uneven distribution of power.

The majority of equipments were BWE, providing a total of 28 six-car trains. Thirteen BTH type six-car trains could be provided, seven with GE69 equipment and six with GE76, but not all these trains could be put into service at once because this total utilised all the six spare motor cars, and there were insufficient trailer cars to make up more than a total of 38 six-car trains.

The 1904 stock, which was entirely composed of BWE-equipped cars, had been provided with nine-core jumper connections down both sides known as the 'Up' and 'Down' sides, enabling individual cars to be turned end-for-end. The turning of trailer cars was rarely necessary, and subsequently trailer cars were provided with the ten-core BTH system on the 'Up' side and the nine-core BWE system on the 'Down' side. Trailer cars so equipped could be operated in either type of train. It was subsequently appreciated that the BTH ten-core, which had to be insulated for 600 volts, was the more important electrically, and could be used for low voltage without detriment if suitable cable adaptors were provided, enabling a nine-core jumper to be coupled into a ten-core socket. The BWE nine-core was then not renewed when any rewiring was necessary, all repair provisions being based on the BTH ten-core arrangement on trailer cars. It was not possible, of course, to use BWE-equipped driving trailers as operating units for BTH trains, but the provision of ten-core jumper sockets enabled them to be marshalled in block six-car formations, with BTH motor cars at the outer ends if necessary.

The motor cars had pressed steel frame bogies with a 7ft wheelbase, and the original cars were fitted with oak shoebeams mounted transversely across the frames. The beams placed at the outer ends of each bogie carried negative as well as positive shoes. In addition, on the inner end of one bogie a short beam carried a negative shoe. The motor cars, therefore, had four positive and three negative shoes. In addition to the control lines a positive and negative bus line was carried down the train to enable the collector shoes to be coupled together, and collector shoes were subsequently fitted to driving trailers. This shoebeam arrangement on motor cars was subsequently altered to the conventional arrangement, having the positive shoebeam mounted between the axle boxes, after difficulty had been encountered on the District section of the Circle.

Both types of train were provided with an 8G2 type Westinghouse compressor, supplying compressed air at 60psi, which was used for the Westinghouse 'quick acting' air brake as well as traction control on BWE-equipped trains. The brakes were applied on each car by means of a large single brake cylinder acting through rigging to the blocks on each wheel. In addition to the driver's brake valve, an emergency valve was provided on each car adjacent to the conductor's or gateman's position.

The door arrangement at the vestibules was rather elaborate. A hinged door was provided over the buffer plate and twin sliding doors between the saloon and the vestibule. The hinged door was subsequently converted to a sliding door and the twin sliding doors removed altogether. The only access to the station platforms was through single sliding doors on each side of the end vestibules. This arrangement proved to be unsatisfactory on the busy Circle service, and the Metropolitan contemplated converting the cars to compartments—compartment stock was considered much superior for quick loading and unloading. In 1911 work began on the provision of centre sliding doors and on altered seating arrangements. The work entailed was considerable and several different versions were produced. The seating capacity of the motor cars was generally reduced to 38 and the trailers to 48. The sliding doors were fitted with self-acting lock mechanisms which enabled the number of conductors carried on the trains to be reduced to two and finally to one guard. By 1927 the traction motors on the BWE trains became a maintenance liability and these cars began to be converted to trailers to operate with new motor coaches. The replacement of the original electric stock did not commence until 1936.

Original Metropolitan electric stock bogie with shoebeams placed at the outer ends.

Electrification of the Circle Lines

Initially, both the Metropolitan and the District provided rolling stock for the operation of the Inner Circle electric service. The Met later became the predominant operator and one of the original 1904 stock trains that would have appeared on the Circle at the time of its electrification is seen on the Met main line. The shoegear fitted is of the original type which caused problems on the District section of the Circle and which had to be modified.

The introduction of electric traction on the Inner Circle was arranged for 1st July 1905. The operation was planned on a similar basis to that which had been worked under steam traction. The Metropolitan would provide all the trains on one rail and some trains on the other because it owned the greater mileage. The Metropolitan's electric service began on 1st July, but was withdrawn later on the same day. The District began its Ealing-Whitechapel service on the same day, serving the southern part of the Circle.

Soon after the service commenced, three 'disasters' occurred which caused traffic through the central area to be dislocated. A derailment at Mill Hill Park and flooding at Hammersmith caused the District main line services to be seriously delayed, while a Metropolitan Circle train overturned the positive current rails in District territory, interrupting the Circle service. This latter incident was attributed to the Metropolitan type shoegear which was mounted outside the bogie frames, allowing the positive shoegear to alter its position relative to the rail on curves. This arrangement had not been properly taken into account on the District section of the railway, and all the Metropolitan trains had to be withdrawn and the shoegear modified. The District trains did not suffer from this malady because the positive collector shoe was mounted on a shoebeam suspended between the axle boxes.

Until the difficulties were sorted out between the two railways the Metropolitan trains were confined to working a shuttle service from Aldgate to South Kensington on its own tracks. This shuttle service worked alongside a restored steam service until September, by which time the Metropolitan had altered the positive shoegear on the 12 trains required to maintain their part of the joint service. The Metropolitan placed two electric trains on the outer rail on 13th September and one on the 14th. The District added two trains three days later, two more on the 19th, and one on the 20th. The full electric Inner Circle service began on 24th September. The last steam train operated on the Inner Circle service on 22nd September 1905.

The traffic did not increase to the desired extent with the introduction of electric traction, and the District announced that it wished to reduce its trains operating the service to four-car formations. As the payments between the railways were adjusted on a car mile basis, the District also wished to raise the additional charges for energy consumed by the six-car Metropolitan trains on the District section on the south side of the Inner Circle between South Kensington and Aldgate. The Metropolitan, instead of agreeing to these increased charges, also reduced the train formation to four cars. This reduced length was retained until 1918, when the formation was increased to five cars.

From 1907 most of the Metropolitan trains were made up with four-car sets, having one GE69 type motor car at one end with a driving trailer at the other. The balance of the Circle trains had to be made up with two motor cars of the GE76 type to give the required performance. The use of the sets with only one motor car caused some difficulty to First Class passengers, whose accommodation was also provided in the driving trailer. It was never possible, therefore, to anticipate whether the next train would be arranged with the driving trailer leading or trailing, and First Class passengers were seriously inconvenienced. Some further difficulties in the provision of the Circle service arose and eventually, after considerable negotiations, the Metropolitan took over the entire weekday working of the Inner Circle service from 4th November 1907. This strained the electric rolling stock position of the Metropolitan which, in turn gave impetus to the conversion of surplus steam stock to electric working.

The District, on the other hand, now had surplus rolling stock and introduced service changes which included the lengthening of a number of District Railway trains.

After the rebuilding of Edgware Road station with four platforms, a Putney Bridge to Edgware Road service was introduced using District rolling stock. This commenced on 1st November 1926 and the operation of District trains on the Inner Circle service ceased at the same time. Three trains continued to operate on Sundays however to enable a nucleus of District crews to be kept familiar with the road.

At the time of the electrification there were two 'foreign' railway services on the Circle tracks; the southern half of the Outer Circle provided by the London & North Western Railway on the District section, and the through suburban trains to the city provided from Paddington by the Great Western Railway on the Metropolitan section.

The Outer Circle service began in 1872 from Broad Street by way of Willesden Junction and Addison Road (now Olympia) to Earl's Court and then over the District tracks to Mansion House. This service was worked entirely by the London & North Western Railway with its own rolling stock and locomotives. To avoid the retention of steam engines on this service the District arranged to provide electric locomotives for hauling the London & North Western trains between Earl's Court and Mansion House. The steam locomotives continued to operate this service until 4th December 1905 when the electric locomotives took over, engines being changed at Earl's Court.

For this duty the Metropolitan Amalgamated Railway Carriage & Wagon Co. built ten electric locomotives which normally worked in pairs. These vehicles, built of steel, weighed 38 tons and had box-like bodies just over 25 feet long to house the traction control equipment. Each locomotive was provided with two sets of traction control equipment which controlled four GE69 type traction motors, each pair being separately operated in series/parallel by the multiple unit control.

On 1st January 1909 the Outer Circle service was cut back to Earl's Court, as the District wanted the train paths for its own services which had been increased when the track improvements were completed west of Hammersmith. The District locomotives were then rendered redundant and three were scrapped in 1911. For a short time some trains were made up with one of these locomotives at each end of a rake of four trailer cars. However, negotiations had been completed with the London, Tilbury & Southend Railway for a through train service to be operated from the western suburb of Ealing to Southend and Shoeburyness. The Tilbury line provided two special train sets to operate this through service, the trains being hauled between Barking and Ealing Broadway by the District locomotives again coupled in pairs. There were now three pairs with one locomotive spare. The through Southend service lasted from 1st June 1910 until 30th September 1939, after the outbreak of the Second World War.

The locomotives were renovated in 1922 when the GE69 equipments, including the traction motors, were replaced by GE260 type surplus from the F stock. This reconditioning work was one of the first such jobs undertaken in the newly constructed Acton Works.

To enable the through suburban services of the Great Western to continue operating from Paddington to the City the Metropolitan also provided some locomotives from the same builders, but these locomotives were required for other duties and their more complicated story requires separate treatment.

The last steam-hauled passenger service through Baker Street on the Circle section was operated on 31st December 1906, when the through Richmond service worked by the Great Western was cut back to Notting Hill (now Ladbroke Grove). On 1st January 1907 electric locomotives began hauling through Great Western trains from Bishop's Road to Aldgate and this type of working continued until the Second World War caused withdrawal of the arrangeent on 16th September 1939.

Neither of these through workings was restored, although Metropolitan locomotives continued to haul 'steam' stock from Liverpool Street over the north side of the Circle on the Metropolitan country services until September 1961.

Below Electric locomotive No. 1A in original condition with plug type tripcock on the truck headstock and not the shoebeam. *Bottom* Interior of District electric locomotive looking towards a driving end. Some of those locos had driving controls at both ends to allow them to be used for depot shunting.

The Hammersmith & City Line

Hammersmith station, Hammersmith & City Railway, about 1870 with Met loco No. 4. Note the provision of both broad and narrow gauge tracks.

In 1861 the Hammersmith & City Railway was incorporated as an independent venture to act as a feeder to the Metropolitan Railway, and made working arrangements with both the Metropolitan and Great Western Railways. It was vested in the two companies jointly on 1st July 1867. The line was constructed of mixed gauge joining the Great Western tracks about a mile west of Paddington. Initially the Great Western supplied broad gauge rolling stock and motive power, beginning a service between Hammersmith and Farringdon Street on 13th June 1864, just 17 months after the Metropolitan Railway itself became revenue earning. The Metropolitan Railway took over the Hammersmith to Farringdon workings with standard gauge trains on 1st April 1865. Meanwhile a branch from the Hammersmith line to the West London line had been built, with the junction at Latimer Road station to enable trains to operate to Kensington (Addison Road). At first through carriages were detached at Notting Hill and later at Latimer Road, but subsequently the Great Western began working the Middle Circle service over this route on 1st August 1872. The trains then operated from Moorgate to Paddington, proceeding over the Hammersmith & City tracks to Latimer Road and so, by way of this new connection, to Kensington (Addison Road) and on to a junction with the District which enabled through trains to continue to Earl's Court and Mansion House. On 30th June 1900 this service was curtailed at Earl's Court, but it was still operated by Great Western trains. On 1st February 1905, however, the service was taken over by the Metropolitan and ran between Aldgate and Addison Road only. From 3rd December 1906 the service was operated entirely by electric rolling stock, but on 31st December 1910 was reduced to a shuttle from Edgware Road to Addison Road. This service ceased to operate on 21st October 1940 when the junction at Latimer Road with the West London Line received severe damage in an air raid, and was not considered worth reinstating under war-time conditions. The service was never resumed, and this connecting link was subsequently removed.

The station at Westbourne Park was not opened until 1st February 1866 and was rebuilt on 1st November 1871. The line at this point actually crossed the main Great Western Railway tracks on the level and as the frequency of the services on the Hammersmith & City Line was increasing an underpass was constructed which was brought into service in May 1878, carrying these trains under the main line to reach Bishops Road where the junction with the Metropolitan Railway was made.

A junction was built at Grove Road, Hammersmith, with the London & South Western Railway's connection to the West London line which had been opened to traffic on 1st January 1869. The Metropolitan Railway began to run trains through from Moorgate to Richmond by way of Grove Road junction and Turnham Green on 1st October 1877. The District had begun working to Richmond on 1st June 1877. One half of the Metropolitan service was taken over by the GWR on 1st January 1894, but after the electrification of the Metropolitan it was cut back to Notting Hill (which became Ladbroke Grove on 1st June 1919) and a half-hourly service was maintained until 31st December 1910. Trains on the Richmond service are said to have been the last steam-hauled passenger trains through Baker Street station, ceasing to operate on this section from 31st December 1906. In any event, during November and early December 1906, the Hammersmith & City Railway services were changed over completely to electric traction—5th November 1906 is the official date for the commencement of electric traction on the line. The District Railway did not encourage the electrification of the Grove Road connection, which would have allowed Hammersmith & City trains to run to Richmond by impressing the London & South Western Railway it could take up all the possible timetable paths available on the two tracks between Hammersmith and Turnham Green.

Trains from Hammersmith ran over the northern section of the Inner Circle to Bishopsgate from 1st July 1875 and then to Aldgate from 18th November 1876, being extended over the East London Railway to New Cross from 6th October 1884. But after electrification, which did not include the East London Railway, this service ceased on 2nd December 1906, and the trains were diverted to Whitechapel. After 31st March 1913, when the East London Line was electrified, a through service began again.

The steam-hauled rolling stock originally used on the Hammersmith & City Railway was supplied by either the Metropolitan or the Great Western. After 1867 the railway was managed by a Joint Committee of the two companies and powers were obtained in 1902 for electrification.

The service over the Hammersmith & City Railway in 1901 consisted of six trains per hour, one of which was extended to Richmond by way of Grove Road Junction. In addition three trains per hour, worked jointly by the Metropolitan and Great Western Railway, operated to Addison Road until 1st November 1910 when the service was cut back to work as a shuttle service from Edgware Road and the Metropolitan Railway provided a double-ended electric motor car for this working.

In the City direction the trains terminated at Aldgate, but after 9th February 1914 three Hammersmith trains (now electric) were extended to New Cross (SE & C) replacing a service which had been worked from South Kensington by way of Baker Street.

The Great Western built a power station at Park Royal and maintained and operated the substations. There were substations at Royal Oak and Shepherd's Bush, and these were equipped with La Cour type converters, a system different from any other traction sub-station then being installed in London. The La Cour converter consisted of two machines which were coupled together like a motor generator set, but also coupled electrically in a circuit known as cascade. The current induced in the rotor of the motor was fed to the armature of the generator and thereby converted to direct current, a system which was in fact half way between a pure motor generator set and a rotary converter.

This system had been adopted because the Great Western power station generated alternating current at a frequency of 50 cycles (hertz) and it was considered that rotary converters for a traction load might be unstable at this frequency. The system was never used elsewhere on the Underground. Another uncommon feature of these sub-stations was the provision of a balancing battery to take up overloads.

This arrangement should have helped the introduction of regeneration to the rolling stock but when such a system came in 1936 it unfortunately proved too fierce and the operation of these substations proved troublesome. Regeneration over the Hammersmith & City section therefore had to be limited.

Returning to 1906, the new electric rolling stock was operated in the name of the Joint Railway, but some vehicles were the property of the Great Western and others the Metropolitan. The Metropolitan, however, maintained all the vehicles and operated the running shed. The rolling stock required for the Hammersmith & City electrification and the through service to Whitechapel consisted of 20 six-car trains. After the extension of the service to the East London line this total proved inadequate, and some Metropolitan rolling stock was transferred to the H & C.

The order for the rolling stock was placed with the Metropolitan Amalgamated Railway Carriage & Wagon Co. and was provided in six-car sets operated in the formation 3M-3T-3/1T-1/3T-3T-3M. The cars were all of the open saloon type and the motor cars were, in the Metropolitan days, provided with small luggage compartments. Smoking was permitted in the motor cars, in the Third Class positions of the composite trailers and one of the First Class saloons. The vehicles were 52ft 7¾ins long (when coupled) and 8ft 9ins wide.

The traction control equipment provided was BTH GE76 type, each motor car being provided with two sets of equipment and four 150hp traction motors. The cars, finished in Metropolitan style, were varnished teak and the cant rail and waist rail in white, but in addition to a monogram with H & C on the side panels they originally had the names of the two railways on the upper panels; it seems that on one side 'Great Western & Metropolitan Railways' was displayed and on the other 'Metropolitan & Great Western Railways'. In 1908/9 provision was made for the division of each train into three-car sets for working in the slack hours. Not only was it necessary to install control gear on the composite cars but additional partitions had to be erected to provide First Class passengers with smoking and non-smoking accommodation in each car. Scarcely was this work completed when complaints arose, as on the Inner Circle, concerning the unpredictable position of the First Class saloon. It was considered undesirable to reposition the control equipment, so the expedient was adopted of interchanging the complete furnishings of the composite and the Third Class trailers. The make-up of a six-car train now became 3M-3/1T-3CT-3CT-1/3T-3M.

The First Class accommodation provided on these trains was withdrawn on 4th May 1936, when the peak-hour service was extended to Barking and some additional new rolling stock of District type was provided to augment the fleet. The 20 six-car trains had been increased by a further four of Metropolitan 150 GE76 type by 1930, and these remained part of the H & C fleet until withdrawn for disposal. Due to war conditions arising in 1938/39 many of these trains were stored or converted for other purposes. In fact four six-car trains, of which 18 cars out of the 24 came from the original H & C stock, were lent to the Mersey Railway from 1942 until 1945 to provide additional facilities for maintaining the vital link under the Mersey in war conditions.

Above left a six-car Hammersmith & City stock electric train as originally built, photographed at Hammersmith depot. These cars carried the title 'Great Western & Metropolitan Railways' on one side and 'Metropolitan & Great Western Railways' on the other. *Left* Side view of an H&C stock motor car when new. Centre sliding doors were added to these trains between 1918 and 1921, the work being carried out concurrently with that on the last of the 1904/5 stock cars to be modified in this way.

The East London Line

A four-car train of saloon stock, with a single 200BTH type motor car, at New Cross (SER) station in 1913.

In 1818 Marc Isambard Brunel patented a tunnelling shield and joined a consortium which formed a new company, the Thames Tunnel Company, to build a tunnel under the Thames between Wapping and Rotherhithe.

Brunel's tunnelling shield was the first of its kind in the world, and the development of this device eventually made possible the building of all London's Tube railways. The building of the first tunnel by this means, however, was an epic of endurance and perseverance, a story which has been told many times, but for the purpose of this history it suffices to record that it was completed and brought into use as a pedestrian subway on 25th March 1843. The intended approach roads for vehicles were never built and at this stage the subway was largely a wasted effort.

In 1865 this tunnel was acquired by the East London Railway Company. Trains first ran through the tunnel in 1869, when a service from New Cross (now New Cross Gate) to Wapping was begun on 7th December by the London, Brighton & South Coast Railway. On 10th April 1876 the line was extended northwards from Wapping to Shoreditch, where a junction was made with the Great Eastern Railway enabling the trains to be run into the Liverpool Street terminal of that railway from south London. The LBSC ran trains from East Croydon, and for eight years from 1876 trains ran between Brighton and Liverpool Street over this route.

There were six intermediate stations, at Deptford Road (renamed Surrey Docks in 1911), Rotherhithe, Wapping, Shadwell, Whitechapel, and Shoreditch. The line was double throughout except at New Cross where only a single platform was provided. The spur to the New Cross station of the South Eastern Railway was opened to traffic on 1st April 1880, and this railway ran trains into Liverpool Street from Addiscombe Road.

The East London Railway obtained powers to build the Whitechapel Junction Railway to join the joint District and Metropolitan Extension Railway, which had been formed to complete the Circle Lines.

The Whitechapel Junction Railway was the first section to be completed and the South Eastern Railway trains on the East London Line were transferred to a new station at St Mary's on 3rd March 1884. Subsequently, on 6th October 1884, Metropolitan steam trains began to work to the New Cross station of the South Eastern Railway, and the District to the New Cross station of the London, Brighton & South Coast Railway. This latter station was renamed New Cross Gate in 1923, after the formation of the Southern Railway. 6th October 1884 was also the day that public traffic began over the last section of the Inner Circle, and on the extension to Whitechapel where the District had built a terminal station above the East London Railway station.

The Metropolitan trains worked from Hammersmith (Hammersmith & City Railway station) to New Cross round the north side of the Circle while the District trains worked from Hammersmith (District Railway station) round the south side of the Circle.

The District steam trains were withdrawn on 31st July 1905 as the East London Railway was not included in the electrification schemes. The Metropolitan steam trains ceased on 2nd December 1906 following the electrification of the Hammersmith & City. Steam passenger services, however, were continued by the two southern railways—the LBSC to Shoreditch and the SER to Whitechapel.

The East London Railway decided that the shuttle steam services were unsatisfactory and wanted to provide through services to the City again, so a decision was made to electrify the line. Part of the agreement on the electrification scheme provided for the District to supply the power from Lots Road Power Station and for the Metropolitan to supply the train service. The East London Railway in fact never owned any rolling stock.

The service, after the introduction of electric traction on 31st March 1913, consisted of a number of four-car trains of Metropolitan open saloon stock from South Kensington round the Metropolitan side of the Circle to New Cross, and two-car shuttle trains operating from Shoreditch. To provide the appropriate accommodation in the two-car shuttles the Metropolitan converted ten of the First Class trailers into composite First and Third Class driving trailers. Three were originally First Class control trailers, four were originally First Class trailers without controls, and the other three were originally Third Class trailers, also without controls. They were numbered 1 to 10 in a new sequence after conversion, as the Metropolitan generally had a separate series of numbers beginning at 1 for each class or type of car. In 1914 the Metropolitan South Kensington trains were withdrawn and the Hammersmith & City service was diverted from Whitechapel to New Cross in their place.

In 1921 the Metropolitan Railway took over management but in 1925 freehold of the East

London Railway was acquired by the Southern Railway (subject, of course, to the 1884 lease). In recognition of this the Metropolitan type nameplates used on the stations were changed from a red lozenge behind the name to a diamond coloured green. After the formation of London Transport in 1933 the line continued to be owned by the Southern Railway. The passenger service continued to be provided by Hammersmith & City rolling stock but the service pattern was altered on 4th May 1936 when first class travel was discontinued on the Hammersmith & City Railway. The through Hammersmith service became peak hours only with the regular East London service being provided by shuttle trains from Whitechapel. On 6th October 1941 the through Hammersmith trains from New Cross stations ceased altogether and St Mary's junction was then closed to public traffic. The spur at New Cross ceased to be used for freight traffic on 1st December 1940, but the connection at New Cross Gate continued to provide an entrance for freight trains until 1st October 1962.

After nationalisation in 1948 the line passed to the control of London Transport completely.

The first District electric trains to work on the East London Line were B stock which began running on the shuttle duties in May 1937. The trains subsequently transferred for shuttle duty on the line were four-car sets of District Line hand-worked door stock, which were eventually designated H class, and the general rolling stock maintenance was transferred from Neasden to Ealing Common. However, one unit used on the service was still maintained by Neasden and was of considerable interest, being a three-car set containing two experimental motor cars having the prototype equipment for the T stock together with the trailer car displayed at the 1924/25 Empire Exhibition at Wembley. This train set continued to work on the East London Line until scrapped.

The transfer of the F stock to the Metropolitan began in 1950 and arrangements were made for this stock to work the East London service. The hand-worked door stock was replaced by F stock by 7th December 1953. These sets had to be adapted by the provision of 'loudaphones' in the single-equipped motor cars, because through communication of this kind was not previously provided in the driving cars normally placed in the middle of an eight-car train. About eight four-car units were available for working the East London service although only six, including spares, were required to be allocated to the line at one time.

The Metropolitan had provided engine and carriage sheds at New Cross for their steam services but these had become disused after the withdrawal of the through trains on 2nd December 1906. This small depot was again brought into use but was only suitable for examination and basic cleaning work as the facilities were minimal. Cars requiring repairs or detailed inspections had to be returned to a major depot. With the advent of the F stock, cars were again returned for maintenance work to Neasden. The F stock was withdrawn from the East London Line in September 1963 when four-car Q stock trains began working on it.

Initially any available four-car set of Q stock could be allocated for duty on the East London service, the four-car sets being returned to Ealing Common Depot in rotation on a daily basis. Subsequently, after delivery of the C69 stock enabled the transfer of sufficient COP stock from the H & C Line to enable the Q stock to be withdrawn from District Line service, seven four-car trains of Q stock made up with the remaining Q38 motor and trailer cars, specially rehabilitated, were specifically allocated for service on the East London Line. An additional hand brake had to be provided at the guard's position on the 'D' motor cars to allow Q38 cars to operate in four-car sets. These sets began working the East London service in May 1971, allowing the older Q stock cars to be withdrawn and scrapped. Subsequently after the transfer of all the CO/CP stock to the District Line five-car units of this stock began working on the East London Line on 18th September 1971 with the maintenance continuing at Ealing Common.

Due to a variety of reasons it became difficult to provide the District Line service requirements out of the allocated fleet of COP and R stock. It was therefore decided to increase the float of rolling stock by withdrawing the five-car units of CO/CP stock from East London Line duty and provide the service with other rolling stock.

With the introduction of new 1972 tube stock trains on the Northern Line, the withdrawal of 1938 tube stock was in progress, so arrangements were made for additional four-car units of this stock to be allocated to Neasden Depot and for this depot once again to supply the operational units for the East London Line. Eight 1938 tube stock units were specifically allocated to provide this duty. Five units were required for service; one was held as a spare at New Cross Depot, and two others at Neasden for general maintenance. While this latter allocation was more generous than previously arranged, it enabled the changeover of units to and from the East London Line and for heavy maintenance to be undertaken without affecting the actual reliability of the train service. On 13th January 1974, four-car units of 1938 tube stock began working the line after some civil engineering work had adjusted platform heights. The use of 1938 tube stock on this service, however, was not popular with the public because passengers had to step down into the vehicles and step up to the platforms, in spite of the raising of the track to accommodate the low tube train height, and because the carriage of bicycles and prams became prohibited by tube train operations.

There had been over the years since the introduction of the A stock to the Metropolitan Line a reduction on the longer-distance services to Amersham, Chesham and Watford and it became fairly obvious that these would not be restored to their past frequencies. Consideration was therefore given to the release of four-car A stock units for use on the East London Line in place of the 1938 tube stock.

It was necessary to restore the track level to surface stock platform height and alter some platform nosings to accommodate the larger A stock. In addition it became necessary to ensure that A stock trains did not pass each other on St Mary's Curve (or Whitechapel Junction) entering or leaving the East London Line because it was not possible to arrange sufficient dynamic clearance for the larger A stock. Four-car A stock trains began working the service on 12th June 1977. Maintenance continued to be undertaken at Neasden Depot.

A train of handworked-door stock on the East London Line at New Cross Gate in November 1953, a month before its withdrawal.

The Whitechapel & Bow Line

Southend through train leaving Ealing Broadway about 1927, composed of Tilbury-type compartment rolling stock. The destination board read 'Southend Corridor Express'.

Incorporated in 1897, the Whitechapel & Bow Railway was constructed to join the District from Whitechapel to the London Tilbury & Southend Railway at Campbell Road junction. The line was controlled jointly by the two companies, and was opened on 2nd June 1902. The last station on the Joint Line was Bow Road. Whitechapel had been the District Railway terminus on a spur from the joint Metropolitan and District Railway extension which connected the Circle with the East London in 1884. At first, Whitechapel itself was not part of the joint ownership, being required as the District Railway terminus. Trains ran through from the District Line over the Tilbury tracks as far as East Ham, and some ran on to Upminster.

The two railway companies bought an equal number of new train sets similar to those already operating on the District to provide the additional service. These trains were known as 'Joint Stock' and normally worked the through service. The Tilbury company fitted at least two locomotives with condensing apparatus to work through the tunnels to Whitechapel. Locomotive changing normally took place at Whitechapel but some District locomotives worked through at least to East Ham.

The projection of the District trains through to East Ham overloaded the existing tracks of the Tilbury line beyond Campbell Road junction, and powers were obtained to widen the lines by two extra tracks. These powers included electrification in order that the through connection as far as East Ham from the District would continue after completion of the main electrification scheme.

Electric trains began running to East Ham on 20th August 1905, and the through steam service to Upminster from Whitechapel ceased on 30th September 1905. The electrified trackage was extended to Barking and the through service to this point began on 1st April 1908.

The Tilbury company arranged to purchase from the District Railway a number of cars to provide the service to East Ham and Barking. A total of 37 motor cars and 37 trailer cars was transferred initially to the Tilbury Company for a sum of £130,000. The cars continued to be maintained by the District and were interchangeable with District-owned cars.

In April 1907 some of the B stock cars were painted in a distinctive green livery as an experiment. As this was about the same time that cars were transferred to the Tilbury Company this change of colour was considered to be associated with the change of ownership, but this colour scheme was not maintained for very long and the Tilbury Cars were completely absorbed in the fleet, not necessarily working on the Barking service or even beyond Whitechapel. This ownership of a number of District Line cars by the Tilbury Railway and its successor, the London Midland & Scottish Railway, continued until nationalisation when the necessity for this special book-keeping ceased. The actual LMS ownership at nationalisation amounted to 57 motor cars and 53 trailer cars.

The transfer and rearrangement of quantities of cars owned by the Tilbury Company occurred from time to time when new rolling stock was purchased or the service beyond Whitechapel increased. The cars owned were indistinguishable from District Railway vehicles except for a small plate carried on the solebar.

In May 1908 a nine-car train was operated on the Barking line and later a ten-car train was worked from East Ham to Whitechapel where it divided into two. The three- or four-car portions of these trains placed at the front end proceeded from Whitechapel non-stop to Mansion House while the six-car portion became a normal District Line stopping train.

Later in 1911 a number of twelve-car trains operated from East Ham to Whitechapel dividing at this point into two six-car trains. The leading portion then proceeded to Mansion House operating on a limited-stop service.

In 1912 the London, Tilbury and Southend Railway was acquired by the Midland Railway, which on 1st January 1923 became part of the London Midland and Scottish Railway. The LMS arranged for the 7¾-mile extension of the track quadrupling from Barking to Upminster and the electrification of the two additional tracks. These came into operation on 12th September 1932, when the District electric trains began running beyond Barking.

Upon nationalisation, on 1st January 1948, the Whitechapel & Bow Railway was vested in London Transport, but the lines beyond Campbell Road junction remained the property of the British Railways Board until 1969, when the two additional tracks together with the stations as far as Upminster became the property of London Transport with the exception of Barking and Upminster stations.

Another interesting rolling stock arrangement concerning the Tilbury line was the provision of the through Southend trains from Ealing Broadway. The Tilbury company provided, in 1912, two train sets of special saloon coaches with sliding end doors and central gangways for this service. These trains were provided with lavatories which were only fitted to the Third Class brake carriages. The lavatories were, in fact, flushing-water closets provided with sewage storage tanks which had drain valves for connection to disposal drains. In spite of this hygenic arrangement to prevent the general transfer of sewage to the tracks, the lavatories were locked when the train changed over to electric working at Barking.

The trains were hauled west of Barking by District electric locomotives coupled in pairs which had been rendered surplus to requirements on the curtailment of the Outer Circle service. This service began on 1st June 1910, but until the special rolling stock was available Tilbury carriages were used. It was withdrawn on 1st October 1939 and not reinstated. Due to war conditions the special coaches were not immediately scrapped, but were found other work for a time.

After the extension of the line to Barking a running shed for the District electric rolling stock was leased between East Ham and Barking. Following the extension to Upminster, and the increase in the service at the eastern end of the line, this accommodation proved inadequate for the additional trains required. Eventually, London Transport constructed a new depot at Upminster to replace the East Ham depot and this opened in 1958. Upminster depot included a number of new features not previously provided in an Underground rolling stock depot. All trains could be washed as they came out of service as twin washing machines were provided on the entry roads to the depot. The movement of trains at the depot was controlled from a control tower using power-operated points. The employment of ground shunters was therefore unnecessary.

A Southend train composed of the special saloon stock provided in 1912 for the through service.

The small sheds at East Ham in 1956, a couple of years prior to their replacement by the new depot at Upminster.

The Great Northern & City Line

Great Northern & City wooden motor car, probably at the bodybuilder's works. The underbody equipment has not yet been fitted.

A company with the title of the Great Northern & City Railway was formed in 1892 to build a tube railway from Finsbury Park (Great Northern Railway station) to the City. A modified method of construction was employed to that used on orthodox tube lines. Although cast iron segments were used in the construction, the lower keys were made of concrete and after the formations had been established the cast iron segments were removed and replaced by brick. The advantage claimed for this method of construction was that it was cheaper and helped to reduce noise levels. The tunnels were of a diameter of 16ft instead of the 11ft 8¼ins used for more orthodox tube lines. When the line was built it was planned that eventually some physical connection would be made with the Great Northern Railway, allowing through services. The final work to achieve this original intention however only began in 1975.

The whole line was only 3½ miles long, and from the outset electric traction was proposed. The BTH Company was awarded the contract in 1901 for the whole of the electrical work, which included the provision of the rolling stock, 11 trains of seven-car length and three spare motor cars being ordered.

The Sprague-Thomson-Houston 'train-control' system was specified. This was a pioneer decision as far as England was concerned, since this type of equipment had only just passed beyond the experimental stage in America. Although the Central London Railway had the honour to have been the first to operate multiple unit trains in Europe, the Great Northern & City made the decision to use such equipment some time earlier. But since passenger service on the line did not begin until 14th February 1904 the railway could not claim that it had the pioneer installation of this equipment.

The controversy between the District and the Metropolitan over the system to be used for joint electrification, which was public property during the construction of the Great Northern & City, highlighted the difficulty of a tube railway in limiting the voltage drop in the running rails to 7 volts. In addition, the Great Northern & City Railway installed the first track circuit automatic signalling arrangement, and felt it desirable to keep the running rails clear of traction current interference. These two factors undoubtedly influenced the adoption of the unique collection system by the Great Northern & City Railway.

A positive and a negative current rail were used, but both were placed outside the running rails, one on either side, positioned 10 inches from the gauge line with the contact surface 2 inches above the running rail. This collection system, although unique, was of course similar to that adopted for the joint trial running of the Metropolitan and District Railways at Earl's Court some years earlier. The decision to place the collector rails outside the running tracks was made to enable the operation of 'electric tractors' proposed for the haulage of through Great Northern suburban coaches over the tunnel section into Moorgate. A clear 'four foot way' would enable these motive power units to be fitted with gearless motors without clearance problems arising. This unique system of current collection employed by the Great Northern & City Railway, which employed an insulated return, pre-dated the operation of such a system by the Underground generally.

The original arrangement continued in service until close of traffic on Saturday 13th May 1939, when the track system was re-arranged and the rolling stock replaced with trains of pre-1938 tube stock from the Northern Line. The new service began on Monday 15th May 1939, using the standard Underground four-rail system with the return rail in the centre of the track.

The line was designed from the beginning for the operation of a maximum train length of seven cars, the platforms being 420ft long.

Driving end of a Brush built steel car.

Interior of a Brush built car.

The original order for rolling stock seems to have been for 77 cars to provide 11 trains of seven-car formation containing three motor cars together with three motor cars as spares. However, this order must have been modified because only 76 cars were built and of these only 32 were motor cars. Trains of seven-car length were not, in fact, operated, the maximum train formation being six cars which were uncoupled to form two-car trains for slack hour workings.

The carbodies were built by two contractors, the Brush Electrical Engineering Co. Ltd of Loughborough and the Electric Railway Tramway & Carriage Works of Preston, and were of two basic types. The majority of the cars were of all teak construction and were referred to as 'wooden' cars. The last eighteen, consisting of six motor cars and twelve trailer cars, were constructed by Brush in 1906 with steel panels and framework, being referred to as 'steel' cars.

On the motor cars the electrical equipment, which was of the electro-magnetic contactor type on the Sprague-Thomson-Houston system controlling two GE66 type traction motors, was housed in a fireproofed compartment behind the driving cab.

The control system connected the two traction motors under hand-notching of the master controller on each motor car in series/parallel with open circuit transition. Until 1906 the controllers were not provided with a dead

Wooden trailer after the formation of London Transport, still in Metropolitan Railway livery but with LT 'Non Smoking' bullseyes in the windows. Originally it was the general practice on the Underground railways to label those cars in which smoking was permitted with the word 'Smoking'. In 1926 the Underground, with the exception of the Metropolitan Railway, standardised on labelling 'Non Smoking' cars instead. The Met continued to differ until taken over by the LPTB in 1933.

man's handle, and assistant motormen were carried. This practice continued for some years on full-length trains after this date, although the two-car portions carried one motorman after the fitting of this safety equipment.

The motor cars were provided with two motor bogies, each carrying only one traction motor. This design, constructed in England to the requirements of the McGuire Manufacturing Co. of Chicago, was unique in Underground practice at the time. The single-motor bogie did not re-appear again until 1935, when it was fitted to the Experimental Streamlined Tube rolling stock.

The trailer bogies, constructed by the Brush Company, were its standard type 'E' design having cast steel side frames, a swing bolster and inside brake blocks.

The air brake originally fitted to the GN & C stock was on the Christensen system, which employed a tripcock device installed on the roof of the motor cars. This worked in connection with an automatic signalling system devised originally by J.E. Spagnoletti.

The multiple unit control line passed down the centre of the roofs of the cars, the jumper couplings being located in this position. There were no through bus lines, however, and each motor car picked up its own current supply by means of four collector shoes, two on the outside of each bogie.

Power was originally supplied from the railway's own power station at Poole Street, Islington, but after control had been acquired by the Metropolitan Railway this was closed down and the power obtained from Neasden Generating Station. This old Great Northern & City power station became the Gainsborough Film Studios.

The cars were coupled by link couplers with centre buffers, an arrangement peculiar to the GN & C. The intermediate ends of all cars were fitted with gates which until the withdrawal of this stock in May 1939 required manual operation by gatemen.

Sliding doors were provided in the centre of the cars, but these were only used at the terminal stations as they could not be opened from inside the cars. Special porters were employed to operate these doors at Moorgate station to speed up the unloading arrangements. The conductors or gatemen on the trains worked the hand-operated spring-locking gates on the end platforms. To start the train the conductor at the rear rang a bell to the conductor next in line. The foremost conductor gave the starting signal for the driver to start the train.

The seating arrangement in the cars was transverse in the American fashion. The wooden trailer cars seated 58 and the steel trailers seated 64. The motor cars of each type seated four less.

Each car was illuminated by 15 lamps of 16-candle power. In 1921 all the cars were provided with an illuminated indicator which gave the name of the next station and there were proposals to extend the system to the Inner Circle and other trains of the Metropolitan. However, it proved unsatisfactory and the equipment was removed from the trains after only a few months.

The railway was not a financial success, probably because the capital outlay required to build 16ft diameter tunnels was excessive for a line which was very short in length. The Metropolitan Railway acquired the assets on 30th June 1913.

Initially an electric locomotive was provided to transfer rolling stock into and out of Drayton Park depot, which in addition to its isolation by having a unique electrical track system had no road access. Stores and heavy material required had to be transferred by rail.

When the original passenger rolling stock on the line was replaced, the locomotive available for disposal was similar in appearance to the original locomotives built by the Metropolitan Amalgamated Railway Carriage & Wagon Company in 1905 for the Metropolitan Railway, and there is some evidence which would indicate that one of the bodies of this group of locomotives was used to rebuild the original locomotive at Drayton Park.

When the Metropolitan Railway acquired control this locomotive was numbered 21 in the fleet; it was subsequently renumbered L33 in the London Transport numbering scheme. The locomotive was finally scrapped on 4th March 1948.

The transfer of the passenger rolling stock to Neasden Works also began in this way, but from the goods yard a main line steam locomotive transferred the vehicles to the Metropolitan Widened Lines at Aldersgate (now Barbican), where a Metropolitan locomotive took over. The dimensions of the Great Northern & City cars, however, were such that they could not negotiate the Finchley Road tunnels and they had, therefore, to be transferred by way of High Street Kensington and Rayners Lane. The District provided a pilotman from High Street to Rayners Lane, where a further reversal was necessary before transfer to Neasden could be completed. This procedure continued until the original rolling stock was replaced, as the Great Northern & City cars never received an overhaul at Acton Works.

The stock originally built for the Great Northern & City remained on the line until tube stock took over in 1939. A wooden-bodied motor car is seen at Finsbury Park shortly before the changeover to tube stock working.

A GN&C steel-bodied motor car towards the end of its life.

When the service was first begun only one class of travel was provided, which was normally accepted practice of a 'tube' type railway. However, soon after the Metropolitan obtained control, First Class accommodation was provided and the carriage of parcels on the trains was introduced.

When First Class accommodation was provided on 15th February 1915 one trailer car of each train set was modified to give 28 seats smoking and 26 seats non-smoking for the privileged class. This facility was withdrawn on 25th March 1934 after the formation of the London Passenger Transport Board. When tube rolling stock from the Northern Line took over the working on 15th May 1939 the original vehicles were scrapped.

In 1930, in order to improve the service on the line, the Metropolitan transferred six Metropolitan BWE150 type motor cars, each with four traction motors, to the line. These cars, together with some existing trailer cars, provided three additional trains but allowed all the other trains of six-car length to be equipped with three motor cars. The service interval was then reduced to 2½ minutes at the peaks. Because of the limited stabling accommodation at Drayton Park, however, the introduction of these six additional vehicles required the withdrawal of six trailer cars from the fleet which were subsequently scrapped at Neasden.

Finsbury Park station was required subsequently to be re-arranged to give an interchange between the Victoria Line then under construction and the Piccadilly Line. The Northern City trains ceased to operate into Finsbury Park from 4th October 1964 and the Northern City was then cut back to operate from Drayton Park to Moorgate. While the construction work was being undertaken for the Victoria Line, a service using hired coaches was provided connecting Drayton Park with Finsbury Park, and the facilities to the passengers were reduced. However, with the opening of the Victoria Line, a new same-level interchange at Highbury was brought into operation on 1st September 1968.

In 1971 authorisation was given for the Great Northern electrification scheme which included the acquisition of the Northern City Line and the projection of suburban rolling stock through the tunnels to Moorgate.

Saturday 6th September 1975 was the last weekday that London Transport trains worked into Moorgate, but until 4th October 1975 a shuttle service between Old Street and Drayton Park was maintained when the London Transport trains were finally withdrawn and the old Great Northern & City Railway lines became part of British Railways. It was an unfortunate quirk of fate that Moorgate was the scene of the worst ever Underground railway accident on 28th February 1975, just over six months before the London Transport service was withdrawn from the line.

The Brill Branch

An Aveling & Porter engine dating from 1872 with a Brill mixed train during the time that the Wotton Tramway was owned by the Duke of Buckingham.

A section of the Metropolitan that could be described as an 'appendage' was the Oxford & Aylesbury Tramroad, commonly known when part of the Met as the Brill Branch. In its earlier days it was called the Wotton Tramway.

It was originally constructed by the Duke of Buckingham to connect Quainton Road station with his estate at Wotton and was opened for private traffic by horse traction on 1st April 1871. It was subsequently extended to Brill, but it was not originally intended for public passenger use, being confined to persons accompanying cattle or merchandise, or estate workmen. Local pressure, however, caused the Duke to obtain a passenger carriage which was duly placed in public service in January 1872, at the same time as the first locomotive appeared.

This locomotive, built by Aveling & Porter of Rochester, was a single cylinder engine and owed its design characteristics more to steam road rollers or traction engines. The drive was by means of a toothed sprocket on the crankshaft driving a chain which was connected to the two pairs of driving wheels. A similar engine was obtained later in the same year. One of these locomotives was subsequently found working in a brickworks by the Industrial Locomotive Society: it was reconstructed and may now be seen in its original colours at the London Transport Museum at Covent Garden.

In 1883 a scheme was promoted to link Oxford with Quainton Road by a railway but these proposals fell through and subsequently a modified proposal, known as the Oxford & Aylesbury Tramroad, came into being with the intention of extending the Wotton Tramway to Oxford.

In 1894 this concern took over the working of the Wotton Tramway and a small amount of rolling stock was acquired for the purpose. Two locomotives built by Manning, Wardle & Co. of Leeds were acquired, one secondhand dating from 1876 and one new. The earlier one was replaced in 1899 by a new Manning, Wardle loco of similar design. These locomotives were 0-6-0 saddle tanks with inside 12 inch diameter cylinders. The driving wheels were only 3 feet in diameter and the locomotives weighed about 18 tons in working order. One of these locomotives subsequently ended its career as a contractor's engine and was used on the construction of the Great West Road about 1929.

On 1st December 1899 the Metropolitan Railway took over the working of the line but never acquired the Oxford & Aylesbury Tramroad. Subsequently, on 2nd April 1906, the Metropolitan & Great Central Joint Committee assumed control of the operations and this body remained in being until nationalisation, the London Passenger Transport Board taking over the Metropolitan functions on this joint committee. It was in the name of the Metropolitan & Great Central Joint Committee that all traffic ceased on the Brill Branch on 30th November 1935.

Sometime prior to the First World War, the Metropolitan transferred two A class locomotives, Nos. 23 and 41, to take over the duties, with one engine in steam. Each engine performed a week's work on the Brill Line. The duty engine took up its duty roster on Monday morning and returned to Neasden on the following Sunday. Locomotive 23 has survived and has been preserved in honourable retirement in the London Transport Museum. The Metropolitan also retained for use on the line five coaches of 1866 vintage built by the Oldbury Carriage Company, consisting of one First Class, one Brake Van, and three Third Class coaches, although the service train complement often only contained one passenger coach. Unfortunately none of these coaches, which were examples of the original Metropolitan Railway rolling stock, was retained after the line closed down.

There were four level crossings, the gates being opened by the train staff themselves. The train was required to cross these level crossings at no more than 2mph.

Above A Manning, Wardle & Company 0-6-0 saddle tank loco bought by the Oxford & Aylesbury Tramroad. The first carriage has two passenger compartments separated by a luggage compartment. *Below* Met locomotive No. 23 and a rigid eight-wheeled coach at Brill in London Transport days shortly before the closure of the Brill Branch in 1935.

Expansion North West

A train composed mainly of eight-wheeled coaches on its way to Harrow behind one of the 1864 batch of A class locomotives. One of the two First Class coaches with the distinctive colour scheme is a four-wheeled vehicle.

The Metropolitan & St John's Wood Railway was a branch line opened to traffic as far as Swiss Cottage on 13th April 1868. It was single track only with passing places at the two intermediate stations, St John's Wood Road and Marlborough Road. A connection with the Metropolitan was provided at Baker Street.

The gradient of the line was steep and five powerful 0-6-0 tank locomotives were built by the Worcester Engine Co. for the service which ran through from Moorgate. The Metropolitan, however, required the paths on the main line section for other services. Through passenger operation over the Baker Street junction was, therefore, withdrawn on 8th March 1869 and not revived until 28th January 1907 after electrification. The original engines were actually too powerful and far too extravagant in fuel consumption so that, after a very short period in service in London, they were sold to railways in South Wales where their characteristics were of more value. Subsequently in 1872 the St John's Wood Railway obtained powers to extend the railway to the Kingsbury/Neasden area. An extension was opened on 30th June 1879 as far as West Hampstead with an intermediate station at Finchley Road, but the St John's Wood section from Baker Street was not completely doubled until 10th July 1882, when a separate tunnel was constructed alongside the old single line tunnel. The Metropolitan Extension Line as it was then called continued to Willesden Green, which was reached on 24th November 1879.

When the line reached Harrow on 2nd August 1880, the district through which it ran was rural. There was no intermediate station between Neasden and Harrow, Wembley Park was not opened until 1894, Preston Road Halt (south of the road bridge, not the present station) in 1908, and Northwick Park as late as 1923. This station was also rebuilt in 1931, as the present island platform.

The Harrow extension was actually constructed by a joint committee of the Metropolitan Railway and the St John's Wood Railway because it was not until 1st January 1883 that the St John's Wood line became part of the Metropolitan Railway.

The first sign of 'expansion' rather than 'extension' was the construction of double tracks alongside the original tracks from Harrow to Canfield Place near Finchley Road. These tracks were leased to the Great Central Railway to enable it to gain access to its new London terminal at Marylebone. The agreement with the Metropolitan included the undertaking that no station would be constructed south of the River Brent so that no platforms were installed on these tracks except for a special wartime arrangement at Neasden in 1940. These tracks are now used exclusively for the diesel train service to Marylebone. Passenger service over the tracks into Marylebone began on 15th March 1899.

The tracks were laid in two distinct sections. The first from Finchley Road to Wembley Park, completed by July 1898, was used by Metropolitan trains for a time to enable alterations to be made to the original Metropolitan tracks. Access to these two tracks was provided south of Preston Road and this junction was used by Great Central trains until 31st March 1901, when the additional two tracks to

Harrow were completed. Harrow station itself was not four-tracked until 1908.

With the opening of the Uxbridge branch from Harrow on 4th July 1904 the Metropolitan became congested, particularly affecting those services operating into the country, and arrangements were made to construct two additional tracks on the north or 'Up' side of the original tracks between Finchley Road and Wembley Park. The first section between Finchley Road and Kilburn was brought into use on 30th November 1913. Further four-tracking as far as Wembley Park began operating in January 1914, with additional platforms at Willesden Green, Neasden, and Wembley Park, but not at Dollis Hill, Kilburn, or West Hampstead. Quadrupling of all sections to Wembley Park was completed by 31st May 1915. The provision of these tracks enabled fast trains to be worked, which were only impeded by the Finchley Road to Baker Street bottleneck. By careful timetabling, the effect of this was reduced.

The passing of the 1929 Development (Loan Guarantees & Grants) Act, making finance available for public works in order to reduce unemployment, enabled the Metropolitan to acquire capital to begin two important projects: the construction of the Stanmore branch from Wembley Park, and the extension of the four-tracking north of Wembley Park to Harrow-on-the-Hill. The four-tracking to Harrow came into full use on 10th January 1932. The rearrangement of the tracks was complicated and it produced two operating difficulties: fast trains had to cross the stopping trains at Wembley Park; and Stanmore trains, when this branch was opened on 10th December 1932, had to cross the fast tracks to reach the branch. The burrowing junction for the Stanmore line was not built until 1938, when further track rearrangements were made.

The Metropolitan realised that some relief to the bottleneck between Finchley Road and Baker Street was required, especially as these two tracks carried the country service of the railway as well as catering for a local service calling at Swiss Cottage, Marlborough Road, and St John's Wood. Plans were prepared for a connection from a point near Kilburn & Brondesbury to Edgware Road, in a 15ft 6ins tube, so that a junction to the Circle Line would be made in the same direction as that arranged at Baker Street.

In anticipation of this connection Edgware Road station was rebuilt in 1926 with four platforms as existing today, utilising the space once occupied by the old Metropolitan Railway engine sheds. The train destination indicators placed on the new platforms for many years contained descriptions such as 'Aylesbury Line' which were never required, because the connection to Edgware Road was never built. The congestion in the bottleneck, however, grew so that the number of stopping trains between Finchley Road and Baker Street was severely limited and subsequently stops were not, in fact, made during the peak periods.

Relief came under the 1935/40 New Works Programme by extending the Bakerloo Line to Finchley Road and re-arranging the tracks so that the Metropolitan fast lines were on the outside with the Bakerloo in the middle. The Bakerloo then took over the operation of the Stanmore branch, including the burrowing junction built north of Wembley Park which eliminated the problems created at this station by the previous expansion.

The Bakerloo service began working to Stanmore on 20th November 1939, stations being provided at Acacia Road (named St John's Wood), situated between the Metropolitan stations of Marlborough Road and St John's Wood (which had been renamed Lords only a few months previously) and at Swiss Cottage. Marlborough Road and Lords were closed when the Bakerloo trains began working, but the Metropolitan platforms at Swiss Cottage remained operational until 17th August 1940. Subsequently, on 1st May 1979, the Jubilee Line was opened to the public which took over the Stanmore services hitherto operated as part of the Bakerloo Line. The re-arrangement of the fast tracks on either side of the slow tracks was extended north of Wembley Park for Metropolitan trains. It was not desirable to rebuild again Preston Road and Northwick Park stations, although a complete rebuilding of Harrow-on-the-Hill station could not be avoided. Unfortunately the conditions imposed as a result of the Second World War interrupted the work and track re-arrangement was stopped north of Preston Road. A flat crossing of the 'Up' or southbound fast line over the slow lines remained in use until 8th March 1948, a few weeks before the enlargement of Harrow-on-the-Hill station to the six-track layout at present in use.

The 1935/40 Programme had also envisaged the duplication of the tracks north of Harrow to Rickmansworth, as well as the extension of the electrification beyond Rickmansworth at least to Amersham. The planning and acquisition of the necessary land was in fact well ahead when work was stopped in the autumn of 1939 because of the outbreak of war. The project then remained in abeyance until 1956 when the work was recommenced. The scheme was then modified but included the electrification to Amersham and the withdrawal of Metropolitan trains beyond that point.

At North Harrow, Pinner, and Northwood Hills the additional tracks were built clear of the existing platforms; the arrangement of having the slow trains between the fast trains was not continued beyond Harrow.

At Northwood, room was not available on the west side of the existing station so that a changeover of tracks had to be arranged and the old station demolished. The first stop for the fast trains north of Harrow was arranged at Moor Park, where a completely new station was built with separate island platforms for the fast and local tracks. The Watford branch junction, opened on 2nd November 1925, was only provided on the local tracks, beyond which the local and fast tracks converged for entry into Rickmansworth.

The first electric train reached Amersham on 15th August 1960 and the last Metropolitan steam passenger train on the Chesham branch ran on the night of 11th/12th September 1960. Electric locomotives continued to haul through Aylesbury steam trains with the locomotive change at Rickmansworth until 9th September 1961, when Amersham became the northern terminus of all Metropolitan Line trains. The four-tracking work including the new stations at Moor Park was not, however, completed until 17th June 1962.

The locomotive change at Rickmansworth. The electric loco is approaching to couple to a London-bound train; the steam locomotive that has brought the train from Aylesbury is returning to the coaling sidings at the north end of the station.

Main Line Electrification

Bogie stock train as converted to electric working, outside the old car shed at Neasden.
Double stepboards are still fitted to the trailer coaches at this time, but they had been removed from the motor cars to accommodate the shoebeams and were soon afterwards removed from the trailers also.

Through trains were worked from Baker Street to Harrow and Uxbridge by electric traction from 1st January 1905, and, with the improved service provided, traffic at intermediate stations began to increase. Consideration eventually had to be given to providing an increase in the available rolling stock so that the train service could be augmented.

The electrification of the lines south of Harrow, however, had rendered most of the steam stock surplus to requirements. At that time, this consisted of four different train compositions: (a) rigid wheelbase 8-wheeled stock, (b) twin carriage stock, (c) 'Jubilee' stock, and (d) 'Bogie' stock. With the exception of the 'Bogie' stock most of the other stock was stored. Even all the 'Bogie' stock was not required to maintain the steam stock service, and arrangements were made to provide two train sets for electric services from this group of stock to be powered by using 150 BWE saloon motor cars.

These sets, which went into service early in 1906, were generally made up with the motor car at the 'Down' end of the train coupled to four 'Bogie' stock coaches. This arrangement was proposed so that the motor car could be uncoupled at Harrow and the rake sent on behind a steam locomotive outside the electrified territory. To enable this train formation to work in both directions the brake van in the set was converted to a driving trailer. Full driver's look-out windows of an unusually large size were provided and the cars were fitted with a BWE nine-core control line and the Westinghouse brake equipment. At the end, coupled to the motor car, a centre buffer was provided but the screw coupling arrangement was retained for attachment to the steam locomotive. These sets were made up as follows: 3CT-3T-1T-3T-3M. It was found in practice that the 150 BWE motor cars were not sufficiently powerful for this duty, and the sets were modified to take 200 BTH motor cars.

With the advent of the 'Dreadnought' steam stock more 'Bogie' stock became available and it was decided to convert two complete train sets of seven coaches for electric working. Four brake coaches were each equipped with four GE69 traction motors, type 200 BTH equipment and new motor bogies of the Fox pressed steel type, with 7ft wheelbase and 38 inch diameter wheels. The coaches of the trains were equipped with traction voltage lighting (five lamps in series) and heating, but through control of this installation was not provided, local switches being fitted at the ends of the vehicles. The BTH ten-core control line was fitted on both the 'Up' and 'Down' side so that the coaches were interchangeable and reversible. The trains were fitted with the Westinghouse air brake.

The passenger compartments on the motor coaches were reduced at first from five to four, to allow the original luggage space to house the control equipment and for one passenger compartment to become a luggage compartment. To afford adequate ventilation for the resistance banks, torpedo-type ventilators were fitted to the roof over the new switch compartment as well as side louvres. Subsequently the passenger compartments were reduced to three, the fourth one being used exclusively by the guard.

The first train of this type in seven-car formation went into service on the Uxbridge line on 11th July 1906. It was originally intended that seven trains should be converted, but only two were completed. The trains were subsequently increased to eight coaches when the platform lengthening programme in the inner area was completed. Some of the platforms were still very short for trains of this length (about 330 feet) and it was at this time that arrangements were made to use another passenger compartment in the motor cars for the guard in order to bring him nearer the centre of the train. A door into the luggage compartment was provided from this compartment.

The trains, when composed of seven cars, seated 400 passengers—280 Third Class and 120 First Class. With the addition of one Third Class trailer but the loss of two compartments converted to guard's compartments, the accommodation was increased by 50 passenger seats. The compartments accommodated only five a side in a body width of 8ft 3ins. The trailer cars were coupled by short links but the motor coaches were coupled to them by screw couplings. These trains were subsequently designated M stock in the Metropolitan timetables and were made up as follows: 3M-3T-3T-1/3T-1T-1/3T-3T-3M. Second Class accommodation was not provided on the electric trains introduced in 1905 and by 17th December 1906 it was withdrawn from the steam service as well.

In 1907 an agreement was reached with the District which required the transfer of saloon motor cars, especially the 200 BTH type, to the Circle service. This depleted the 'semi-converted' sets of their motive power, and it was then decided to add four more 'Bogie' stock coaches to the rakes and fully convert them to electric working, making two six-car trains. These trains were designated N stock in the Metropolitan timetable classification.

The vehicles converted to motor coaches were the two driving trailers and two vehicles which had been stored after being used in the Wembley Park electrification experiment. They were fitted with the 150 BWE equipments which had been taken into storage after orders had been placed for BTH equipments. All the trailer coaches were fitted with BTH ten-core control lines so that they were generally interchangeable with the other trains of this type.

The BWE motor cars with their nine-core control were coupled by means of special jumper connections. The two six-car sets were

Bogie stock train after the formation of London Transport. One extra car had been added to these trains about 1925.

Bogie coach of 1900 converted in 1921 to electric working as a driving trailer.

made up as follows: 3M-3T-3T-1T-3T-3M providing a seating capacity of 330 with 270 Third Class and 60 First Class. These sets were worked on the Uxbridge service until 1932 when, with the opening of the Stanmore branch, they were reduced to four-car formations for this service until it was taken over by Bakerloo tube stock in 1939.

Arising from the train formation then operating on the Circle, some trailer saloon cars were rendered redundant and, with the delivery of the new electric locomotives, three trains of five vehicles were made up for operating local trains to Neasden. Having end doors only and fewer seats than the other trains then operating, these trains were unpopular and caused public complaint. In 1909 three sets of 'Jubilee' stock were taken out of storage, each set consisting of nine coaches providing 390 seats, 80 First Class and 310 Third Class. These were fitted with traction type lighting and heating. Shoebeams were fitted to the brake coaches to provide the supply to lighting and heating but the bus line provided was not suitable for traction current and was not connected to the locomotive, so that gapping of these trains was not infrequent. These trains were successful in meeting the traffic needs so that it was decided to provide a further three trains. These were composed of six vehicles of old straight-sided eight-wheeled non-bogie stock which had been stored, and were given similar treatment in being provided with traction lighting and heating. The trains of this make-up hauled by electric locomotives ran in service until 1912/13, when it was possible to rearrange the service with more modern rolling stock.

Metropolitan Electric Locomotives

No. 1 locomotive of the Westinghouse batch with a bogie stock train, showing the large destination blinds originally fitted.

Unlike the District Railway, which arranged for the complete electrification of its system, the Metropolitan envisaged dual working arising from the services extending well into the country area. The Metropolitan decided, therefore, to build some electric locomotives capable of hauling the heaviest steam passenger trains over the electrified tracks, as it was considered desirable to eliminate all steam working into Baker Street.

The first ten locomotives were ordered from the British Westinghouse Electric & Manufacturing Company and built by the Metropolitan Amalgamated Railway Carriage Company at Saltley under sub-contract. All these locomotives were delivered and ready for service by April 1906. They were double bogie vehicles with central cab having bonnets at each end, a type of locomotive normally described as 'camel backed'. The length over buffers was 35ft 9ins with bogie centres at 17ft 3ins. The bogies of pressed steel had a wheelbase of 7ft 6ins and each carried two type 86M nose-suspended traction motors, driving 36-inch diameter wheels through spur gearing with a ratio 22/60. These motors were of the Westinghouse split-frame design, without interpoles but with plain split sleeve bearings. The advantage of this type of motor was that the armature, which required a great deal of maintenance in these early years, could be removed without lifting the vehicle. These motors were expected to work under very arduous conditions and cooling was increased by a motor-driven blower.

Each pair of motors was controlled by 15 electro-pneumatic switches in the form of a turret actuated by a low voltage supply, powered by a 14-volt battery. A single small master controller was originally installed to control both sets of equipment, but was not arranged for automatic acceleration because of the amount of shunting the locomotives were expected to do. The provision of only one control position was found to be unsatisfactory for locomotives requiring to travel in both directions with equal facility without recourse to a turntable, since the driver was badly placed for good visibility in one direction of travel. An additional master controller was fitted soon after delivery of the vehicles.

The locomotives were fitted with an electrically-driven air compressor and two exhausters. The compressor provided compressed air for the Westinghouse brake equipment and the pneumatically-operated control gear. The locomotives were designed to haul trains fitted with either the Westinghouse or the vacuum brake and were themselves dual fitted. The Gresham & Craven or Reavell exhausters were provided in tandem working at full and half speeds. When coupled to a vacuum-braked train, the exhauster on half-speed worked continuously to maintain the vacuum against normal train line leakages while the full-speed machine was switched in when a brake release was required. On the locomotive only one brake block on each wheel was provided, but this was actuated by either system of brake operation.

The bogies were each originally fitted with transverse beams at the outer ends but located on the axle boxes to carry the collector shoes, positive on the outside with a negative in the middle. This type of gear gave trouble on the car stock (as non-compartment stock was called) working on the Circle, so all vehicles were later modified to the conventional arrangement with the positive shoebeam between the axle boxes and the negative beneath the motor casing at its outer end.

One very distinctive feature of these locomotives was the large roller destination blind displaying 12 inch lettering carried at both ends, extending the whole width of the body. The blinds must have given trouble because they were removed at an early stage in the life of the locomotives. Automatic couplers were not fitted, coupling to trains being by link and screw, the standard main line practice.

The 'turret' type control system on both the car stock and these locomotives was not satisfactory and was replaced by individual electro-pneumatic contactors. The 14-volt battery was also replaced by a motor generator set. This work was not completed on all locomotives until 1911.

Following the experience with the first ten locomotives a contract was placed in 1906 for a further ten vehicles from the same carbuilders, but this time BTH electro-magnetic traction control equipment was specified. In addition a box-like body with the driver's controls at the outer ends was arranged. These vehicles were lighter at 47 tons and shorter, being only 33ft

Westinghouse locomotive No. 2 in the 1920s with a rake of Dreadnought coaches and a more manageable destination board. The photograph was taken at Harrow-on-the-Hill.

6ins over buffers against the 50 tons of the BWE locomotives, which were over two feet longer. This batch also had destination blinds, but much smaller.

Two sets of type 200 BTH (GE69) equipments were provided; the master controllers were fitted with deadman's handle, although it was always the practice to carry two men in the electric locomotives and this feature was rarely used in service. Although multiple operation of two locomotives of the same type would have been feasible, through control lines were not provided on either type. The BTH locomotives were provided with buck-eye couplers as well as the standard screw coupling. The latter was removable, being carried in the cab when not required. The first BTH type locomotive entered service in September 1907.

Experimental haulage of steam trains by electric locomotive began in 1906, and by 1st November of that year all trains were hauled electrically from Baker Street as far as Wembley Park where engine changing was arranged. Harrow-on-the-Hill station was reconstructed to four platforms on 21st June 1908, and from 19th July of the same year the locomotive exchange was transferred to this point. This remained the end of the electrified territory until 5th January 1925 when the locomotive exchange point was transferred to Rickmansworth on the extension of the electrification. This remained the transfer point for locomotive-hauled stock until electric locomotives were withdrawn from passenger service in 1961.

The equipment of the BTH locomotives proved very satisfactory, requiring no modifications at all, but in 1913 this equipment was removed and fitted to new car stock then being constructed, and ten sets of BWE equipment ordered for these cars were fitted to these locomotives. This was done, it was said, to maintain a rolling stock balance between BWE and BTH equipped trains.

The replacement work included the transfer of trucks and traction motors. The new bogies had 86M type split-frame traction motors fitted with a wheelbase of 7ft 9ins. All 20 locomotives now had similar equipments but different appearance.

In 1919 it was decided that it was necessary to improve the power available for hauling steam trains as these were becoming heavier by the provision of longer trains with improved amenities. As part of the plan of re-equipment of the Metropolitan Railway it was decided to rebuild the 20 electric locomotives giving them an improved performance. Two locomotives, No. 6 of the 1904 batch and No. 17 of the later batch, were rebuilt and in addition to the provision of new bogies, the solebar was extended to accommodate the increased body length. This proved to be a weakness because it was considered that the modified frames were prone to fracture. Consequently, new locomotives were ordered instead and these started to arrive in 1922 from Vickers Ltd of Barrow. Metropolitan-Vickers, the successor to British Westinghouse, was the main contractor supplying the new electro-magnetic control gear and the MV339 type traction motors, each with a nominal rating of 330hp. The 86M motors supplied in 1913 had been rated at 215hp on the comparative one-hour basis. The MV339 motors were, in fact, the largest ever to be used on London Transport service. As originally built they were provided with sleeve bearings but had interpoles and solid frames. In 1953, because of the postponement of the electrification plans beyond Rickmansworth, a sufficient number of these motors was modified and fitted with roller bearings when a renovation of 15 remaining locomotives was undertaken at Acton Works. The fitting of roller bearings was a necessary step in the reduction of maintenance procedures as grease-lubricated roller bearings could run up to 12 months without regreasing, whereas oil-lubricated sleeve bearings required attention every few days and renewal under 12 months. Because of the size of the traction motors, the new bogies were arranged with larger diameter wheels—43½ inches when full size. These were the largest wheels apart from steam locomotive driving wheels used by London Transport and some special arrangements were required to turn the tyres on conventional wheel lathes especially when this process was transferred to Acton Works. The gear ratio was 23/57. The locomotives were much heavier than the earlier types; 61½tons in working order. Screw couplings were normally provided, but buckeye couplings could be fitted and were carried inside the locomotives.

No. 11, the first of the BTH locomotives, at Willesden Green.

Locomotive No. 15 was placed on view at the Wembley Empire Exhibition in 1924 and was given a nameplate recording the fact. In 1926 it was decided to name all the locomotives and cast-bronze plates were fitted with the various names bestowed on the locomotives. This was completed the following year. In 1943, as a result of a suggestion to help the war effort, it was decided to remove these bronze plates for scrap, but there was considerable reluctance to do this immediately because extensive renovation work was necessary after removal of the plates. The work could only be adequately carried out when the vehicles passed through Acton Works for overhaul, with the result that the last plate was not removed until 1948!

In 1953, 15 working locomotives were left in the fleet and a complete renovation was undertaken at Acton Works. Nameplates were again fitted! In addition to the fitting of roller bearings to the traction motors mentioned above, the Metro-Vick traction control equipment was replaced by BTH electro-magnetic type available from the scrapping of District Line cars. More modern compressors were also fitted. These locomotives were fitted with exhausters, a vacuum brake control line, brake valve and vacuum brake cylinders, but this brake was used only for controlling the train. The Westinghouse brake was normally used on the locomotive itself. As originally installed, both the Westinghouse and vacuum brake cylinders had actuated leverages which applied the brakes on both trucks together. Following the renovation work at Acton it was considered desirable to alter this arrangement because of the necessity for these vehicles to work as single units. To avoid the possibility of a dangerous brake failure when operating as a single vehicle the main brake beam was divided, each part being separately actuated so that each truck was virtually independently braked. Only one locomotive was not given back its original name; Locomotive No. 2, which had been *Oliver Cromwell* was renamed *Thomas Lord*. The recent war against dictators had left its mark! The full name William Ewart Gladstone was curtailed on the appropriate new nameplate to *W.E. Gladstone*.

The locomotives were principally used for hauling the Aylesbury, Verney Junction, and Chesham trains within the electric territory, but saw many other duties as well. They hauled the through passenger trains composed of Great Western coaches from Paddington to the City until 16th September 1939, when due to war conditions this service ceased. At one time three such trains were worked in the morning and evening peaks. There were some goods train workings to Vine Street Goods Depot, between King's Cross and Farringdon, and of the coal train to feed the boiler house at Chiltern Court.

'William Ewart Gladstone', No. 10, with original nameplate.

Although the electrification to Amersham was completed on 12th September 1960, through trains to Aylesbury continued for another year. Locomotives were still changed at Rickmansworth to avoid providing facilities for the locomotives at Amersham. However, through Chesham trains were electric locomotive-hauled all the way during this time until replaced by multiple unit stock.

Four locomotives were retained for shunting duties, one each at Acton Works, Neasden, Ealing Common, and Ruislip. After the final delivery of the A stock the locomotive at Ruislip, No. 3 *Sir Ralph Verney*, was scrapped. The remaining three locomotives continued to perform various duties for several years. Locomotive No. 1 *John Lyon* was brought up to exhibition standard for the Metropolitan Railway Centenary at Neasden in 1963, but was not in a satisfactory working condition, so No. 5 *John Hampden* hauled the commemorative special. It has subsequently been placed in the London Transport Museum at Covent Garden. No 12 *Sarah Siddons*, allocated to Acton Works, became a test platform for trials of new brake blocks, as well as running on miscellaneous duties. These include leaf-clearing on the Metropolitan Line each autumn.

Right The driver's controls of a 1900-type locomotive. These locos had two sets of brake equipment. The vacuum brake handle is to the left of the Westinghouse brake handle. *Below* An Aylesbury to Liverpool Street train leaving Rickmansworth in February 1952 with loco No. 14.

The Rothschild Saloons and the Pullmans

The Rothschild saloon in the train shed at Neasden.

The extension of the Metropolitan line from Chalfont Road to Aylesbury was opened on 1st September 1892. Wendover, one of the stations on this line, was near the country seat of the millionaire Ferdinand de Rothschild. He began to patronise the new railway facilities, reserving a First Class compartment for his requirements. In 1895, however, the Metropolitan Railway ordered from Brown Marshalls, two special saloon vehicles which could be formed into a special train to accommodate this First Class passenger and his entourage.

These vehicles were 32 feet long and were provided with six wheels equally spaced; the only Metropolitan vehicles ever to be built with this arrangement which was considered to provide a very smooth ride. One of the Royal Trains of this period was also provided with six-wheeled coaches for the same reason. At one end of one saloon there was a six-foot wide compartment and lavatory. There was a luggage section at the other end. The saloons themselves were provided with settees and two armchairs, together with gas lighting. A special train containing these two vehicles was regularly operated for a number of years, but following electrification at the Baker Street end of the line with increased track occupation, it was suggested that this special train should work into Marylebone. In 1905 these two vehicles went into Neasden Works for extensive overhaul and reconstruction. The old bodies were spliced together to make one vehicle some 58 feet long over the buffers containing two saloons. The virtually new vehicle was provided with four-wheel bogies and Stone's electric lighting system. The saloons were refurnished with movable chairs and tables in place of the fixed settees. This vehicle was known for many years as the 'Rothschild Saloon', and in its later years was used by the Chairman and Directors of the Metropolitan Railway for line inspections. The last official use of the vehicle was to convey the Chairman and officers of the London Passenger Transport Board on an inspection of the Brill Branch before its closure. This saloon was withdrawn from the active stock list in 1935, but remained available at Neasden for over ten years before it was scrapped. There was a genuine reluctance to break it up.

The Metropolitan Railway felt that the competition from the better-equipped Great Central Railway trains running over the same tracks might cause a depletion of the First Class traffic from the outer areas. As a special inducement to this traffic a ten-year agreement was drawn up in 1909, with the Pullman Car Company for the introduction of a Buffet Car service.

Two vehicles were built by the Birmingham Railway Carriage & Wagon Company for the Pullman Car Company, but were fitted out to the requirements of the Metropolitan Railway. The cars were just over 59½ feet long over the buffers and had bogies with 7ft 6in wheelbase. The wheels when new were 40⅝ inches in diameter for maximum riding comfort commensurate with the curvature of the track.

Accommodation was provided in each car for 19 passengers in upholstered armchairs, the saloon itself being divided into three sections containing eight, seven and four seats. In addition to the provision of a small pantry a lavatory was also provided. The lavatory was locked and not available for use in the tunnels south of Finchley Road.

When equipped with seating and furnishings the vehicles weighed 29 tons, and were finished in the Pullman livery of the time—umber bodywork with upper panels of light cream and gold lining. The interior decoration of the two cars, while similar in treatment, was distinctive but of 18th-century style. One of these handsome cars had a mahogany finish with inlaid satinwood and green upholstery. The other had an oak finish and crimson upholstery. Eight glass-topped tables with portable electric table lamps typical of the standard Pullman design, were also provided. The outside appearance of the cars contained six square side lights with an oval window at each end. Access to the cars was obtained from the end vestibules.

The cars were coupled in the trains by means of the centre screw link and standard side buffer arrangement. The cars themselves were provided with end doors but these were never used on the Metropolitan, access to the cars being obtained from the station platforms.

The names which were chosen for the two cars, *Mayflower* and *Galatea*, do not seem to have had any special significance to the Metropolitan Railway, and the reason for the choice of names is obscure. These were the two contestant yachts in the 1886 America's Cup.

A Baker Street to Aylesbury Pullman car train, with Westinghouse loco No. 10 and Bogie stock soon after the introduction of the Pullman service. On the right is a Great Central train.

The Pullman service began on 1st June 1910, and was the first electrically-hauled Pullman service in Europe. Initially the vehicles were formed in trains of 'Bogie' stock necessitating the coupling vehicle being provided with long buffers and screw couplings. Subsequently the vehicles were reformed in trains made up with 'Dreadnought' vehicles, and they remained in these formations until finally withdrawn on 7th October 1939. They were equipped with through electrical bus lines so that the trains containing these vehicles operated under normal conditions when hauled by electric locomotives in the electrified territory. The braking system was, of course, vacuum, to conform with the standard steam rolling stock.

The supplementary fare charged for the use of the Pullman facilities was 1/- beyond Rickmansworth and 6d for any distance between Aldgate and Rickmansworth. The trains worked from Verney Junction, Aylesbury, and Chesham to Baker Street, certain workings being extended to Liverpool Street or Aldgate. Light refreshment was served, including breakfast, on the London-bound morning trains. A light supper was served on the late train from Baker Street to cater for the theatre traffic. The supplementary fare was reduced in 1915 for a time to 6d, all the way. When the Pullman cars were withdrawn for overhaul, the Rothschild saloon was used as a substitute to maintain the continuity of the service.

Following the 1922/23 overhaul of the vehicles the external colour scheme was changed to a crimson lake all over, as the light cream was difficult to maintain under the tunnel conditions of the Metropolitan, and this livery was retained until the coaches were withdrawn. They received only one overhaul, at Acton Works in 1935, after the formation of the London Passenger Transport Board.

Below Pullman car 'Galatea' in original livery at the carbuilder's works. *Bottom* Interior of a Pullman car.

The 1913 Metropolitan Stock

First Class trailer of 1913 stock. This stock was used primarily on the Circle Line and broke away from the initial American influence on the design of electric rolling stock bodywork.

Following the rebuilding of Baker Street station enabling the through running of trains to the City, and the electrification of the East London Railway, the Metropolitan required some additional rolling stock. An order was placed with the Metropolitan Carriage Wagon & Finance Company for 23 motor cars and 20 trailer cars. The motor cars were all Third Class but the trailers were equally divided between Thirds and Firsts and, in accordance with then existing practice, the First Class cars were driving trailers.

The distinctive feature of these cars, which were 52ft 10ins long overall, was the elliptical roof with raised ventilators. The motor cars seated 38 passengers and had a small luggage compartment directly behind the driving cab. The saloon was designed with one pair of hand-operated sliding doors in the centre of the car, together with one end sliding door at the opposite end to the driver's cab on each side. All the trailer cars, both Thirds and Firsts, seated 48 and were also provided with the middle and end doors. The Third Class had, of course, additional doors where the driving cab door was arranged on the First Class cars.

To equip these cars 23 sets were purchased of duplex 200 BWE type traction equipments for controlling four traction motors, but only 13 of these equipments were fitted to these new motor cars at Neasden Works. The remaining equipments were fitted to the ten BTH type electric locomotives releasing the 200 BTH (GE69) type equipments for the remaining ten new motor cars.

This division of equipments provided new rolling stock in both types of saloon trains operated by the Metropolitan. These new vehicles were not segregated from the earlier clerestory-roofed stock, and mixed trains of earlier and later built cars were made up in both 200 BTH and 200 BWE type rakes.

The BTH-equipped cars received the bogies from the electric locomotives so that there was some difference in the running gear of the two types of car.

The gear ratio of the BTH cars with GE69 traction motors and 38-inch motor wheels was 19/64, while the BWE cars had 86M traction motors, 36-inch motor wheels and a gear ratio of 22/60. The Fox type pressed-steel trucks from the electric locomotives had a wheelbase of 7ft 6ins while the plate frame trucks taking the 86M traction motor had a wheelbase of 7ft 9ins. The trailer trucks provided were similar to those fitted to earlier vehicles, which were pressed steel with a 7ft wheelbase.

Most of these new cars entered service on the Inner Circle which now included additional workings to provide the East London service, with four through trains per hour from South Kensington over the Metropolitan side of the Circle. The East London service was actually 12 trains an hour of which eight were shuttle operations from Shoreditch. The car stock on the main line at this time consisted of a number of trains made up into six- and seven-car formations, whereas on the Circle working the maximum length of a train was usually of four cars.

The traffic on the Metropolitan Railway increased considerably during the war years, and at the end of hostilities there was insufficient rolling stock to meet the needs of all the services. For a time some Great Western vehicles were borrowed and used on the Uxbridge service until additional rolling stock could be obtained. Some time later the luggage compartment was converted for passenger accommodation on 16 of the twenty-three 1913 motor cars. The seating capacity of the cars was raised from 38 to 46 by this means, as well as providing additional standing room. The luggage compartment doorway was sealed up. Normal side lights were not fitted at this time, which made this area somewhat cell-like in appearance, and it was not until the reconditioning work undertaken by London Transport for the improvement of the Circle Line trains that this section of these cars was completely rebuilt.

Most of this stock became part of the fleet used for the Circle working, together with the later 1921 stock, and continued in service until 1952. In order that reference can be made subsequently to the history of some of these cars the following table of the motor cars will be of assistance.

Type of Equipment	*Metropolitan No.*	*London Transport No.*
200 BTH (GE69)	83-92	2587-2596
200 BWE (86M)	93-98	2581-2586
	99-105	2546-2552

Third Class 1913 stock trailer No. 82.

The reason for the split in the renumbering from the Metropolitan to London Transport arose because the cars working on the Main Line were separately numbered from those working the Circle services. The cars numbered from 2581 to 2596 were retained on the Circle service, but 2589 was severely damaged in a bomb incident in 1941 and the body was replaced by one from an earlier batch of cars, although the number 2589 was retained. Car number 2552 of the batch of cars operating on the main line was transferred to the Circle working after the Charing Cross collision of 17th May 1938, when car number 2546 (a 1921 stock car) was damaged beyond economical repair.

The cars retained for Circle working received a number of modifications before being finally withdrawn in 1950. The cars working on the main line were withdrawn in 1938/39.

A 1913 stock motor car in its final condition, working on the Inner Circle with 1921 stock in the late 1940s. The 1921 stock had a different door arrangement.

The Metropolitan Shuttles

Shuttle car No. 46, later No. 2768.
The traction equipment was placed under the solebar, thus no switch compartment was necessary.

In a dense fog at West Hampstead on 26th October 1907, a serious accident occurred when one six-car train ran into the back of another. The force of the collision was considerable; there was extensive damage to the colliding vehicles, and three passengers lost their lives in the wreckage. The leading motor car of the colliding train, No. 46, received very severe damage and was stored pending a decision to scrap. No. 46 was a 150 BWE type vehicle.

There was another accident on 6th October 1908 when a severe fire broke out in No. 69, badly damaging its bodywork, and this car was also stored pending a decision to scrap. This car was a 200 BTH type motor car.

In June 1909 No. 46 was used as a gauging car to check clearances for the introduction of the new Pullman coaches which were designed to be rather longer than coaches then in service. A temporary wooden bolster was fitted at one end of the under-frame to enable the bogie centres to be increased to 39ft 9ins from 35 feet. A temporary buffer beam was also fitted to give an equivalent car length of 60 feet.

In 1910 these two cars were converted into double-ended shuttle cars by the Metropolitan Carriage, Wagon & Finance Company, for use on the Uxbridge line from Harrow.

The bodies, 52 feet long, had elliptical roofs with torpedo ventilators and two driving cabs. There were, between the two driving cabs, six compartments and a luggage section with two doors. Two Third Class compartments were placed on either side of the two First Class compartments. The two adjacent Third Class compartments were connected by a central gangway and were not divided by a partition; the middle seating had a luggage rack common to both sides. The passenger accommodation provided for 36 Third Class and 16 First Class —only 50% of each class were smoking. Both cars had a similar appearance but had different electrical equipment.

Car No. 46, which became 2768 in London Transport's numbering scheme after its formation in 1933, had 150 BWE equipment with which it had originally been provided. This car retained its 50M type traction motors until scrapped.

Car No. 69, which became 2769, was originally equipped with 200 BTH type equipment. This equipment, being more powerful, would have been wasted on a single shuttle car, so it was interchanged with that of a 150 BTH car, the GE69 traction motors being interchanged for GE76 type. Both these cars were provided with electrical couplings so that they could be attached to a driving trailer, enabling a two-car train to be formed when necessary.

These cars were used on the Uxbridge shuttle service until 1918, when they were transferred to the Addison Road shuttle from 12th May of that year. This worked from Edgware Road and had previously been worked by three-car sets of H & C stock. The cars had to be modified at this time because the driver's cab door, as built, had opened outwards like the compartment doors; this was not considered good practice in tunnel operations and these cab doors were altered so that they opened inwards.

After the opening of the Watford branch and the electrification to Rickmansworth these vehicles operated a shuttle between Watford and Rickmansworth round the north curve. This service operated from 2nd November 1925 to 21st January 1934, when the vehicles were transferred to operate the off-peak shuttle to Stanmore from Wembley Park. A service by these single units was provided from 21st January 1934 until 27th November 1938, but thereafter, as traffic seemed to have increased, a driving trailer was added permanently to 2769. This worked as a two-car set until the introduction of the Bakerloo to Stanmore on 20th November 1939.

No. 2768 having the less reliable equipment was withdrawn for scrapping in February 1938, but 2769, although not used again in passenger service after November 1939, was retained in reserve until 1942.

It had been intended to provide, under the 1935-40 New Works Programme, seven shuttle cars by converting motor coaches 2700-2706 to double-ended vehicles. In addition to the provision of an additional driver's cab, one of the equipments was to be removed. Presumably these coaches would have been used on Chesham shuttles and possibly between Watford and Rickmansworth; as they were compartment cars it is unlikely that they would have been used on the Addison Road service. This plan was not proceeded with. After the war it was considered that 2598 and 2599 should be made into single shuttle unit cars on their release from the East London Line, but this also was not proceeded with.

The 1910/1913 District Stock

C stock motor car as delivered in 1911.

Between 1908 and 1910 a number of important engineering works were undertaken by the District Railway, thus enabling an increased service to be operated which, in turn, required the provision of additional rolling stock.

With the introduction of electric traction a new rolling stock depot was opened at Ealing Common and the workings to and from this yard, together with the operation of the South Acton branch, made the track layout at Mill Hill Park (opened for steam operations in 1879) totally inadequate. A new three-track layout with a flyover arrangement west of the station (enabling the Ealing service to avoid conflicting with the Hounslow trains, many of which worked from South Acton) was brought into use on 20th February 1910. The station was renamed Acton Town on 1st March of the same year.

Until 3rd December 1911 the District Railway had used its running powers over tracks belonging to the London & South Western Railway between Studland Road junction, just west of Hammersmith, and Turnham Green junction. This double-track stretch of railway was used by both the London & South Western Railway trains from Richmond to Kensington, and by Great Western trains to Richmond as well as by the District. After electrification of the District the sharing of these tracks with steam trains was very unsatisfactory. The District then arranged for the construction of additional tracks alongside the original London & South Western Railway tracks for its exclusive use. As these would be on the south side of the existing lines, a flying junction for the Ealing trains to cross the LSWR tracks at Turnham Green was also included in the proposals.

A new station at Stamford Brook was opened on 1st February 1912, but served by the District trains only. The new track arrangement enabled an improved District Line train service to be operated from 11th December 1911. Subsequently it was considered that all the expense of the additional trackage had really been wasted, because the London & South Western Railway reduced its train service and finally withdrew the Kensington service altogether on 3rd June 1916. The Great Western service from Notting Hill (now Ladbroke Grove) was withdrawn on 31st December 1910 so that these tracks were then virtually unused. However, this lack of use paved the way for the adoption of these tracks by the Underground, so that the four-tracking arrangement as in use today was established, enabling the Piccadilly Line to be projected west of Hammersmith.

Another burrowing junction was constructed at Earl's Court to enable the Wimbledon services to be segregated from those proceeding to Hammersmith. This junction was brought into operation on 4th January 1914.

In addition to the need to provide more trains arising from these major operating improvements, some trains were increased in length from seven to eight cars. The installation of automatic electro-pneumatic signalling in the congested area enabled a considerable reduction in headways to be achieved, and advantage was taken of this to introduce into the timetables the so-called 'Non Stop' trains. This system commenced on 16th December 1907 and was a feature of District Line working in some form until 1964. It was said that when this arrangement was introduced the journey time for some trains from Mansion House to Ealing Broadway was reduced from 48 to 30 minutes. This improvement in timing, however, could only be achieved by some trains, and required careful timetabling and timekeeping. Frequently the 'Non Stop' trains did not stop at the station but had to stop subsequently in the tunnel. The term 'Non Stop' was also a misleading description as the trains stopped at most stations, only passing a few in an accepted pattern. The cars were provided with 'Non Stopping' boards on the sides near the doorways which displayed names of the stations at which the trains did not stop. These boards continued to be a feature of all District rolling stock until the R stock in 1947.

To meet the increase in rolling stock required to gain full advantage of these improvements, cars were obtained from three different carbuilders. This group of cars, although generally similar, had a number of distinctive features. In spite of these, in later years this whole group were known as 'Hurst Nelsons' although only the first batch came from these Scottish carbuilders.

An order was placed in 1910 with Hurst, Nelson & Co. of Motherwell, Scotland, for 32 motor cars and 20 trailers. These cars, designated C stock, were delivered in 1911. Both the motor and trailer cars were similar in appearance and construction, and in 1928 the 20 trailers were converted at Acton Works into motor cars. Although the cars were basically constructed of steel, a great deal of wood was used in the bodywork.

The vehicles were 49ft 6ins long with a pair of narrow doors in the middle and single end doors as well. The interior was provided with a clerestory roof and the cars resembled the B class.

The electrical equipment originally supplied by the BTH was of the non-automatic electromagnetic type similar to that already established on the B class rolling stock. In fact a number of the cars were fitted with secondhand equipments. Six came from three of the double equipped electric locomotives which had been withdrawn and two further equipments came from two breakdown locomotives converted to flat wagons having been replaced by two battery locomotives. However the GE69 type traction motors fitted were subsequently replaced by a new type designated GE212 which had interpoles. These were the first such motors to be supplied to the Underground and probably the first such motors to be used in England.

The motor truck was of pressed steel construction and designated 'B' type while the trailer truck which had a 7ft wheelbase was designated 'L' type.

The second batch of cars, 30 in all consisting of 22 motors and 8 trailers, ordered from the Metropolitan Amalgamated Railway Carriage & Wagon Company, were similar in general design. These cars were built in 1912 and were designated D stock. The motor bogies were again 'B' type but a new trailer truck, the 'M' type was introduced. The eight trailers were also converted to motor cars at Acton Works in the 1928 Reconstruction Programme.

The third batch, the E class or 1913 'Gloucester' stock, was delivered in 1914, again being a total of 30 cars: 26 motors and four trailers which also became motor cars in the 1928 reconstruction programme. The appearance of these cars was very different because for the first time an elliptical roof construction was provided instead of a clerestory. When first delivered they had small torpedo-type ventilators in the roof which were later removed because they caused too much draught, resulting in passenger complaint.

The Gloucester cars were provided with a new type motor bogie, the 'C' type, with 7ft 3ins wheelbase, while the trailer bogie provided was the 'M' type.

The general arrangements of the C, D and E classes of rolling stock were similar, and

A 1913 E class motor car built by Gloucester.

Interior of a Gloucester-built car.

A 1910 Hurst Nelson motor car on the traverser at Acton Works in the 1920s.

although various different types of bogies were originally provided they were all interchangeable, and some mixing of these inevitably occurred when repairs were undertaken. The original bogies gave a great deal of trouble and between 1910 and 1922 at least 60 new motor bogies were provided.

The last batch of these cars was received in time for the District Railway to provide a service of trains from Earl's Court to Willesden Junction, on behalf of the London & North Western Railway, from 1st May 1914 to 22nd November 1914 when the North Western rolling stock was delivered following the electrification of this line. This was the remaining portion of the Outer Circle service which continued in operation until 1940 when the service was withdrawn, although the Olympia shuttle does cover a small part of this route now.

At this time all cars were interchangeable in duty and formation with the exception of the original A stock. The A stock was confined to the shuttle services at the west end of the line to South Harrow (to Uxbridge from 1st March 1910), and from South Acton to Hounslow.

As briefly mentioned earlier in this book, in May 1908 a nine-car train formation was operated on the Barking line, consisting of four motor cars and five trailers. The three leading cars proceeded from Whitechapel as a 'Non Stop' train to Mansion house; the remaining six cars continued as a normal train. In 1910 some 12-car trains dividing into two six-car trains were similarly operated. A nine-car train was still running from East Ham to Whitechapel in 1918.

The success of the longer trains at the eastern end of the District Line caused a number of such operations to be tried from Ealing Broadway. In 1914, a nine-car train was operated, with the extra car in charge of a special attendant with passenger access available only at Ealing Broadway, Acton Town, Turnham Green, Hammersmith and Mansion House. This train operated from June 1914 until the start of the First World War.

Although at this time most platforms west of Whitechapel were capable of accommodating only seven-car trains, it was decided to operate a number of eight-car formations and to alter the platform length on the important stations. At others, by accurate stopping with half the front car and half the rear car in the tunnels, such trains could be worked without too much difficulty, but some doors had to be locked.

After the end of the First World War numerous platforms west of Mansion House were adjusted to accommodate eight cars. The short platforms east of Mansion House were provided with cat-walks in the tunnels, but these were always considered unsatisfactory. They are not needed now as eight-car trains no longer operate.

The trains of six- and eight-car length were usually made up with an equal number of motor and trailer cars. The formation arrangements, however, were complicated by the need to provide both First and Third Class accommodation as well as smoking and non-smoking sections. The motor cars were generally all Third Class, while some trailers provided First Class smoking and non-smoking accommodation. The ninth car on the long Ealing Broadway trains provided both First and Third Class accommodation.

A 1910 District Railway motor car in London Transport days coupled to a Q35 trailer. Many trains with handworked doors had them left open in the summer, as seen in this view.

Metropolitan Post-War Electric Stock

Experimental motor car 198 with the switch compartment behind the driver.
This was the forerunner of the MW stock.

At the close of the 1914/18 war, the Metropolitan Railway had to increase the rolling stock fleet. The saloon versus the compartment controversy became of paramount importance because the operation experience with the open saloon cars without centre doors had been very unsatisfactory. Several designs were considered including arrangements for the conversion of the existing saloon cars.

Some sample cars were, in fact, converted at Neasden Works to test the effect of different arrangements especially so far as cost was concerned.

Car No. 32 (LT No. 2501) was the first compromise design. It was reconstructed with a single sliding door of about three feet in width in the middle of the body. The seating of the vehicle was reduced from 48 to 46. The car concerned was a 150 BWE type motor car and all the seating was Third Class and smoking.

Car No. 14 (2513), another 150 BWE motor car, was also reconstructed to provide a single sliding door behind the luggage compartment in addition to a pair of centre doors. This rearrangement reduced the seating capacity of the car to 38.

Neither of these two designs was accepted as the answer to the problem, but the cars remained in this modified condition until withdrawn for scrapping just before the Second World War: 2513 in 1936 and 2501 in 1939.

In 1919 a contract was placed with the Metropolitan Carriage Wagon & Finance Co. to rebuild one six-car train. The cars selected for this experiment were 150 BWE motor cars Nos. 36 and 44, First Class trailer cars 53 (6535) and 55 (6555), and two Third Class trailer cars 35 (9516) and 67 (9531). The two motor cars were converted in 1931 to trailer cars and renumbered 197 and 198 before the formation of London Transport, when they received the numbers 9588 and 9589 respectively. The Metropolitan trailer cars were numbered in a separate sequence to motor cars and these numbers should not be confused with the experimental MV153 motor cars built in 1925.

When returned from the Saltley Works (where the conversion was carried out) these cars had a completely changed appearance, including the provision of elliptical roofs instead of clerestories. The main feature on this train, however, was the provision of five swing doors on each side of the trailer cars and four on the motor cars to improve passenger circulation. A similar arrangement is now common practice on British Railways diesel multiple-unit trains. The swing doors, however, on these experimental cars, did not open between seats but in separate vestibules which were provided with draught screens. The seating capacity of the Third Class trailer cars was raised to 58, although the motor cars which still retained a small luggage compartment had only 41 seats and the First Class control trailers 44.

Numerous innovations to the Metropolitan Railway's method of operation were introduced on this experimental train which earned it the soubriquet 'Hustle train'. The lighting and heating switches for the first time were placed under the direct control of the guard, by means of through control lines, and not switched on each car individually. The driver was provided with an automatic window wiper, but this equipment was found to be unreliable and was converted subsequently to hand operation.

Although a considerable amount of publicity was given to this train when it first went into service, a special press inspection being arranged at Baker Street on 18th December 1919, it did not fulfil the expectations and no further cars of this kind were acquired. In 1931, as part of the programme of reducing the number of 150 BWE equipments in service because of the maintenance problems, the motor cars of this experimental train were converted to trailer cars. The driving cabs and luggage compartments were removed and the space used to provide additional passenger accommodation. The train was then formed into an eight-car set by providing either two motor cars of 1913 stock or the two 1925 experimental MV motor cars as the motive power units. These cars were withdrawn for scrapping in February 1941. This set was known as the 'S' train in the Metropolitan timetable nomenclature.

In 1921 seven new six-coach 'Dreadnought' trains were put into service for the steam workings. This enabled a number of 'Bogie' stock vehicles to be withdrawn and converted for electric working. Actually, in 1921, the Metropolitan obtained 101 new vehicles, of which 42 were steam stock. The electric car stock was similar to that purchased in 1913, having elliptical roofs, but the trailer cars of this batch were provided with three pairs of double doors down each side. These doors were hand-operated and gave an opening four feet wide.

The motor cars were provided with a small luggage compartment and had a narrower pair of double doors adjacent to this compartment, the other two pairs of double doors being the same size as those provided on trailer cars. There was no through communication from car to car.

The order covered the provision of 20 motor cars, 33 Third Class trailers, and six First Class control trailer cars. Most of this stock was used to provide improved service on the Circle workings, a number of the trailer cars being used to increase the length of the trains from four to five cars.

The motor cars were all equipped with 200 BWE equipments and 86M traction motors, which had been recovered from the 20 electric locomotives being replaced by the new Metro-Vick type. The motor cars were, therefore, divided into two classes—one slightly heavier than the other because the pressed steel bogies recovered from the original BWE locomotives were lighter than those fitted to the BTH locomotives, which had plate frame type. There was no difference in appearance but the different bogies had 7ft 6ins and 7ft 9ins wheelbases respectively, and the unladen weight was 45 tons against $46\frac{1}{2}$ tons.

The motor cars had a seating capacity of 37, the First Class trailer cars 45, while the Third Class trailer cars seated 50. The First Class cars, in addition to having a driving compartment, had a partition dividing the accommodation into smoking and non-smoking. These cars survived in Circle workings until 1947, when withdrawals for scrapping commenced.

A First Class control trailer similar to the 1921 stock was constructed in 1923 for display in the Palace of Engineering at the Empire Exhibition at Wembley in 1924/5. This was the last car type trailer vehicle built for the Metropolitan Railway. This vehicle did not become part of the Circle fleet. It was numbered 6557 in the London Transport fleet and was used subsequently as part of a three-car train operating on the East London shuttle service.

Top Interior view of experimental car No. 198. *Centre* Control trailer car No. 55 after conversion by Metro-Carriage at Saltley in 1919. *Bottom* Interior of 'Hustle' train trailer car, showing partitions at doorways. The layout is similar to that used in the C69 stock built fifty years later. The Metropolitan Railway favoured leathercloth upholstery instead of moquette in saloon cars.

The MW Stock, Later Known as T Stock

A seven-car MV stock train heading for Rickmansworth.

Arising out of growth in the Extension traffic following the electrification to Rickmansworth and the opening of the Watford branch on 2nd November 1925, additional rolling stock was required.

Fortunately the rolling stock was not immediately necessary as initially the Watford service was shared with the London & North Eastern Railway which provided half the service, steam-hauled, with through trains to Marylebone. The service to Marylebone was withdrawn within a year and the Metropolitan then provided the entire service with electrical multiple-unit rolling stock.

At this time the Metropolitan management was still undecided whether to order additional saloon or compartment rolling stock for the lengthy journeys now required by the electric stock on the Extension services.

Two experimental motor cars were ordered in 1925 from Metro-Carriage Company, provided with entirely new equipment designed by Metropolitan-Vickers. The bodies of these cars were substantially the same as the 1921 car stock, but the passenger saloon was shortened by the provision of a switch compartment to accommodate the new type of control equipment. This equipment was electro-pneumatic in operation. The control instructions from the master controller were electrical but the mechanical operation of the individual switches was made by means of pneumatic cylinders actuated by the electrically controlled valves. The advantage of this system was basically that the electrical power required for control was small and could be achieved from a low voltage supply, because the mechanical work of operating the switch gear was provided by pneumatic power.

The control supply was provided at 110 volts obtained from a potentiometer across the 600-volt supply. This potentiometer was carried in the roof of the cab behind the driver. The control gear itself was centrally placed in a rack in the special compartment behind the driver. There were two separate sets, each of which controlled two MV153 traction motors in series-parallel. These traction motors were of 275hp at the one-hour rating which, with a gear ratio of 21/62, made these cars the most powerful multiple-unit vehicles in Europe at the time.

The seating in the vehicles received special consideration and studies were undertaken to obtain the best shape for passenger comfort.

The trucks were of heavy construction, formed of plate and angle, and the axles had journals measuring 11×7 inches, the largest so far used on multiple-unit stock. The vehicles weighed just over 49 tons. After the motor cars of the 'Hustle' train were converted to trailer cars these vehicles were generally used to complete the eight-car formation of this set, which was designated S stock. These two cars were numbered 198 and 199 (2598 and 2599), and later ran on the East London Line as a three-car shuttle train together with the 1924 Exhibition trailer car.

These cars were considered successful and the equipment worked exceedingly well. However, the passengers on the line preferred compartment stock and this fact, together with the length of time taken at terminal stations (especially Baker Street) to unload a crowded train, induced the Metropolitan management to concentrate on compartment stock.

For delivery in 1927 an order was placed with Metro-Carriage for 12 new motor coaches, having five passenger compartments, seating five a side, 50 Third Class passengers in all, a luggage compartment, and a switch compartment as well as accommodation for the driver and guard. These cars were of two types to work with existing trailer stock, because at this time no new trailer cars were bought to run with them. The cars were provided with similar Metropolitan-Vickers control equipment, and four MV153 traction motors with a gear ratio of 21/62 giving a balancing speed of 65mph.

Coaches numbered 200-205 (2700-2705) were provided with Buckeye couplings and no side buffers, which gave an overall length of 53ft 9ins. These coaches were fitted with the Westinghouse brake and were used to replace car stock motor cars working with 'Bogie' stock trailers forming the W stock trains. The rakes of 'Bogie' stock had been provided with Buckeye couplings at the outer ends and BTH-type ten-core through control cables, which was satisfactory for the 110-volt system of the new motor coaches. There were three trains made up in this formation.

Coaches numbered 206-211 (2706-2711) were provided with side buffers, screw couplings and vacuum brakes. They had an overall length over couplings of 55ft 5ins, although were virtually similar to 200-205. These coaches were used with five coaches of steam stock of the 1920/23 types converted for the purpose to make up three trains of seven-coach length. The conversion consisted of providing a through control line for multiple-unit operation, but in addition six coaches were turned into control trailers by reducing the number of compartments from nine to eight. This enabled

Above A four-coach MW stock train in Metropolitan Railway livery led by a motor coach built in 1930 by the Birmingham Railway Carriage & Wagon Company. It is seen passing Willesden Green station. *Below* Interior of a First Class compartment of MW stock.

the trains to be uncoupled into three- and four-coach sets. The three trains made up in this way were designated MV stock. The conversion work undertaken at Neasden was not completed until 1929.

The MV trains of seven coaches were 378 feet long, while those of eight coaches of 'Bogie' stock, the W trains, were 354 feet long. The trailer coaches on the MV trains could still be formed into steam-stock trains if required, while the motor coaches on the W trains could be replaced by open saloon-type motor cars, which gave a limited amount of flexibility when repairs were necessary.

These coaches were considered to be very successful and in 1929 a further batch of coaches were ordered from the Birmingham Railway Carriage & Wagon Co. The total order this time was for 55 vehicles of which 30 were motor coaches with similar Metropolitan-Vickers traction equipment. The 25 trailer cars were made up with ten of the motor coaches into five seven-coach trains which became known as MW stock. The 'W' stood for Westinghouse to make a distinction from the MV stock which, although similar in appearance, had vacuum brakes. All the new cars were provided with centre buffers, and Buckeye couplers so that, in fact, the motor coaches were interchangeable with the first batch of the 1927 stock vehicles.

Coaches numbered 212-241 (2712-2741) were, therefore, interchangeable in duties with the original six. Arrangements were made for four of the new motor coaches to be used on W stock trains so that all the trains of this type, of which there were five, were now propelled by the same means, the car stock being released for other duties.

No. 229, a Metro-Vick equipped coach built in 1930.

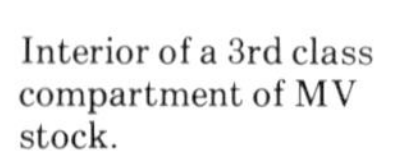

Interior of a 3rd class compartment of MV stock.

Ten of these latest motor coaches were fitted with roller bearing axle boxes, being the first batch of cars for the predecessors of London Transport with this type of equipment. A number of traction motors too were fitted with roller bearings for the armature, but the motor was axle-hung mounted on the well-tried sleeve type bearings, using the usual waste packing to carry the lubrication to the bearing surface.

In 1931 the last batch of compartment stock for Underground services was ordered from the Birmingham Railway Carriage & Wagon Co. This order consisted of 65 vehicles; 18 motor coaches, 14 First Class trailer coaches, 14 control trailer coaches with Third Class accommodation, and 19 plain Third Class trailer coaches. These vehicles were used to make seven complete trains of eight coaches, which had a length of 428 feet, and five of the Third Class coaches were used to increase the existing five MW type train to eight-coach length.

In addition to the fact that these coaches—numbered 242-259 (2742-2759)—were built by a different car builder, the equipment was manufactured by the General Electric Co. However, it was also electro-pneumatic in operation and designed to work in multiple with the Metro-Vick equipment of the earlier cars. The motor bogies were fitted with two motors of type WT545 provided with a gear ratio of 20/62. All axle boxes and traction motors were fitted with roller bearings. Although this arrangement was designed to work in multiple with the MV153 motor having a gear ratio of 21/62, this did not prove satisfactory in practice and these GEC coaches had to be kept segregated.

At the formation of the London Passenger Transport Board there were, therefore, 60 motor coaches, of which a set of six and a set of eighteen were not interchangeable in duties or with each other. So it became necessary to arrange greater interchangeability for better stock utilisation. The Metro-Vick gear ratio was changed from 21/62 to 18/65. This arrangement, when applied to the MV153 traction motor, made them compatible with WT545 motors in service which retained the original gear ratio of 20/62.

The three vacuum brake-fitted MV trains were converted to Westinghouse brakes when they passed through Acton Works during 1935. In addition three steam-stock trailer coaches from the 'Dreadnought' fleet were converted to electric working so that these trains could be lengthened from seven to eight coaches.

There were then 17 eight-coach MW stock trains together with 26 motor coaches, which were used as the motive power with other stock in W and VT stock trains. When these trailer cars and coaches were replaced by the introduction of P stock in 1938 seven more steam-stock coaches were converted at Acton Works. The MW stock was then made up into nine eight-coach and ten six-coach trains, and this group of stock was then given the designation T stock in London Transport nomenclature. This rolling stock provision, however, only required 38 motor coaches whereas 60 had originally been built.

At this time it was intended that the additional electric trains required for the extension of the electrification beyond Rickmansworth to Amersham and Chesham would be obtained by converting the 'Steam' stock (the 'Dreadnoughts') to electric working, the motive power being provided by the surplus T stock motor cars. The advent of the Second World War postponed this programme which had also included the fitting of electro-pneumatic brakes to the T stock. All the motor coaches were kept in running order during the war years so that this work could be completed at the cessation of hostilities.

The provision of through heating and lighting controls was also a feature of the proposed renovation programme. One of the operating disadvantages of the T stock was the fact that heating and lighting switches were operated from the platform by rods at the ends of the vehicles on each coach. One train was actually converted to through controls. The end, however, was in sight, because two of the motor coaches were withdrawn for scrapping before the end of the war. The underframes of these coaches were used for experimental cars 17000 and 20000.

The electrification to Amersham was postponed again, and when replacement stock began to be delivered in 1961 the fleet of motor coaches had been gradually reduced to 44. The last T stock train ran in passenger service on Friday 5th October 1962. Two coaches were retained for the Metropolitan Centenary celebrations before being scrapped. These were 2711 and 9724. Two of the motor coaches, 2758 and 2749, both from the 1932 batch, were converted into a double-unit sleet locomotive for use in winter weather, being renumbered ESL118A and ESL118B respectively.

A T stock train (originally MW stock) at Northwood in the closing years of its operation. Until the end of T stock frequent problems occurred with doors being broken off trains entering Finchley Road tunnel. In September 1956 an open-door detector was installed on the southbound platform at Finchley Road which consisted of a mechanical arm located 60 feet beyond the starting signal. When this was struck by a compartment stock door it triggered six flashing white lights along the tunnel wall to alert the guard to stop the train. Compartment stock doors were normally hung so that the forward movement of the train at double platforms tended to close the door. Where island platforms were in use, the doors opened on the wrong side for this to occur and an open door tended to blow back further.

Renovation of the Circle Stock

The first five-car Circle train with BTH-type 1913 motor cars renovated at Acton Works.
The trailer cars date from 1921.

At the formation of the London Passenger Transport Board in 1933 the Metropolitan Railway passenger rolling stock transferred to the new organisation consisted of:

1. 'Steam' stock, and 20 electric locomotives for working the Aylesbury Line services from the City and Baker Street.
2. Three seven-coach trains of MV stock, compartment-type electric stock with 1927 motor coaches fitted with vacuum brakes.
3. Twelve eight-coach trains of MW stock also compartment type with 1927/30/31 motor coaches but fitted with Westinghouse brakes.
4. Five trains of 'Bogie' stock powered by motor coaches from the MW pool and designated W stock.
5. Five eight-vehicle trains and three seven-vehicle trains also powered by MW type motor coaches, but having saloon trailers marshalled between them. These trains were designated VT stock.
6. One eight-vehicle train made up with the two experimental motor coaches, Nos. 198 and 199, together with the experimental six cars with swing doors like compartments. This train, known as the 'Hustle', had the official designation S stock.
7. Twelve seven-car trains made up with motor cars having either of the 200 BWE or 200 BTH equipments together with saloon trailer cars. The motor cars had, of course, to be used in pairs as the two different types could not be used with each other. These trains were designated V stock.
8. Two eight-coach trains, provided with motor coaches fitted with 200 BTH equipments, converted from 'Bogie' stock in 1908. These trains were designated M stock.
9. Two four-coach trains, having the motor coaches fitted with 150 BWE equipments. The trailers of these trains were coupled by short links but the motor coaches were coupled to the rakes by means of screw couplings. These trains were known as N stock.
10. Twenty-three six-car trains for Hammersmith & City services which included the original H & C cars, plus 18 additional cars from the Metropolitan fleet.
11. Eighteen five-car trains for Circle service, some with BTH and some with BWE equipments.

After the formation of the Board a plan for the renovation of the Circle stock was introduced. During 1934 ninety cars were selected from this duty and were passed through Acton Works for modification. The most striking change was the repainting of the vehicles in a red and cream livery, which altered the appearance of the cars considerably. All the 59 cars of 1921 stock were taken for reconditioning, the remainder being cars of earlier vintage. The selected fleet of 90 vehicles consisted of 36 double-equipped motor cars, 18 control trailer cars and 36 trailer cars. The 18 trains selected were of two basic types, five with 200 BTH motor cars and 13 with 200 BWE motor cars. The control trailers were not required to be used as such, and the equipment was removed. The 86M type traction motors on the 200 BWE motor cars were not in very satisfactory condition, and it was decided to replace these with secondhand GE212 type motors available from District cars recently scrapped. These motors had solid yokes, interpoles, and had been converted to roller bearings. However, because these replacement GE212 motors were rather more powerful than the ones being displaced, it was decided to reduce the actual number of motors on a train from eight to six by converting half of the motor cars to single equipments. These motors had become available from two sources, some from the Watford Joint Stock withdrawn in 1930 and the remainder from District motor cars being converted to trailer cars.

The BTH cars had GE69 motors, which were in better condition because they had solid yokes and were not of the split-frame type which had proved very vulnerable to excessive wear in the bearing housing. The GE69 motors were replaced later by GE212 type when further supplies became available by the introduction of Q stock to the District Line. The gear ratio employed on both types was 19/64.

The motor cars with 200 BTH equipment were numbered 2587-2596 by London Transport, having previously been the Metropolitan's Nos. 83-92. The 200 BWE motor cars were divided between 1914-built cars and 1921-built cars. The Circle cars from the 1914 batch were Nos. 93-98, renumbered 2581-2586, while the 1921 batch were Nos. 106-115, renumbered 2561-2580. The cars converted to single equipments were 2584-2586, 2561, 2562, 2573-2580.

The programme of work included refurnishing of the interior of the cars; loose cushion type upholstery was provided in the First Class and fixed moquette-covered seats in the Third Class. The control trailers had been retained in the formations because these vehicles provided the First Class accommodation. Lighting fittings were re-arranged and fitted with bell-type shades similar to those used on tube stock at the time. Previously the Metropolitan cars had had unshaded bulbs. The luggage compartments were eliminated, thus increasing the seating accommodation. To bring the vehicles in line with standard practice on the District, communicating doors were installed between the cars so that through detrainment of passengers in an emergency could be arranged.

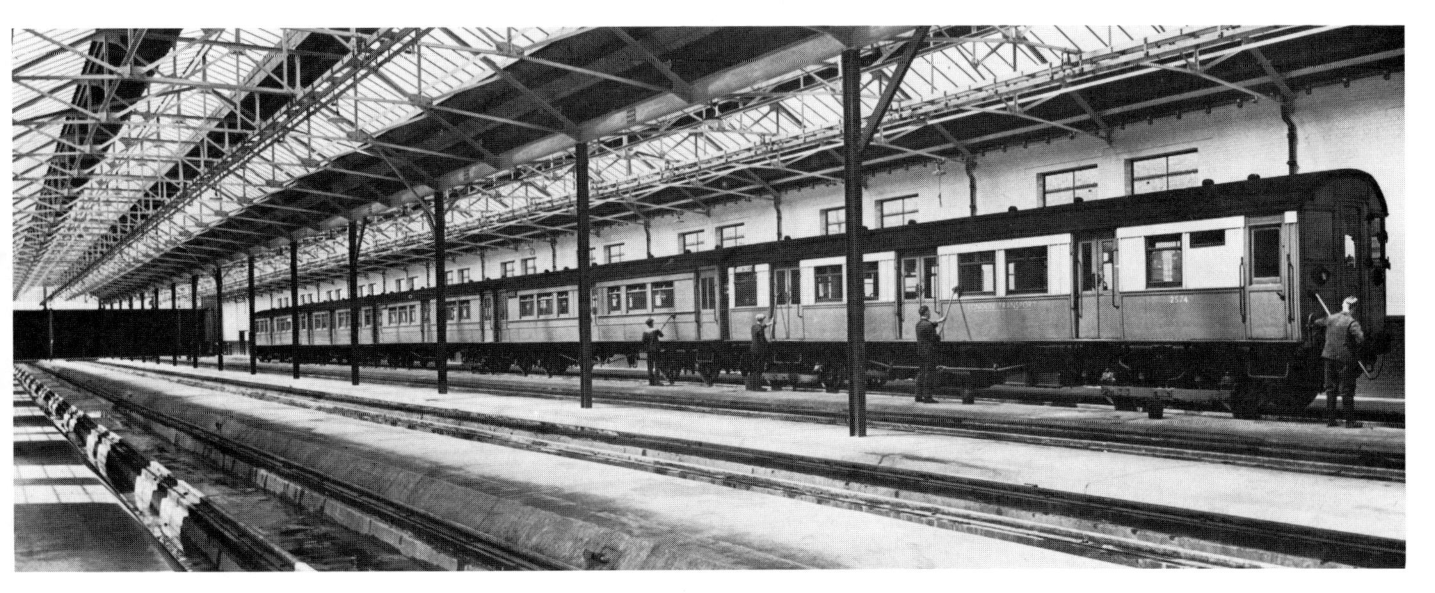

A Circle train in the cleaning shed at Neasden Depot. Car No. 2574, a BW 1921 stock car, is still in the two-colour livery.

In addition some of the cars were fitted with K2 bogies in the trailing positions, as this type of bogie had become available from the scrapping of District Line cars. They were much superior to any other trailer bogie then in service. As K2 bogies became available they were not only fitted to Circle stock but also to some 'Steam' stock coaches. These bogies had the advantage of providing double block brake rigging against the single blocking previously employed on these trailer cars.

The traction equipments remained unaltered; the BWE type had electro-pneumatic contactors actuated by a low voltage 24-volt supply obtained from a small motor generator set carried in the driver's cab. The contactor notching under the control of a master controller was provided with automatic acceleration by a notching relay. The BTH cars, on the other hand, had electro-magnetic contactors actuated by 600-volt circuits under the control of a master controller, the driver having to hand-notch through the control sequence without the overriding control of a notching relay.

The cars were at first finished externally in a red and cream livery, and internally in the standard Underground colour scheme of that time of cerulean blue and cream. Subsequently at later overhauls, to reduce the painting costs, the cream upper panels were painted red to provide the overall red colour scheme which the cars retained until scrapped.

The successful repainting of the Circle stock which, without doubt, enhanced the appearance of the cars concerned, caused consideration to be given to repainting all the Metropolitan stock which was to be retained for further service, because the varnished teak finish was an expensive process. Rakes of 'Steam' stock during 1936 received treatment, one set being painted olive green, another Underground red, but both these were uninspiring. The last colour experiment was the painting of a train bright green with a waistband of red. This was particularly horrible and the brown finish, resembling as near as possible the original teak, was decided upon as the best compromise which did not alter materially the general appearance of the vehicles.

Five-car P stock trains began to operate on the Circle service in February 1947, and the last Circle Stock train was withdrawn on 31st December 1950.

Interior of a renovated Circle car.

Circle stock train at Moorgate in the late-1940s near the end of its working life.

The F Class (1920 Stock)

A five-car F stock train outside Ealing Common Depot. The elliptical cab windows were unique to this design of stock.

After the end of the First World War, considerable industrial difficulty arose as manufacturers changed over from munition supply to peacetime requirements. The Government of the day provided some assistance in the transition period. One of the benefits to the District Railway from this policy was the provision of 100 new cars. The actual financial arrangement concerning these vehicles is not entirely clear, but they were certainly much more lavish in equipment and appointments than could have been provided by the District Railway finances alone.

The cars were built by the Metropolitan Carriage, Wagon & Finance Company at its works in Birmingham and were known officially as 1920 Stock and given the designation letter 'F'. They were known at first as 'Dreadnoughts' but were immediately nicknamed 'Tanks'. Whether this name came from the fact that they were built in shops which had only recently been building parts for such vehicles, or because of their construction almost entirely of steel, will never be resolved. The cars retained this nickname to the end of their days and are still remembered by this name by those who knew them. The first train went into passenger service on 23rd December 1920.

These cars were additional to the existing fleet and were always incompatible, being made up into separate trains. From the beginning they were intended to provide additional facilities because some increase in the service had been made possible by the introduction of colour light automatic signalling. The trains were provided with a high performance as well as a high carrying capacity. The acceleration provided was of the order of 1·5mph/second which was superior to anything previously operated on the District. It is difficult to appreciate now how this improved performance was to be fully utilised operating among trains which did not have the benefit of these improvements. However, it was considered that they could be utilised to enable the 'non-stopping' services to be improved where the improved performance could be of benefit in short bursts at least. There was also a scheme proposed for the increase of power on all eight-car trains of 'standard' stock by changing their composition to five motor cars and three trailers, but this never materialised.

The original formation was of eight-car length, M-T-T-T-M+CT-T-M, so that it could be divided into two portions, one of five-car length and the other of three-car length, which could operate separately. At one time, during the peaks this train formation was split at Acton Town so that the three-car portions went to South Harrow while the five-car portion went to Ealing Broadway. This arrangement ceased in 1932 when the South Harrow service became part of the Piccadilly Line.

The motor cars as originally delivered were double equipped, having four traction motors. These were of a new type designated GE260 and provided with a tapped field system which enabled higher speeds to be achieved. In these motors part of the field windings themselves was cut out to reduce the number of coil turns, rather than reducing the current flowing in the field coils. These were the only motors to be operated by the Underground with this system for increasing the motor speed. On all other stock, increases in top motor speed were obtained by a field divert system (generally described as a shunt field system, which is technically incorrect), in which the reduction in field strength of the motor to give the higher running speed was obtained by diverting or shunting a proportion of the current through resistances in parallel with the main motor fields.

The BTH control system was electro-magnetic with individual contactors providing multiple-unit control by means of a hand notching master controller. It is surprising that this advanced rolling stock was provided with a system of control which had already been technically superseded by automatic notching under the control of an accelerating relay. In fact the equipments provided on these trains were obsolete within five years, but in spite of this gave excellent service for 40 more years.

The gear ratio of these high-speed motors, which were axle hung, was 19/64. Each pair of motors was controlled in series-parallel by an independent set of equipment, two sets being carried in each car. The trains were intended to be operated at 45mph on non-stop runs. In the event they were found to work up to speeds in excess of this and were considered to be over-powered, consuming too much electricity. Because of this, arrangements were made for 14 of the motor cars to be reduced to single equipments which would help to reduce the maximum current at starting. Fourteen of these equipments, together with the traction motors, were then fitted to the seven electric locomotives used on the through Southend trains, improving their performance. Subsequently, about 1928, a fifteenth motor car was converted to a single equipment.

A First Class F stock trailer car. The indicators by the centre doors were to show those stations at which the train was not stopping. All the names are displayed in this posed view for the photographer.

The motor bogie had a long wheelbase of 7ft 10in, while the trailer bogies were of 7ft 3in wheelbase. These trucks, designated 'E' and 'N' type respectively, were of rolled steel construction, remaining virtually in their original condition for the whole of their life with the exception of the springing. This was considered to be too lively and was replaced subsequently with springs with greater damping. These trucks were provided with clasp brake rigging, the first on the District to be fitted with two brake blocks per wheel.

The actual cars were of all steel construction and were built to templates, so that sections were interchangeable from car to car and very little individual tailoring was incorporated in their construction. The cars were 11 inches wider than previous stocks, the width being increased from 8ft 8in to 9ft 7in. The body width was extended almost to the limit of the step board of the earlier stock; the sides, however, were slightly inclined above the waist-rail, making the body width at cantrail level 9ft. In addition, the body was 8 inches longer at 49ft 8ins while the overall length over buffers was 50ft 5¼ins. The double-equipped motor cars were heavy, weighing 44½ tons. The whole interior of the cars was of steel, but the panels and mouldings were finished to resemble woodwork. As originally delivered the floors were not provided with the usual wood lagging, being covered with linoleum and concrete.

The seating capacity of a motor car was 40, a control trailer 44 and a trailer 48. The seats themselves were mainly facing; cross seats were only provided at the end bays. Vertical grab poles were originally provided for the convenience of standing passengers, but in practice these poles were found to be an obstruction and were removed.

Six large ventilators of an improved pattern were fitted in the roof. These were found to be exceedingly draughty and uncomfortable when entering tunnels, and were soon sealed up. During the Second World War the operating handles were found to be useful for attaching the 'reading lights' which were fitted to provide a very slight glimmer of light in the open sections during the hours of darkness as part of the air-raid precaution arrangements. In these cars reading light battens were fixed to the ventilator handles instead of the ceiling. After the reading lights were removed the handles were cut off at ceiling level also. The square-type roof ventilator ducts outside on the roof, however, remained a distinctive feature of the external appearance of these cars. Another special distinctive feature was the eliptical windows at the car ends, including the driver's look-outs.

Three pairs of double doors, narrower than those used today and hand-operated, were provided on each car and the trains soon received a well-deserved reputation for clearing large crowds quickly from platforms, and were always in demand for services to cover the football matches at Chelsea, Fulham and West Ham.

The 1920 stock was the last to be provided with gap protection between the cars. To prevent passengers falling between carriages, earlier stock had been fitted with pantograph barriers, but on the 1920 stock this protection was provided by means of leather covered chains. When the practice of connecting these to the adjacent car ceased, they remained in position and came to be used as grab handles instead. The cars themselves were designed to reduce the gap by chamfering the ends and the chains were felt to be unnecessary.

The 100 cars originally ordered were divided into 40 motor cars (12 westbound and 28 eastbound) and 60 trailer cars, of which 12 were control trailers with the control equipment at the westbound end. These control trailers were composite, having both First and Third Class accommodation, as were 12 other ordinary trailer cars, leaving 36 as Third Class cars.

When originally delivered, control and bus line jumpers were duplicated on each side of the headstock so that F Stock could virtually be formed into any formation, including turning if necessary. The reconstruction programme beginning in 1928, which included the fitting of the electro-pneumatic brake requiring additional through control lines, caused the cars then to become handed because the control jumper on one side was used for the e.p. brake wires while the traction control used the other side. The fleet allocation of driving positions then became 12 double-equipped westbound, 15 single-equipped eastbound and 13 double-equipped eastbound motor cars, with 12 westbound control trailers. Three of the single-equipped motor cars retained two motor bogies, since only 12 were required to equip the control trailers. The trailer bogies released were used at the idle ends of the other single-equipped motor cars. Up to this time, all motor cars had been provided with shoegear on both bogies. On those converted from control trailers, however, shoegear was not provided on the trailing end bogie, reducing

the amount of new power cabling that had to be installed. The reconstruction programme was completed by June 1930 but the first operation of a train with the electro-pneumatic brake was in June 1928. The train formation at this time was DM-3T-1T-SM-CT-3T-DM and as the control trailer provided First Class accommodation, this formation gave a symmetrical train in this respect.

The 'F' stock was chosen for the extended trial of the electro-pneumatic brake equipment which had been developed in America, because this block of stock could be kept segregated.

At the time of this reconstruction the lino flooring was replaced with the normal wood lagging, as this was found to be more serviceable.

One train was at first equipped experimentally with the American Westinghouse Type 20 driver's brake valve based on the electro-pneumatic design then in use in New York. Between 1928 and 1930 all the F stock was equipped with the Type 21 brake controller which incorporated the full electro-pneumatic control. Subsequently when this equipment was applied to other Underground rolling stock following the success of this trial the American nomenclature was abandoned and the controller used in London Underground became known as the 'A' type. During the third rehabilitation of the 1920 stock in 1950 the Type 21 brake controllers were replaced with type 'A' controllers, many of which had become redundant from the tube stock control trailers no longer required.

In 1938 the second rehabilitation of the 1920 stock was undertaken. The principal work being carried out at this time was the conversion of the control trailers to single-equipped motor cars and the fitting of air-operated doors with passenger push-button control.

The control trailers were converted to motor cars by the transfer of equipment from the scrapped 'Southend' locomotives.

The guard's control panel for the air-doors was only provided on the double-equipped motor cars and the train formation was altered to DM-3T-1T-SM-SM-3T-3T-DM. The west-facing single-equipped motor car was provided with First Class accommodation, having been converted from the control trailer car.

The final rehabilitation programme for the F stock came in 1950 with the advent of the R stock on the District. This caused some re-allocation of rolling stock, enabling the 1920 stock to be transferred to the Metropolitan Line. Because of its speed it was very suitable for working the semi-fast Harrow and Uxbridge

Top Original interior of F stock, with vertical grab poles. *Centre* Interior of F stock in its final form with additional light fittings at the cant rail. The centre grab poles have been removed and the seating has been provided with armrests. *Bottom* An F stock train with guard demonstrating new starting bell arrangements introduced in the early-1920s in connection with a reduction in the number of guards carried on each train of six cars or more from two to one.

services. The first renovated train went into service on the Metropolitan on 27th February 1951. In addition arrangements were made for four-car sets to work the East London shuttle services with the maintenance based on Neasden Depot, replacing the hand-worked door stock based on Ealing Common. This change took place on 7th December 1953. The use of four-car units of F Stock in passenger service created an additional problem because the guard's door control had only been provided on the double-equipped motor cars. The guard was therefore required to operate always from the same position, whichever direction the four-car unit was working. A double battery arrangement with alternate charging was therefore incorporated on those double-equipped motor cars that could be allocated to the service. Ten four-car units were altered to be available for East London service although only six units were required at any one time to be on duty on the line.

When 'Drico', the driver-to-controller communication system, was added to F Stock this too was only fitted to the double-equipped motor cars for operation on eight-car trains, but the ten units suitable for operation on the East London service had this equipment fitted to the single-equipped cars also.

At this time the most important work undertaken was the renewal of all the electric power cabling and control wiring, and the installation of 'A' type electro-pneumatic brake controllers.

Another innovation which has since become standard equipment on the more modern stocks was the provision of mercury-type door interlocks. The door interlock, an important safety feature provided with air-door installations, ensures that doors are properly closed before the starting signal is given. Until this time these were copper contact 'make and break' switches which required regular cleaning to ensure proper functioning. The mercury switch, having no open contacts and working on the tumble principle, requires little direct attention.

In addition some improvements were made to the bogie springing by the fitting of 12-plate laminated springs instead of 7-plate. Additional lighting fittings were provided in the car interior to increase the illumination.

The original doors were of wood covered with steel panels and these were beyond reasonable repair, so new doors of aluminium alloy were fitted at this time. Although the passenger push-button control was retained and brought into use on the Uxbridge service on which the trains were now running, this equipment was soon withdrawn from use. The transfer of this stock released P stock for operating the Circle service which in turn enabled the old Metropolitan Circle stock to be scrapped.

The last F stock passenger train was a four-car on East London service on Saturday night, 7th September 1963. The last train on the Uxbridge service ran on 15th March 1963.

An eight-car F stock train passes a four car CO/CP stock train near Eastcote in later life.

The G Class (1923 Stock)

G class motor car when new. It carries a new livery of lighter red body with original dark red doors.

In 1923 it was decided to purchase some new motor cars. The new cars were known as G class and enabled some of the original wooden trailer cars to be scrapped by converting the equivalent number of 1905 motor cars to trailers. The equipments released from the converted motor cars were used to fit out the new cars which were then compatible with the original stock. Forty-two 1904/5 motor cars were converted to trailer cars and eight motor cars were scrapped, providing the GE69 equipments fitted to the new G class cars at this time.

A total of 50 car bodies was ordered from the Gloucester Railway Carriage & Wagon Company, together with new motor and trailer trucks. More trucks were ordered than necessary to equip the 50 car bodies so that a number of the original 1905 type bogies which were unsatisfactory could also be replaced. These new bogies were designated 'A2' and 'K2'. The 'A2' motor bogie was of plate-and-angle construction with a 7ft 10in wheelbase.

The original 'K' bogie was of equaliser bar type with a wheelbase of 5 feet, and this bogie had proved very unreliable, requiring frequent maintenance. The new 'K2' bogie was of plate-and-angle construction, with a wheelbase of 7ft 3in and 42 of the 1904/5 motor cars were converted to trailers and fitted with 'K2' bogies. These converted cars were at this time designated H class.

In 1925 the rolling stock maintained for general passenger service on the District Railway was listed by the Records Office at Acton Works to be as follows:

	Type	*Motor*	*Trailer*	*Control Trailer*
1904/5	B	147	150	26
Hurst Nelson	C	32	20	—
Metro	D	22	8	—
Gloucester	E	26	4	—
Metro	F	40	48	12
Gloucester	G	50	—	—
Electric locos	—	7	—	—
Converted 1904/5	H	—	42	—

Interior of a 1923 Gloucester-built car with original grey 'lozenge' moquette.

Of this total 37 motors and 37 trailers of B class and eight motors and eight trailers of D class were owned by the London Midland & Scottish Railway to cover the mileage operated on the section between Campbell Road Junction (east of Bow Road station) and Barking, which was controlled by this railway.

Although subsequently 33 of the G class faced west and only 17 faced east, this was a result of the 1928 reconstruction programme. As delivered the air hoses were under the coupler, as on the B stock, the control and bus line jumpers being duplicated at the car ends so that they could be turned if necessary. However no turning facilities were provided at Ealing Common Depot for adjusting train make-ups. The only method available for turning cars was to run round the Cromwell Curve triangle, reversing at High Street Kensington and again at South Kensington, or vice versa.

These G class cars were similar in appearance to the earlier District Railway cars, with clerestory roofs and straight-sided bodies. The clerestory roof, however, was carried forward to the end of the car body and not rounded off as in the American style, and this construction gave the cars a box-like appearance.

The driver was given a totally-enclosed narrow cab across the whole width of the driving end, the practice of providing driving facilities at one end only having now been firmly established as a general operating principle. This cab was narrower than that provided on subsequent stock, and in the later days these cars came to be referred to as 'horse boxes'.

On the G class cars the driving cab was unavailable to passengers when not in use by the driver. This facility existed in the older cars, where the driver's controls were locked in a 'cupboard' making it possible for the driver's vestibule to be available for passengers when not required by him. The side cab doors were of the hinged type, being locked when not in use. The passenger doors were placed in pairs and were sliding hand-operated, originally being provided with a safety catch and indicator denoting whether the catch was 'locked' or 'unlocked'.

A B class car converted to run with new G class motor cars being lowered onto K2 bogies in the lifting shop at Acton Works.

A 1923 steel stock motor car coupled to a wooden trailer converted from a B class motor car, photographed in December 1934.

In 1928, when the first District Line rolling stock reconstruction programme was undertaken, the G class motor cars had GE69 traction motors and equipment (which was secondhand in any case) removed and replaced by WT54B type traction motors, together with the latest type of BTH electro-magnetic control equipment using an accelerating relay which eliminated hand notching of the controls.

About ten years later, under the 1935/40 New Works Programme of the London Passenger Transport Board, the G class cars were converted to join the Q stock fleet, being fitted with air-operated doors and electro-pneumatic brakes at Acton Works. When the Q stock fleet was reduced after the advent of the A stock for the Metropolitan Line in 1960/62 as many G class cars as possible were withdrawn, but 14 west-facing cars had to be retained to provide the eight-car formations which only required one west end motor car.

Although no trailer cars of the G class were originally built, 14 of them ended their days as trailer cars, being converted in 1959 to replace Q38 stock trailer cars removed from the Q stock fleet at this time to augment O, P and R stock fleets. These 1923 stock cars, however, were among the first to be scrapped in 1962, when the Q stock fleet was reduced upon the introduction of the second batch of A stock on the Metropolitan Line.

Two G stock cars were converted in the 1938 rolling stock reconstruction programme to operate the South Acton shuttle and these were provided with some special features. The two cars chosen for this duty were 4167 and 4176, and the similarity of the numbering made the cars easily recognisable by all concerned. The removal of 4176 from the Q stock fleet, however, upset the balance of cars and one east end motor car was turned to west end to compensate, and renumbered.

The South Acton service became a shuttle from Acton Town on 15th February 1932, shortly before the projection of the Piccadilly Line trains west of Hammersmith, which took place on 4th July 1932. Before this a South Acton to Hounslow service had been operated, with the permanent way on the South Acton branch double-tracked. This was reduced to a single track on 14th February 1932, when Acton Town station was rebuilt, in anticipation of the Piccadilly extension, with five platforms, one of which was very short and used exclusively for the shuttle train to South Acton. B class motor car No. 37, one of the batch originally built at Lunéville in France, was converted to a double-ended car which could be operated as a single unit. In addition to providing control positions at both ends of the car, two brake cylinders were installed to ensure independent braking of the two bogies to reduce the possibility of a brake failure. This car was replaced from time to time by a motor car and control trailer of B stock when No. 37 required maintenance.

Originally in the 1935/40 programme it was intended to retain No. 37 on this duty, but the provision of a substitute after the scrapping of the B stock would have presented a problem since all the control trailer cars were also being scrapped. It was decided, therefore, to convert two 1923 stock cars for this duty, one in service and one as standby. The work on these cars included the fitting of duplicate brake cylinders and triple valves and the provision of a driver's cab at both ends. The work, which was carried out at Acton Works late in 1939, also included the fitting of air-door control but the cars, being intended for one-man operation, had a special interlock circuit which prevented traction control being obtained until the driver had shut himself in the cab. After operating for a number of years with full series-parallel notching, it was considered that this provided too high a speed potential for the short curved track between Acton Town and South Acton. An alteration to the control circuit was therefore made, limiting the notching to series only. Because the train service was one-man operated, a pair of emergency telephone wires, normally installed only in tunnel sections, was erected alongside the shuttle track in 1938. This enabled the driver of the shuttle to take off the current in an emergency without having to leave his cab.

The South Acton shuttle service ceased to operate on 28th February 1959, and the track was completely removed. The bridge which carried this line across Bollo Lane was also later removed, so that practically all trace of this service has now disappeared.

The Acton Town to South Acton shuttle at South Acton in the 1950s.

The 1927, 1931 & 1935 Stocks

One of the 101 Birmingham-built motor cars of the K class, photographed when new in 1927.
This car was for a time owned by the LMS railway, as indicated by the M painted after the K on the soleplate.

A complete review of the District Line rolling stock position was undertaken in 1926, and arising from this 101 new cars (the K stock) were ordered from the Birmingham Railway Carriage & Wagon Company—81 were required as replacements and 20 to provide additional services. As all the cars purchased were motor cars this meant another re-arrangement of the existing fleet, because, at the same time, a total of 263 sets of BTH electro-magnetic equipments, together with their appropriate WT54B traction motors, were also purchased.

The District Line's rolling stock requirements would be met as follows: 40 motor cars and 60 trailers provided by F stock incompatible with any other stock; 263 motor cars (52 C class, 30 D class, 30 E class, 50 G class and 101 K class) and 248 trailers provided by 'standard' BTH stock, or 'Main Line' stock as it was then called; and 37 motor cars and 18 control trailers to be provided by stock still equipped with GE69 type traction equipment (but now fitted with GE212 traction motors), known as 'Local' stock.

The provision of this total number of motor cars entailed the conversion of 32 of the 'C', 'D', and 'E' trailer cars to motor cars which had been anticipated in the original design.

The 248 trailer cars required were provided by the 42 'H' class trailers already converted from 1905 motor cars, together with a further 110 similar conversions. The remaining 96 trailer cars required were wooden 'B' class trailer cars fitted with the appropriate through control lines. Apart from 18 control trailers of 'B' class kept to run as 'Local Stock', all the other wooden 'B' class trailers were scrapped. Most of the B and H trailers could work with the main line motor cars because the control lines were available in a suitable position for coupling and the air connections could be made with adaptors. The net result of all this work was to increase the District Line fleet by 42 cars.

The 'Local Stock' was required to operate the shuttle-type services then running from South Acton to Hounslow, and from Acton Town to South Harrow and through to Uxbridge over the Metropolitan tracks.

Of the 101 new cars delivered at this time 91 were delivered complete with bogies, two with new trailer bogies only and eight without any bogies at all. Ten 'A2' type motor bogies and eight 'K2' type trailer bogies were recovered by the conversion of motor cars to trailer cars and the scrapping of some 'B' class cars.

At the end of this programme the District Line had three types of stock in service which were incompatible, because they had different traction control systems using different type traction motors GE 260, WT 54B, and GE212. This unfortunate condition continued for over 40 years, providing operating problems on the District Line which were not entirely eliminated until the completion of D 78 stock deliveries in 1983.

Externally the 'K' class cars had a less box-like and much smoother appearance than the earlier 'G' class, the corners and lines being rounded off. This improved the looks of the cars considerably. The main side lights were made larger and the end of the clerestory was curved down to the cant rail. Four additional seats were provided in the guard's gangway,

Interior of K class motor car looking towards the guard's end.

which could be folded away when not in use. These proved to be rather an obstruction and were later removed.

The five headlights, or marker lights, were contained in a single panel on the opposite side of the front of the car to the driver, instead of being exhibited as single lamps distributed widely over the front. The display of the marker lights was controlled by shutters adjusted from inside the cab, instead of movable fan-plates swivelled from the outside.

In addition the destination box placed above the marker light panel was accessible from inside the cab. Previously, destination plates had been inserted externally in brackets. These cars were about 49 feet in length overall, slightly longer than previous stock. The extra floor area was used to improve the space available to the driver and the guard's gangway at the trailing end of the car. The driver's cab in particular had been considered to be too small on the G stock. They were somewhat lighter than the G class however, weighing about 34 tons compared with 35 tons.

On the earlier stock the guard's gangway had been separated from the car saloon on the trailing end of motor cars by a metal screen. These new cars were provided with a glass draught screen. The guard's door, however, was still of the hinged inward opening type and could not, therefore, be used by passengers when not required by the guard. The car saloon seated 40 passengers and some folding companion seats were provided. These cars were designated the 'K' class.

With the introduction of K stock, the District adopted the 'shuttle' or 'handed' train formation whereby the cars normally faced in one direction only and were not turned except under abnormal conditions. The inter-car air hoses were placed at waist level, the main pipe or compressor line on one side of the car centre line and the Westinghouse brake pipe or train line on the other. These air hoses in the earlier stocks had been placed adjacent to and just below the centre coupling, so that both ends of the car were virtually the same and reversible coupling was possible by the provision of duplicate electrical connections. On the K stock all the electrical connections were brought to the outer ends of the car body headstock, the control with ten wires on one side and the auxiliary, containing lighting and heating circuits, on the other. On the earlier stock the lighting bus line had been carried across the roof, while the control jumper had been arranged near the coupler.

A six-car District main line train of 'standard' BTH stock during the second world war, showing the mixed car formation which was anything but standard in appearance. It is seen at Ealing Broadway alongside Central Line tracks with the three rail system. The leading car is a 1927 motor car and it is followed by a wooden B class trailer.

A 1931 L class motor car built by the Union Construction Company. From this stock the doors were painted in the same shade of red as the rest of the car.

Interior of L class trailer car with the First Class partition door fully open.

As it was necessary for the K stock to run with older stocks, arrangements were made for these to be modified to conform to this new formation. The C, D, E and G classes of rolling stock were altered as they passed through Acton Works, and so were some of the earlier B stock cars which had been converted to trailers and reclassified as H stock. The alterations included the replacement of the GE69 type equipment and the fitting of WT54B type traction motors. The entire programme was not completed until January 1930.

About the time of the introduction of this class of stock to District Line service, a new type of train-starting equipment was tried, and subsequently adopted, continuing in use until the introduction of air doors. A twin wire arrangement was suspended at car-roof height on the station platforms at the guard's end of the trains. These wires were shorted together by a metal ferrule provided on the end of the guard's green flag handle. This action caused a bell to ring at the driver's end of the platform and for an illuminated S (for start) to appear within the driver's vision. This arrangement superseded the system of passing a signal from car to car with the trains carrying a number of conductors instead of just a single guard at the rear. For a number of years after the introduction of this new starting device, two guards continued to be provided on eight-car trains because of the limited platform clearances at a number of District Line stations.

The $7\frac{3}{4}$-mile extension to Upminster beyond Barking came into operation on 12th September 1932. The London Midland & Scottish Railway had constructed two additional tracks alongside the old Tilbury & Southend line, so that six stations beyond Barking could be served by District Line trains. A seventh station, Upminster Bridge, was added on 17th December 1934, and an eighth at Elm Park on 13th May 1935.

In 1932, in anticipation of the additional cars required for the Upminster service, 45 new vehicles designated 'L' class were ordered from the Union Construction Co. of Feltham, a subsidiary company of the Underground group. Of this number only 8 were motor cars, the remaining 37 were trailer cars. The 'L' class motor cars were the first surface stock to be provided with a sliding door at the guard's position.

The number of new cars purchased at this time for the District Line was small because some District trains were being replaced by the extension of the Piccadilly Line west of Hammersmith. A full service of Piccadilly Line trains began running to Hounslow West on 13th March 1933, with only a few District trains operating in rush hours to this destination subsequently; these were withdrawn in 1964. District Line trains ceased to run on the Uxbridge service after 22nd October 1933.

The trailer cars had the passenger compartment divided into three sections separated by a glazed partition to provide First and Third Class accommodation, and also to divide the First Class into smoking and non-smoking sections. The glazed partitions were provided with swing doors which were returned to the closed position by spring door checks. These trailer cars were of 'lightweight' construction, since complete with bogies they weighed only 23 tons although constructed of steel.

The bogies for the cars were built by Metropolitan Cammell, the electrical control equipment by BTH, and the WT54B motors by GEC to match the equipment obtained for the 1927/28 conversion programme. The traction motors for these cars, however, were delivered with roller bearings, while the earlier motors of this type had to undergo a conversion programme at Acton Works to change from white metal to roller bearings. This change was one of the major labour-saving innovations at this time. Before the advent of roller bearings on the traction motors, oiling of the motor bearings had to be undertaken at least once a week. Now, with the introduction of grease-lubricated roller bearings, the period was extended first to 3 months and later to 12 months, while today consideration is being given to even longer periods between lubrication of this type of equipment.

All eight motor cars of this class faced west, but the overall service requirements at this time needed the addition of six eastbound cars and only two westbound. To balance the stock requirements, therefore, six of the 1910 'C' class were turned at Acton Works from west to

Above N class motor car of 1935. This was the last stock to be delivered with hand-operated doors; the M class built at the same time and to the same general design was fitted with air-operated doors. A short-lived innovation was the application of the line name to some stock in addition to the London Transport lettering. *Below* Interior views of an N class motor car (left) and an N class trailer (right) with First Class compartment.

A six-car train of 1935 M stock, with air-operated doors, outside Hammersmith (Met) station.

east. The physical turning was, of course, accomplished round Cromwell Curve, but the work at Acton consisted of changing control connections and air lines for coupling purposes and other minor equipment alterations.

These eight 'L' class motor cars were, in fact, owned by the London, Midland & Scottish Railway, as the mileage operated arising out of the extension to Upminster called for an increase in its ownership of vehicles. The total ownership by the LMS was raised at this time to 57 motor cars and 53 trailer cars, or the equivalent of 13 trains plus a few spare cars. However, these cars were never specially worked together, and no distinction was made as to their operating routes. For operating purposes they were part of the District fleet and the ownership arrangements were purely financial. Nationalisation in 1948 removed the necessity for any joint ownership of rolling stock.

At the completion of these modifications and the new stock deliveries the District train formation was made up with a four-car main portion having either one or two 'East End' portions added so that the trains could be operated either as four-car, six-car or eight-car trains.

The London Passenger Transport Board's creation in 1933 had the effect of amalgamating the Metropolitan and District Railways, and some consolidation of the services provided was inevitable. One of the first effects of this was the projection of Metropolitan trains to Barking in 1936. This service was provided from Hammersmith at first but then between 17th July 1939 and 6th October 1941 an Uxbridge to Barking service with eight-car trains was operated. This improved the frequency of the services over this section in addition to providing a route to the north of the City from the East End without the need to change.

In order to obtain some new vehicles quickly it was decided to repeat the design which was available. Orders were placed for 28 cars, 14 motors and 14 trailers from the Birmingham Railway Carriage & Wagon Co., and a further 26 trailer cars from Metro-Cammell. Although the designs were almost identical and similar to the 'L' class, the 28 cars were given the classification 'M' and the Metro-Cammell cars the class letter 'N'.

Out of the 40 trailer cars built, only 5 were plain Third Class trailers, the other 35 were composities, identical with the 'L' class, having three sections with glazed partitions.

Twenty-four of the Birmingham cars were delivered in four six-car train sets and operated in block formations; that is, the same six cars were kept together in each train. The reason for this was that this group of cars was fitted with electro-pneumatic brakes and two of the trains were experimentally fitted with air-operated doors. These were the first surface stock trains to operate with air-door equipment since the unsuccessful pneumatic door equipment was taken out of use on the B stock in 1908. The cars were equipped at this time with passenger-operated door buttons so that only those doors through which the passengers wished to board or alight were opened. This was the first use of this equipment on Underground trains. The trains went into service on the Hammersmith & City Line, providing the extra operating trains required for the extension of this service to Barking. Some trains worked from the H & C Line to East Ham from 30th March 1936, but when First Class accommodation was withdrawn from the Hammersmith & City and East London Line service on 4th May 1936, eight trains an hour out of the twelve provided at the peak periods began working through to Whitechapel and Barking. The provision of First Class accommodation on the new trailer cars was, therefore, short-lived, although this class was reinstated when these cars were later transferred to the District Line on completion of the delivery of the O stock specifically for the Hammersmith & City service.

On 1st February 1940 First Class accommodation was withdrawn except to Aylesbury and the Watford Joint Lines, where it survived until 6th October 1941.

When the cars were transferred to the District the electro-pneumatic brake had to be temporarily disconnected and all doors converted to hand operation, because at this time it was necessary for the trailer cars to work with the 1910/13 motor cars which were not suitable for conversion to air-doors.

There were originally 112 motor cars of 1910/13 stock retained in 1938 and, together with seventy-seven 1931/35 stock trailer cars, they formed the 'H' class stock. This was the second use of the letter 'H', as none of the original 'H' stock trailer cars were now left. 'H' now conveniently stood for 'hand-worked' door stock.

Of the 112 motor cars, one was damaged beyond repair in the Charing Cross collision in May 1938, and during 1938/39 fourteen were converted to trailer cars, so that the fleet of 'H' stock became 97 motor cars and 91 trailer cars. All this work, however, formed part of the 'Q' stock programme which began in 1937 and was not completed when the Second World War broke out in 1939.

The O & P Stocks and the Metadyne

The first Gloucester-built two-car unit of O stock at Ealing Common depot. The leading car carried the metadyne machine.

At the time that new stock was being considered for Metropolitan and District Line replacement requirements, a new system of control was being developed by Metropolitan Vickers known as the metadyne system. Arrangements were made in 1934 for a six-car experimental train to be tested to see whether this system could be used on the new rolling stock.

The six cars chosen for this experiment were old Metropolitan motor cars built between 1904 and 1907. The cars were converted at Acton Works during 1934, being fitted with metadyne traction control equipments and externally finished in a red and cream livery similar to that applied to the reconditioned Circle cars.

The metadyne system involved the provision of a rotary transformer (metadyne means 'conversion of power') placed between the line supply and the traction motors. This machine was able to supply four traction motors and in order to conform to the accepted practice of having only two traction motors to each car the experimental cars were converted in pairs. One carried the metadyne machine and control gear and the other was provided with the auxiliary equipment which included a motor generator set to supply low voltage for control and lighting.

Two traction motors on each car were supplied from one metadyne machine so that the cars could not be worked singly and always worked in pairs. Each pair of cars could be operated separately having a driving position at the outer ends. Test trains could, therefore, either be worked in two-, four- or six-car formations. When this test train had completed its trials the cars were scrapped, but the metadyne equipment was removed and fitted to three battery locomotives, also now scrapped.

The metadyne system was attractive for several reasons:

(1) one set of control equipment could control two motor cars;
(2) the system was inherently regenerative so that an economical braking system could be developed;
(3) no starting resistances were needed and the acceleration was smooth.

One of the principal developments achieved with this experiment was the successful blending of air and electric braking, so that initially the motors provided all the braking effort, but when more was required than they could provide, air braking was gradually applied to the trailing axles. At low speeds, as the electrical effort faded away, or if the line became unreceptive to regenerated current (because no other trains using current were in the section at the time), then air braking took over as required on the motored axles also. All this was performed without the passenger being aware of what was being done, and without the driver having to take any special action to achieve it.

As a result of the tests carried out during 1935 and 1936 over practically all the electrified tracks of the Metropolitan and District lines, and later tests in passenger service, it was decided to equip most of the new stock with metadyne control.

For surface stock renewal at the time of the 1935/40 New Works Programme, 573 cars were purchased. These vehicles were built by two carbuilders, the Gloucester Railway Carriage & Wagon Company and the Birmingham Railway Carriage & Wagon Company, starting in 1936 and consisted of three different classes – the O, P and Q stocks. The last of the cars were delayed by the outbreak of the Second World War and delivery was not completed until March 1941. All the cars were similar in general construction and the trailer cars were so built that they could be converted into motor cars at a later date if necessary.

The original order covered the purchase of rolling stock to replace the Hammersmith & City trains and consisted of 116 cars, all motor cars, equally divided between the two carbuilders and to be formed into two-car units. These were designated O stock. The stock ordered to replace the Metropolitan car stock was designated the P stock, and that required for the District replacement the Q stock.

The O stock trains at the ordering stage were known as the Hammersmith & City Replacement Stock and, as they were designed to operate in two-car units, the 116 cars could be made up into 19 six-car trains with one two-car unit spare. Together with 4 six-car trains of 1935 stock already operating on this service, this made a total of 23 six-car trains which equalled the number of old stock previously required to provide the Hammersmith service, including maintenance spares. Subsequently trailer cars were provided to make all the O stock units into three-car sets, which meant that a total of 29 six-car trains could be provided. The 1935 stock was then transferred to the District Line and some of the O stock began to be used on the Met main line.

This new stock was different in appearance from any which had previously been built. Each car body was just over 51 feet long and, apart from the equipment fitted to the underframe, each car of the pair was in general layout a mirror image of the other. Each car was provided with one single and two double passenger doors each side of the passenger saloon, and because these cars were built for the Hammersmith & City service only one class of travel was now provided. As originally built the 'A' end motor cars were virtually divided into two compartments by glass partitions reaching full body height, but without a swing door, providing smoking and non-smoking space. No door division was provided because the double glass partition which formed the air intake for equipment cooling made a natural division of the car. This air intake ventilated the interior of the vehicle and also provided clean air for cooling the metadyne machine carried on the 'A' car.

The O stock did not go into service immediately on the Hammersmith Line, the first use in service being between High Street Kensington and Putney Bridge with a four-car unit on 13th September 1937. The first six-car train composed of three two-car units went into service on the Hammersmith Line on 10th December 1937.

The O stock cars were fitted originally with semi-loose cushions covered with moquette, but these were later converted to standard interior sprung seats as fitted to subsequent stock. Each car had seating for 40 passengers with, in addition, two tip-up seats provided on the trailing end bulkheads. The sliding doors were pneumatically operated and when built were fitted with passenger door control. The push-buttons were fitted to the body door pillars and not on the door frames themselves as arranged on the original 1935 stock fitted with this equipment.

The guard's door controls for these air-operated doors were placed in the driver's cab because the guard on Hammersmith & City stock had always worked from the rear cab, and at the time of placing the orders for the stock this was still the practice.

Externally the car windows were flush with the body. This was effected by the use of rebated glass. The side panels were flared at the bottom and the lower end of the sliding doors followed this contour. This was done to take the place of the side running boards provided on the earlier stocks and avoided having gaps at platforms. It was useful to avoid providing running boards with air-door stock because of the hazard if foolhardy passengers hung on to the outside after the train started with the doors closed. This arrangement gave the cars a very pleasing appearance, which was spoiled as far as the Q stock was concerned by the need to operate some formations with stock of new and old designs.

In addition to the original 116 cars of O stock a further 457 cars were ordered from the same carbuilders, making a total of 573

Interior of an O stock motor car.
The partitions in the centre bays had two panes of glass with a space in between for the metadyne air intake.

vehicles of which 287 were motor cars. All except 25 of these motor cars were provided with metadyne equipment and formed into two- or three-car units. The 25 motor cars not metadyne-equipped were part of the Q stock order for the District Line. The three-car units included a trailer car. The cars of the units were close-coupled, with a bar coupling not normally disconnected. The units themselves were made up into train sets of four-, five-, six-, seven-, or eight-car lengths by coupling appropriate combinations of two- and three-car units together by means of a Wedglock automatic coupler which coupled them together pneumatically, electrically and mechanically. Although the Wedglock couplers themselves at both ends of the units were identical mechanically, the electrical connections were not duplicated on each side of the centre line, so the cars continued to be handed. In addition the west end or 'A' car was fitted with a solid buffer while the east end or 'D' car was fitted with a spring buffer. Under normal coupling arrangements an 'A' and 'D' were coupled together but in an emergency two 'A' cars could be coupled. Two 'D' cars could also be coupled but had to be provided with an emergency "adaptor".

The second batch of metadyne-controlled cars, designated P stock, was required for the replacement of all the car stock on the Metropolitan Line, where eight-car formations as well as six-car formations were required. It was therefore decided to adopt the formation M-T-M+M-T-M-M-M; that is, an eight-car train made up of two three-car units and one two-car unit. The units were close-coupled with automatic couplers at the outer ends. The automatic couplers provided were similar to those adopted for the 1938 tube stock ordered at the same time, providing mechanical, electrical and pneumatic coupling. The first P stock train entered service on 17th July 1939.

Although the P stock had a similar external appearance to the O stock, they differed from O stock cars in several respects. The door controls operated by the guard were provided on the P stock in the then conventional tube stock position at the end gangway of the motor car. The metadyne cooling intake provided in the 'A', or west end, cars on P stock was placed under the middle companion seats without the provision of double glass in the partition.

MD53-type metadyne machine from the regulator and exciter end on the ventilating duct side. This machine weighed about 3 tons and was suspended along the centre of the car underframe.

Guard's control panels in a P stock car. On the O stock the guard's controls were situated in the driver's cab.

P stock trailer. The hinged door at one end was provided so that the trailers would be easier to convert to motor cars at a future date.

A train of P stock on the Met main line at Rayners Lane in the early 1950s.

Interior of a P stock trailer car when new.

Some O stock cars were subsequently fitted with centre grab poles in the middle of the double-door gangways to provide additional support for standing passengers. This feature lasted for several years, but was later removed because the pole in the middle of this standing area proved to be an obstruction tending to restrict the free flow of passengers under crowded conditions.

The bogies were of welded steel plate construction and were asymmetric in design, that is – the axles were unequally spaced about the pivot point. The axle nearer the centre carried the single traction motor fitted to each motor bogie. In this way a greater proportion of the car weight was available for adhesion. The bogie was designed for good riding qualities, having the bolster springing and the swing links placed as far apart as possible. The wheels were 36 inches in diameter with full-sized tyres, and the gear ratio provided was 16/65. The motor axle had a roller bearing sleeve on which the MV145AZ type traction motor was mounted. Previous surface rolling stock had been provided with plain white metal bearings for mounting axle-hung traction motors on the axle. The wheels were fitted with either SKF or Hoffman parallel roller-type axle boxes, a feature of this type of axle box being the ease of removal from the axle journal.

The trailer bogies were almost identical with the motor bogies but did not carry a traction motor and, therefore, neither axle had a suspension sleeve. Two brake cylinders were provided, one which actuated the brake blocks on the motored wheels or their equivalent on a trailer bogie, and the other on the trailer wheels. This arrangement enabled a differential braking system to be installed in connection with the metadyne control which included the provision of regenerative braking.

Each two- or three-car unit of O and P stock was fitted with one compressor and one 5kw motor-generator set which provided a 50-volt DC supply for control and lighting. The lighting was provided by incandescent bulbs along each side of the roof line, and the bulbs were originally covered by shovel-type lamp shades. These shades were removed in later years when a higher lighting standard was considered necessary, and unshaded antiglare-type bulbs were fitted to provide an increase in the illumination.

The cars of similar construction for the District Line services were known as Q stock and, with the exception of 25 motor cars, were all trailer cars. These cars had to work with existing older rolling stock not equipped with 50-volt lighting circuits. The interior appearance was the same but the lamps were energised from a 600-volt supply having five lamps in series. As a safety measure the shades were not removed from these cars in case unauthorised persons tampered with the lamps in these high-voltage circuits.

Of the 573 O, P and Q stock cars, 286 were trailers. They were constructed so that they could, in fact, be converted to motor cars, because it was considered that at some time in the future – after the improvements to the power supply had been completed – a higher performance would be required from the rolling stock in the way of acceleration, and this could only be met by increasing the number of motored axles on the trains. The cars were built 'handed'. Provision was made for a driving cab at either the 'A' or 'D' end in equal numbers. At the position where the driving cab would be provided the cab door of the hinged type was fitted but locked up, and the four extra seats in trailer cars were provided against the car end. The end corridor door at this position was not provided with a droplight as it was the equivalent of a driver's leading cab door.

Although only a few of these trailer cars were converted to P stock motor cars, advantage was taken of this provision when the R stock was purchased after the war.

When the O stock first entered service in 1937, technical problems arose through the maximum demand and the effect of regeneration with a train entirely composed of motor cars, and it was decided to dilute the train formation by the insertion of trailer cars into the units. To do this, 58 further trailer cars were ordered from the Gloucester Company, to make each of the two-car units into a three-car set. The problem was virtually one of timing as it was considered that sometime in the future trains composed all of motor cars would be necessary to meet the traffic demands, and these trailer cars were designed in such a way that they could easily be converted into motor cars at a future date. The first train with trailers went into service on the Hammersmith Line on 18th July 1938.

The O and P stocks were compatible both as to control and coupling arrangements but there were a number of fundamental differences so that equipment itself was not interchangeable. In particular the metadyne machines were not interchangeable. This machine, which weighed about 3 tons, consisted of three rotating machines known as the exciter, the regulator, and the metadyne machine itself, mechanically coupled together. The electrical connections of the machine were different and they were not interchangeable between O and P stock cars. This was a serious disadvantage in later years when a spate of major defects requiring extensive repairs arose. This epidemic was one of the reasons why consideration was given to the withdrawal and replacement of the equipment. Some spare 1938 tube stock PCM (pneumatic camshaft mechanism) equipments were available at the time, and as the operation of this equipment had exceeded all expectations in reliability, it was decided to convert one metadyne train operating on the Circle Line service to PCM control. This, in the first instance, provided additional metadyne spares for metadyne equipments by cannibalisation, but in addition enabled the conversion costs to be assessed.

The first converted train, which became known as CO/CP stock as it contained both O and P stock cars, went into service on the Circle on 31st March 1955 and subsequently all the O and P stock was converted. Individual motor cars were classified either CO or CP and trailers were classified COP.

Another difference of a fundamental nature between O and P stock was the operating position of the guard. In O stock the door control boxes were provided in the driver's cab so that the guard worked from the extreme rear of the train, which conformed to the previous operating practice of the Hammersmith & City Line with hand-operated doors. The P stock, however, had the door control boxes placed on the end gangway conforming with previous Underground practice where air-doors were fitted.

With the introduction of trailer cars into the O stock two-car units, 19 units were released from H & C service for operation elsewhere. Apart from the Hammersmith & City services, the requirements for the Metropolitan Line at this time could be fulfilled by the provision of 64 three-car and 28 two-car units. The problem which then had to be overcome was that the O stock units could not be operated at the end of 8-car trains in the central area platforms because of the length limitation which would leave the rear end cab in the tunnel with the guard unsighted for his platform duties.

Subsequent adjustments to the stock allocation made it necessary to purchase 73 P stock units which, together with the 19 units of O stock, made the total of 92 units required. As 28 of these were to be of two-car formation without trailer cars, it was arranged that the A-end 'O' and O stock cars (those numbered from 13xxx) were placed at the west end of 19 of these units; these would then normally be attached to the east end of six-car formations to make eight-car trains. Having placed these cars in a position where the door control equipment was virtually unused, it was then further arranged that six of the new motor cars of P stock which would also be 'A' end cars should not be provided with door control boxes. The decision to have six of these cars without door control boxes instead of nine arose because the service requirement was 25 eight-car trains, not 28 trains, so that the remaining three units were spares. In theory, therefore, the provision of door boxes enabled these cars to be utilised as spares for either type of operation. This theoretical decision was not, in fact, very helpful in practice, because splitting of any unit which was bar-coupled to change from a two-to three-car was an engineering operation not achieved by a simple shunting process. These cars without guard's control panels were coded 'P1'.

The 'D' end O stock cars (those numbered from 14xxx) were placed in three-car units and were only at the ends of six-car formations, and could be accommodated at all the stations where such formations were operated.

The effect of this programme was disastrous to the carefully prepared numbering scheme which had been devised to pair the 'A' and 'D' motor cars with the 13xxx and 14xxx numbers matching, and thereby simplify the recording requirements.

The O stock formations operated as six-car sets and provided the Hammersmith & City service to Whitechapel and Barking, while the mixed O and P stock maintained mainly the Metropolitan Line's Uxbridge service until the introduction of 'R' stock enabled the old Circle stock to be replaced by a re-arrangement of duties of F stock and O/P stock.

The O/P stock fleet suffered badly from war damage. At the end of the war the fleet was short of two 'A' or west end cars and five 'D' or east end cars, so to restore the balance three 'P' stock trailer cars were converted to 'D' end P stock motor cars by the Gloucester Railway Carriage & Wagon Company at the same time as the R stock was being built.

One other interesting conversion was undertaken during the war when car No. 14233, which had been severely damaged in an air raid on 18th September 1940, was repaired by using half of another car, Q stock trailer No. 013167 damaged at a later time. This car was returned to service on 29th September 1941 and for a number of years afterwards it carried a card with photographs showing the work involved. The car is now preserved by the Quainton Railway Society.

The transfer of F stock to the Uxbridge service enabled O/P stock units to be released to make up five-car sets of one three-car and one two-car unit to take over the Circle workings. The first five-car P stock train began operating on the Circle service in February 1947, but it was nearly four years before the complete service was provided by this stock. Although it was hoped that this change in the rolling stock would improve the reliability of the service, this was only marginally satisfactory. The Circle service is particularly arduous, each train making journeys of over 350 miles each day, stopping and starting every half-mile. This began to take its toll of the metadyne equipment, and the decision was then made to convert the trains working the Circle service to 'PCM' control.

The first converted train began working on 30th April 1956 and after conversion the first digit of the car number of the motor cars was altered from '1' to '5', so that the 'A' end cars became 53xxx and the 'D' cars 54xxx.

Subsequently 17 five-car trains were converted allowing only three spare trains against four previously held. This indicated to some extent the measure of the improvement of reliability which it was expected would be gained by the conversion. These spare trains, however, were now confined to Circle workings and did not form part of a greater fleet which could be used on the Metropolitan Main Line, where other O/P stock still operated. Improved reliability was in fact achieved, so it was decided to convert all the O/P stock to PCM in two stages, first the Hammersmith & City fleet and then the Metropolitan Main Line fleet. This latter conversion was arranged to

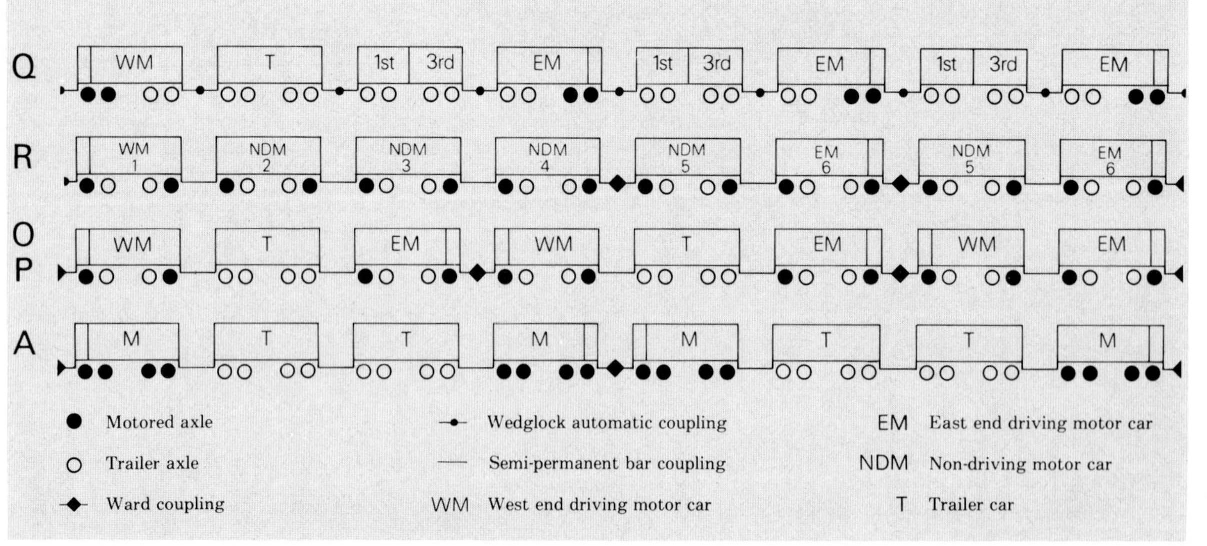

Diagram of eight-car train formations

CO stock train at Earl's Court in 1980. On the original O and P stock designs the driver had to leave his cab if the tripcock had to be reset, but in the early 1960s the tripcock resetting cord was extended so that it ended by the front door, as seen in this view.

coincide with the release of the P stock for transfer to the District Line upon the introduction of the second batch of A stock.

The five-car Circle trains were overcrowded in comparison with the District and Hammersmith & City six-car trains so it was then decided to increase the train length by the insertion of a trailer car into the two-car unit. The transfer of P stock to the District service enabled some of the Q stock trains to be replaced and the fleet reduced. Seventeen Q stock trailer cars were, therefore, converted to work as COP trailers. The conversion involved the alteration of the lighting from the 600-volt series to the 50-volt parallel arrangement, and the couplings from Ward to bar. The work of converting these cars was carried out at Acton Works during 1959/60. The first six-car train operated on the Circle service on 15th June 1959.

The lengthening of the Circle trains to six cars and the conversion of the H&C trains to PCM made it possible to integrate these two services so that the maintenance of all the CO/CP stock working Metropolitan services was concentrated at Hammersmith, enabling Neasden to concentrate on the enlarged A stock fleet. When the Metropolitan P stock fleet was first released for working on the District Line, only six-car formations were required because the R stock at that time could provide all the necessary eight-car workings. A further eight Q38 trailers were therefore converted to make two-car units into three cars during 1961/62.

Upon the introduction of the A62 stock to the Metropolitan Line, the bulk of the CP stock was transferred to the District Line. Almost the whole of the CO stock remained on the Hammersmith & City and Circle services until delivery of the C69 stock in 1970 allowed transfers to begin. The use of CO stock on the District Line's eight-car formation presented a similar problem to that encountered when O stock was first lengthened to eight cars before the war, because the guard travelled in the rear cab on the trains. This was acceptable in six-car formations but a number of District Line platforms only just accommodated the passenger door span of eight-car sets. Arrangements were made, therefore, to re-form three-car and two-car units to make sure that CO stock could not be placed at the extreme ends of eight-car formations.

The train formation of the CO/CP stock eight-car train on the District was arranged to be:

M-T-M M-T-M M-M
1-2-3 4-5-6 7-8

Originally the CO/CP stock was arranged so that the 53xxx numbered cars were classified 'A' end or west-facing and the 54xxx were 'D' end or east-facing cars. When the first batch was moved to the District Line the 54xxx cars were placed at the west end of the units. This was done to ensure compatibility of coupling with the Circle Line trains which were also composed of this stock, and which was 'right way' on the Metropolitan side of the Circle, but was 'wrong way' on the District portion.

So when the units were reformed the CO 54xxx cars were placed in two-car units, in this way providing the No. 7 position in an eight-car train. The CO 53xxx cars were placed at the east end of three-car units, forming either the No. 3 or No. 6 position.

One of the difficulties of running a service which uncouples (where the peak-hour trains are longer than those used at 'off-peak' times) is to ensure that the proper sections are available to make the appropriate marriage at the right time and place. This problem is increased, of course, when the service uses different stocks which have coupling incompatibility. The District Line management throughout its long history had had to cope with this problem.

Following the completion of the transfer of the whole of the CO/CP fleet, the case for running District Line seven-car trains over the whole of the operating day (rather than some eight-car sets mainly in the peaks, with six-car trains at all other times) was urged. As this arrangement would greatly simplify the operation of the service, it was decided to proceed. Some six-car trains were still necessary because of short platform lengths on the Edgware Road service, north of High Street Kensington. The CO/CP stock units, however, lent themselves to both six-and seven-car train formations as long as more two-car sets were maintained than three-car units. This position was achieved by scrapping some trailer cars. The seven-car formation was then made up in this way:

M-T-M+M-M+M-M

with the 6-car continuing as before:

M-T-M+M-T-M

The acceptance of the seven-car formation made it simpler to place CO stock cars at any position in the train. A new problem arose, which was solved by turning the units to face the other way. The CO/CP stock had remained 'wrong way' on the District Line as long as similar stock worked the Circle service but two emergency couplers were needed, a D-to-D to engage with the east end of an R stock, and a Ward-to-Wedglock to engage with the west end of an R stock. By turning the CO/CP stock, the provision of the D-to-D emergency coupler was no longer necessary because an 'A' end Wedglock would always meet a 'D' end whether the train was composed of R or CO/CP stock. The only problem which then remained was that of the Ward coupling fitted at the 'A' end of the R stock trains for which a Ward-to-Wedglock coupling adapter was required (already carried on R stock trains). Turning the CO/CP stock began on 26th March 1972. A special timetable was used, and six weeks later all the units required for passenger service had been dealt with.

Scrapping of some CO/CP stock transfer cars began as trains were reduced from eight to seven cars. But motor cars also became available for disposal when this stock ceased working the East London Line.

Delivery of the C77 stock enabled C stock to operate the six-car Edgware Road service of the District Line and further CO/CP stock was selected for scrapping. D stock deliveries began in 1979 and these trains started to replace CO/CP stock on the main District service from January 1980. The last seven-car CO/CP stock train was operated on 18th March 1981, while the last CP stock ran in passenger service on 31st March 1981, when two six-car trains were operated on special workings. These were the last red surface stock trains and were outlived only by the 1938 tube stock on the Bakerloo Line, which lasted three years longer.

The Q Stock

The Q stock trains made up of converted cars of 1923/27/31/35 stocks and newly-built cars of similar appearance to the O and P stocks had a very odd look to them. This Q stock train at East Ham in the early 1950s has a G class (Q23 stock) motor car leading with three Q38 stock trailers in its formation. The diamond by the tail light indicated that the train was fitted with passenger door control.

In 1938 work began on rehabilitating the District Line rolling stock built from 1923 onwards. This included the provision of pneumatically-operated doors, the fitting of electro-pneumatic brakes together with retardation control, and a number of other minor alterations. The stock retained the 600-volt power bus line which ran from end to end of the train, connecting all the collector shoes together and retained the electro-magnetic traction control gear operating with WT54B type traction motors.

The 1910/13 motor cars were not suitable for conversion. These cars were, therefore, retained as hand-worked door stock working with more modern trailer cars. There were originally 112 motor cars of 1910/13 vintage, but there were only 77 modern trailer cars of 1931/35 types. The 112 motor cars were reduced by 15, one being damaged beyond economical repair in the collision at Charing Cross in May 1938, and 14 being converted to trailer cars to augment the seventy-seven 1931/35 types to form an equitable balance of hand-worked door stock. This stock, which later became known as 'H' class (for hand-worked doors), was made up with an equal number of motors and trailers into six-car trains, the formation being M-T-T-M-T-M with the four-car portion at the west end of the train.

At this time some of the more modern trailers which had been operating on the Hammersmith & City service had the air-door equipment removed, the doors converted to hand-operation and the electro-pneumatic brake equipment disconnected, because the hand-worked door stock was only provided with the Westinghouse air brake.

Confining all the modern trailer cars to work with the 1910/13 motor cars meant that a new fleet of trailer cars had to be purchased to run with 173 motor cars of 1923, 1927, 1931 and 1935 vintage after their conversion to electro-pneumatic brakes and pneumatic doors. A total of 183 trailer cars similar in design to the O/P stocks were provided and in addition, 25 new motor cars. This new stock was given the designation 'Q' and the rest of the District Line fleet, when converted to air-doors, became known as Q-converted stock.

Fifteen of these new motor cars were given secondhand electrical equipment salvaged from the fourteen 1910/13 cars converted to trailer cars and the one which had been scrapped. At this time, therefore, only ten new equipments of the old-fashioned electro-magnetic type were purchased.

The first Q stock train, consisting of converted motor cars and new trailer cars with pneumatic doors and electro-pneumatic brakes, entered service on the District Line in November 1938.

The Q stock eight-car train formation was:

M-T-M M-T-M M-M
1-2-3 4-5-6 7-8

The air-doors included the 'passenger open' feature which allowed the passengers at certain stations to open individual pairs of doors without the whole of the doors on the side of the train being opened. This feature was discontinued during the black-out imposed by the Second World War.

This train formation required one 'A' end motor car and three 'D' end motor cars in positions 4, 6 and 8. All these cars were Third Class, but of the 183 new trailer cars purchased 125 were composite providing three sections, First Class smoking and non-smoking at one end, and Third Class in the remaining half of the car. Composite trailer cars were provided in positions 3, 5 and 7 in the train formation. Only position 2 was a full Third Class car.

Another formation problem beset the Q stock after operation commenced. This arose from the practice of uncoupling the eight-car trains to six cars for the off-peak running. The two cars, known as east end portions, placed in the 7 and 8 positions, had to be shunted over considerable distances at depots and sidings during coupling or uncoupling with the trailer car leading. Some special fittings including emergency brake handles and grab poles for the use of the shunter had to be installed on these trailer cars, which were then confined to the No. 7 position in the train formation.

At this time the District Line required 47 six-car and 37 eight-car trains for service. Eleven of the eight-car trains were normally provided by F (1920) stock and 27 of the six-car formations by hand-worked door stock. The remainder of the six-and eight-car formations, the latter being those which uncoupled, were made up of Q stock. This was the general arrangement during the war years 1939/45. The hand-worked door stock was restricted to the minimum of duties, especially under black-out conditions, as this door arrangement mixed with air-operated door trains was thought to be dangerous. After the war the introduction of the R stock enabled the hand-worked door stock to be withdrawn from service and the F stock to be transferred to the Metropolitan Line. The District Line service was thereafter provided by Q stock and R stock.

Far Left Q stock train with experimental door-control system, in which the operating controls were placed outside the car body. The guard travelled in the middle of the train in this experiment. *Left* Q stock trailer fitted with door-interlock lights to provide an indication to the guard of doors not fully closed. These were incorporated into the design of the R stock which followed.

The R stock programme utilised the original conception of the O/P/Q family of cars in that all the trailer cars could be converted to motor cars. In the first batch of R stock a total of 82 Q stock trailer cars were converted to driving motor cars, and their place in the 'Q' stock trains was taken by the conversion of the seventy-seven 1931/35 stock trailer cars to pneumatic doors and electro-pneumatic brakes. This substitution naturally resulted in an imbalance of motor cars, so that to match the trailer car position the eight Feltham-built 1931 stock motor cars and the 14 Birmingham-built 1935 stock motor cars were converted to trailer cars. This, in turn, upset the balance of east and west facing cars so that, in addition, seven 1927 motor cars were turned from east to west.

This conversion work was not completed until 1955 and for a time a number of motor cars ran in trailer positions with the control equipment rendered inoperative. To distinguish these cars from driving motor cars they appeared with a 'O' prefix to the 4xxx number. At the same time, the 8xxx numbered trailer cars were operating in both H class and Q class trains. Those converted for working Q class trains had the numbers also prefixed with a zero.

By 1951 there were only half a dozen six-car trains of H class operating in service and this was then reduced to three retained for a few years for the Olympia shuttle service. The trailer cars were obtained by converting some 1910/13 motor cars to trailers as all the more modern trailer cars had by this time been converted to operate in Q stock trains. This provision enabled two trains to operate, with one spare. However, when any exhibition was scheduled which required a 'good shop window' for Britain, an effort was usually made to provide the service with more modern stock. Use of this was often achieved at the expense of the Putney Bridge to Edgware Road Service because the 1910/13 stock was no longer operated in service on anything other than the Olympia shuttle. In 1954 the number of trains kept for this service was reduced to two, and three years later the 1910/13 stock was finally withdrawn, although some of the motor cars remained operational as pilot and service motors for a little while longer.

The second batch of R stock took a further 43 Q stock trailers and then, in 1959, a further seven were required. Another 17 Q stock trailers were modified to become COP stock for lengthening the Circle trains from five to six cars. This again upset the balance of motors to trailers in the Q stock fleet, and fourteen 1923 stock motor cars were now converted to trailer cars. The work was complete by January 1960.

A further depletion of Q stock trailers then took place, a total of 13 being required to ensure that all the remaining CO/CP stock two-car units released from the Metropolitan Line on the introduction of the A stock were built up to three-car units. The transfer of these CO/CP stock trains to the District Line then enabled the scrapping of the Q stock to commence. To summarise, a total of 183 Q stock trailers were originally constructed and these were subsequently distributed as follows:
132 Converted to R stock motor cars;
17 First conversion to COP trailers;
8 Second conversion to COP trailers;
(number reduced from 13 planned)
3 Damaged beyond repair during the war;
23 Remained as Q trailers.

In the first phase of the Q stock displacement as many of the 1923 stock cars as possible were scrapped, but to retain the balance of east and west end cars without the necessity to turn further motor cars, 14 of these older vehicles at the 'A' or west end of the trains were retained.

By 1967 only 203 Q stock cars remained in service, of which only 25 motors and 23 trailers were actually of Q38 type. Until this time Q stock cars fitted with Ward couplings at both ends and hand-inserted control jumpers had been coupled indiscriminately. When the size of the fleet was restricted, however, it was decided to form cars into semi-permanently coupled units as they passed through Acton Works for their last overhaul. After they had been coupled in block four-car main portions and two-car east end portions they had a letter 'B' painted on the car ends.

When the C69 stock was introduced to the Hammersmith & City and Circle Lines this enabled all the remaining CO/CP stock to be transferred to the District so that the Q stock could be scrapped. However, 28 cars were retained for operation on the East London Line which had been worked by four-car units of Q stock since 9th September 1963. These 28 cars were made up into seven four-car units using 14 of the 25 Q38 type motor cars and 14 of the Q38 trailer cars. The cars concerned were given a reconditioning overhaul at Acton Works. An additional hand brake was fitted to the 'D' motor cars to ensure an adequate parking brake if these units had to be held on an incline.

These units continued to operate the East London service until September 1971, when five-car CO/CP stock replaced them.

The R Stock

R stock when new, fitted with passenger door control.
This first post-war stock was almost identical to the pre-war O/P/Q stocks,
the main visible differences being the fitting of door-interlock lights and the use of a destination blind rather than plates.
The area below the cab window previously used for the destination display was now occupied by the train number.

At the end of the Second World War it was felt desirable to withdraw all the hand-worked door stock, so the Circle stock and the District C, D, and E had to be replaced.

New stock, which was designated R, was ordered for the District. The initial delivery was to replace the hand-worked door District cars, and subsequently in addition to enable the F stock to be transferred to the Metropolitan Line. This transfer in turn enabled the hand-operated door stock on the Circle service to be replaced.

The new trains of R stock were composed entirely of motor cars but the general design of the bodywork was similar to the P stock. This design feature made it possible to convert existing Q stock trailer cars to motor cars as had been envisaged in the original arrangements when they were purchased.

All but six of the driving motor cars, therefore, were obtained by converting the appropriate handed Q stock trailers to driving motor cars. This conversion work was mainly undertaken by the Gloucester Railway Carriage & Wagon Company, although at the end of the R stock programme some were converted at Acton Works. The newly-built cars of the first batch were designated R47 stock and all were non-driving motor cars. They were built by both the Gloucester and Birmingham Carriage Companies. The use of non-driving motor cars in the train formations on surface rolling stock was a new departure copied from the tube stock arrangement introduced in 1938. Although all the cars in the trains were motor cars, only 50% of the axles were in fact motored. Only one traction motor was carried on each bogie, continuing the practice of the O/P/Q family of cars. The bogie itself was again asymmetric, with a greater proportion of the weight on the axle carrying the traction motor. The bogies were however of a new design, incorporating side frames of all-welded construction but with the transverse members riveted to them to provide some flexing, the absence of which in the earlier designs had produced cracking of side members from time to time. Individual brake cylinders for each brake block were provided, similar to the practice established for tube stock cars, but the converted cars retained the metadyne arrangement, having two brake cylinders mounted on the bogie, one applying pressure to the trailer wheels and the other to the motor wheels. This was arranged to avoid any major modification to these bogies.

The trains of R stock were designed to be operated in only two formations, six or eight cars, with the ability to uncouple an eight-car set to form a six-car. This followed the District Line operating practice at that time with Q stock trains.

In order to economise in driving positions and keep to a minimum the Q stock trailer cars to be converted to motor cars, the train formation provided was the most inflexible yet devised. Each car in a six-car formation had a specific position with the last two cars repeating to form an eight-car train. The eight car train formation was: 1-2-3-4+5-6+5-6 with car No. 1 being an A-end driving motor car and the two type 6 cars being D-end driving motor cars. Nearly all cars of this second type were rebuilt 'Q' trailer cars of 1938 vintage.

One of the problems at this time was in releasing sufficient cars for this work to be undertaken, as there were no additional trains available at the beginning to provide a working float. The position did improve when R stock trains began operating in service, but the inflexible train formation made up with cars from different car-builders also caused serious difficulties. At one particular time in the programme there were as many as 40 R stock cars delivered to London Transport but it was not possible to make up a single R stock train because one type of car was missing.

R stock driver's cab.

The conversion work consisted of fitting a driver's cab where provision had already been made for it, thereby reducing the seating capacity from 44 to 40, and the fitting of door control boxes with appropriate wiring at the other end for the guard. The lighting arrangements now consisted of two-foot fluorescent tubes placed along the car lines of the roof, eliminating the 600-volt series wiring from the Q stock trailers. It was the first batch of Underground rolling stock to be fitted throughout with fluorescent lighting. A total of 24 tubes was provided in each car, supplied in parallel circuits from a 110-volt a.c. supply obtained from a motor generator set. This motor generator set (a 600-volt/50-volt d.c. converter) had, in addition to the 50-volt d.c. winding for control and emergency battery charging, an auxiliary winding on the pole faces. This winding generated the 110-volt a.c. supply at a frequency of 850 cycles, which powered the fluorescent lighting. At the ends of cars inside the saloon, some battery-fed tungsten lamps were provided which acted as an emergency lighting supply in case the motor generator failed. The motor generator set was fitted to four cars out of the eight on a full-length train, in positions 1, 4, and 6, and proved to be very reliable in operation, but unfortunately the a.c. winding produced a high-pitched humming noise which made the machine undesirable for tube working, and this arrangement was not repeated on other types of stock.

Collector shoe gear of a new design incorporating a retractable feature operated by a capstan-type hand wheel was fitted to both types of car. This shoe gear was originally mounted on the truck frame independent of the axle boxes, and had to incorporate a compensating bracket to allow for changes in wheel diameter. This shoe gear was unsatisfactory in operation and after a number of years was modified to accept a shoebeam for the positive gear, but still retaining the retractable feature which used a modified hand wheel device placed on the side of the truck frame to lift the negative shoe.

Two successful innovations were introduced on the R stock. One was the provision of tilting mercury-type door interlocks instead of direct contact switches. A successful trial of this type of switch had been carried out on the F stock previously, so that it was decided to incorporate this in all future air-door arrangements. The other was a door indicator light fitted on each side of each car, which was illuminated whenever any door interlock contact on that car was not 'made', indicating that a passenger door was 'open'. In this way the guard and platform staff could quickly detect the car which was causing the failure of the guard's pilot light and bell circuit, and so minimise train delays. This feature had been tried out on Q stock trailer 4200 and has been incorporated in all new tube and surface rolling stock.

Original shoegear arrangement of R stock, without shoebeam but with shoe lifting device.

Another innovation, which was only partially successful, affected the guard's door control. To avoid inadvertent operating of door-opening by push buttons which were always alive when the position switch was placed in the operative position, a double key arrangement was introduced. While the position switch key livened up the operative guard's position, a second key was required to work a 'turret' controller on the door panel on each

Right R stock guard's control panels as originally fitted. Handbrake gear was provided on the 'A' end cars, seen here. *Below Right* R stock guard's panels as subsequently modified, with push button controls instead of lever controls.

side to open and close passenger doors. This key had to be moved from side to side as the platform side altered and could not be operated except by a very direct rotary motion. The door-open button could not then be selected by accident.

Problems arose after years of continuous operation since a mechanical device of this kind required intricate and expensive maintenance to avoid malfunctions and subsequent train failures. A return was made to the simpler push button arrangement which had proved satisfactory in its modified form on the 1938 tube stock. As the 1938 tube stock was withdrawn from service for scrapping, push button control boxes became available and work started at Ealing Common Depot and Acton Works (according to circumstances) to modify the driving motor cars. The work began in 1973 and was completed on all the driving motor cars by the end of 1978.

The first batch of R stock cars to replace the hand-worked door stock on the District Line comprised 225 vehicles — 143 new cars and 82 converted cars — sufficient to make up 31 trains of both six- and eight-car formations. The new cars were designated R47, although they did not enter service until 1949, and the converted Q trailers were known as R38/1 cars. Fifty-four of the new cars were built by Gloucester and 89 by the Birmingham Railway Carriage & Wagon Company.

It was at first considered desirable to convert a block of numbers of Q stock cars, but subsequently it was decided to send cars of the correct type which were due or nearly due for overhaul. The cars scheduled for conversion, therefore, have no relationship to the numbering sequence except that from 013xxx they were converted into No. 1 cars only and from 014xxx were converted into No. 6 cars only. A greater number of 014xxx-numbered cars was converted, because more No. 6 cars than No. 1 cars were required.

In the second stage of the programme, to allow the Circle stock to be replaced, a further 17 trains consisting of 133 cars were required of which 90 were new cars. All but six were non-driving motor cars, and were designated R49. The Q stock trailers converted to run with these were designated R38/2.

At the time the R49 cars were ordered it was decided that the underframes and bodies of the new cars should be constructed of aluminium alloy of a corrosion-resistant type. These cars were built by Metropolitan-Cammell. A light alloy was used to reduce the car weight. The weight of a fully-equipped car was, in fact, reduced by 5·4 tons to 38·4 tons by the use of this material. The first light alloy vehicles went into service in May 1952. One car (No. 23567, a No. 5 position car), was left unpainted for a special test. All the other cars were

The first complete train of unpainted aluminium stock photographed on its first day in service, 19th January 1953. It is seen at South Kensington.

Steel-bodied R38 stock car 22663 was repainted silver to run with the original unpainted aluminium R49 stock car 23567. The rest of the cars in the train containing this two-car unit remained red initially, but during the 1960s all red-painted R stock trains were painted silver to avoid mixed formations of red and silver trains. This photograph was taken in February 1957.

painted in the standard red livery. This single vehicle ran some months in service to ensure that none of the adverse cleaning difficulties which at the time were predicted arose. It was then decided to form a complete unpainted eight-car train, using three of the six new driving motors to provide the driving positions as all other driving motors of R stock were steel cars converted from Q stock trailers.

The eight-car train with unpainted exterior, finished in bright aluminium alloy and a red waistband, went into passenger service on 19th January 1953. This train was kept as a block train formation for a number of years until sufficient experience had been gained to justify the subsequent purchase of all new rolling stock externally finished in unpainted light alloy. The train formation was: 21146-23247-23346-23446-23581-22679-23582-22680.

Because the R stock was virtually formed into block trains, automatic couplers were only provided at the uncoupling positions, so that cars Nos. 4, 5 and 6 had this equipment at one end only. The car at the No. 1 position was not fitted with an automatic coupler, only a Ward type, for use in an emergency only. A Ward-to-Wedglock adaptor was carried to enable this car to couple to another R stock or an O/P stock train in emergency. Coupling with a Q stock which had the Ward coupling on every car could be made directly.

In 1959, in order to release Q trailers to increase the Circle trains from five- to six-cars, it was necessary to provide an additional eight-car and two additional six-car trains, so the fleet of R stock was enlarged by 20 cars, 13 being new and seven being further conversions. These conversions, designated R38/3, were carried out this time at Acton Works and not by carbuilders. The new cars were of unpainted light alloy and were designated R59, and the converted steel cars were now painted in aluminium to run with the new cars. By 1957 a No. 6 position R38 car (No. 22663) had been painted aluminium to run with the original unpainted car No. 23567 to make a 'silver' east-end pair.

One of the R59 cars, No. 23584, was sent to Strasbourg in France in June 1960 for the International Aluminium Exhibition. R Stock cars have in fact featured in a number of exhibitions. Non-driving motor car No. 23231 from the R49 batch was exhibited at the Festival of Britain Exhibition on the South Bank in London in 1951. Another R49 stock car, this time one of the aluminium driving motor cars No. 22680, was exhibited at the Willesden International Railway Exhibition in 1954, and in the following year another non driving motor car, No. 23567, of the R49 aluminium stock was on display at an aluminium exhibition in London.

During 1953 controlled tests were undertaken on the test track between Acton Town and Northfields to compare the power consumed by an all-aluminium constructed train with an identical train of steel. The results of the tests justified the higher expenditure incurred in purchasing the lighter aluminium cars. Leaving the cars unpainted was estimated to save, on an eight-car train, a further two tons.

R stock car No. 22680, one of the experimental unpainted cars, on the traverser at Acton Works.

R stock train at Upminster depot. The leading motor car is an R38/3 car painted aluminium to match the unpainted R59 cars.

Interior views of R47 stock (left) and R49 stock (right). On the R49 stock the fluorescent light fittings were moved to the other side of the handgrips.

After the delivery of the R59 cars, mixed aluminium and red cars would appear in many trains due to the uncoupling procedures, and it was decided that as the R stock cars passed through Acton Works for overhaul all the stock would be painted aluminium. This decision was also taken to assist staff to distinguish easily between R stock and CO/CP stock cars which had a similar physical appearance. The painting of all R38/47 stock in aluminium was undertaken between 1963 and 1968. The eight original unpainted cars lost their red waistband during this period.

Another distinctive feature of the R stock was the re-introduction of the use of a roller destination blind instead of enamelled plates. This blind was placed at the top of the windscreen opposite the driver's position. On the CO/CP stock the destination plates were carried above the marker-light cabinet.

The R stock was provided with the well-tried PCM type traction control equipment, one equipment controlling two traction motors of type LT111. These motors of 110hp were manufactured by three different manufacturers, GEC, Crompton Parkinson, and Metro-Vickers, and incorporated a pressure fan, a new feature which was fitted to the motor on the leading bogie of the driving motor cars. The fan operated a fluid-type speedometer in the driver's cab. While this arrangement was ingenious and fairly robust it had the weakness of being difficult to calibrate accurately, and it was not easy to read at the lower speeds when the driver required help for safe working.

In order to provide some experience with an alternative equipment to the PCM, the seven 'R38/3' cars were fitted with a GEC camshaft equipment which was designed to run in multiple with the PCM. However, these equipments did not achieve the standard of reliability of the PCM and when some spare PCM equipments became available these cars were converted to PCM; the last car of this type was converted at Acton Works during 1969.

The R stock numbering scheme had been intended to be helpful and simplify recording because the trains operated in block formation, but unfortunately the conversion and delivery programme was too complicated to enable car numbers to give the guide for entry into service. 21xxx cars were west-end driving motor cars and 22xxx were east-end driving motor cars, while 23xxx cars were non-driving motor cars. As each R stock car took up a specific position in a train the middle number or third digit would indicate this.

A six-car train would then read from west to east:

211xx-232xx-233xx-234xx+235xx-226xx
1 - 2 - 3 - 4 + 5 - 6

and it was hoped that the last two digits of the 1 to 4 cars would have been the same and similarly the last two digits of the 5 and 6 cars. Once this alignment was broken down it was not possible to correct and very few formations of four or two cars worked with the numbers in proper sequence. The experience with this train formation encouraged the view that future rolling stock should be formed into interchangeable train units with a simpler numbering arrangement.

Starting on 4th October 1971 all District Line trains, except those required to work the Edgware Road service, were re-formed into seven-car formations, and uncoupling of service trains on the District Line was withdrawn after almost 75 years. The R stock presented some special problems, however, because two different formations were necessary to obtain the maximum number of trains for service.

These two formations could be represented in this way:

211xx-233xx-234xx+235xx-226xx+235xx-226xx
1 - 3 - 4 + 5 - 6 + 5 - 6
or
211xx-232xx-232xx-233xx-234xx+235xx-226xx
1 - 2 - 2A - 3 - 4 + 5 - 6

The first formation was an eight-car set (which lost a No. 2 car) and the second formation was a six-car set (which gained an additional No. 2 car). The first formation was made up with a three-car unit and two two-car units while the second was a five-car unit linked with a two-car unit. Where this extra No. 2 car had been inserted into the four-car unit to make a five-car unit the additional car number had the letter 'A' added underneath because some modification to the wiring was necessary. The reformation of the stock actually rendered 21 No. 2 type cars surplus to requirements and these were scrapped during 1973/74. Initially there were 15 trains with five-car units and 36 with three-car units but two of the three-car units were scrapped during 1977/78 after fire damage.

Regular scrapping of R stock took place after the withdrawal of the last CO/CP stock in March 1981. The last R stock train ran in passenger service on 5th March 1983.

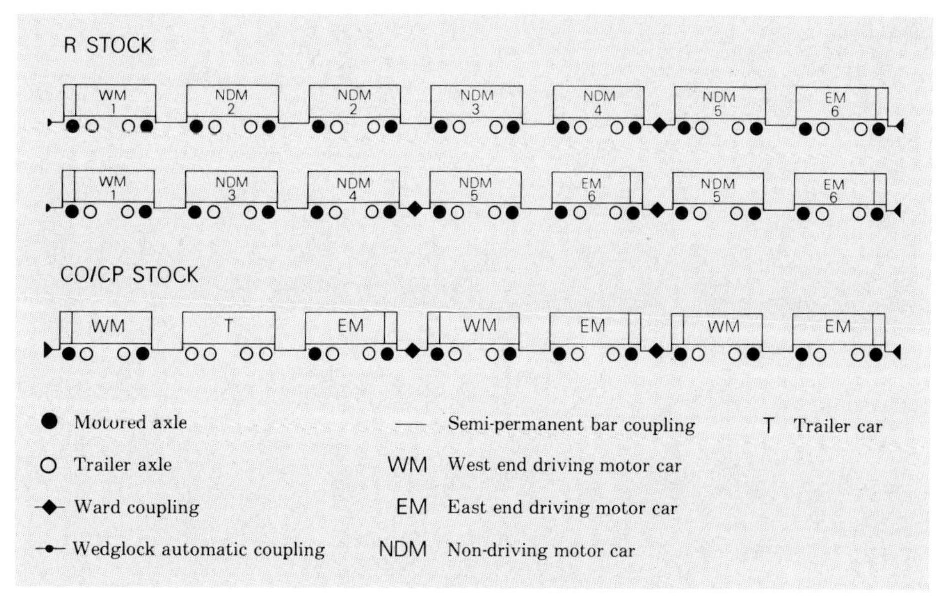

Diagram of seven-car formations including the two R stock versions.

An R stock train gets the go-ahead from the semaphore signal at BR's Gunnersbury station on the Richmond branch of the District. The photograph was taken in 1974.

Met Electrification Experimental Stock

No. 17000, the first of the experimental cars built in connection with design work on Met electrification stock, was completed at Acton Works in 1945. Heating and lighting control rods were fitted at the body end so that the vehicle could operate in a T stock formation.

Included in London Transport's 1935/40 New Works Programme were the projection of the Bakerloo Line over the Metropolitan tracks to Stanmore, the four-tracking of the Metropolitan from Harrow to Rickmansworth and the extension of electrification to Amersham.

Originally, it was intended to provide additional electric stock by the conversion of further 'Dreadnought' steam stock to T stock, but progress on the Met electrification was prevented by the outbreak of the Second World War. Various plans were tentatively discussed for the construction of buffet car semi-express EMUs which could work fast services from Aylesbury to London in 45 to 50 minutes. These plans did not get very far — not even to the outline drawing stage, but they were well documented in memoranda between the LPTB's Chief Mechanical Engineer and the Board.

Various schemes for achieving the advantages of electrification without the cost of converting the line beyond Rickmansworth were also proposed. Suggestions were made for the use of either 'mobile power houses' (lightweight diesel-electric locomotives) or diesel-electric tenders which could be attached to existing multiple-unit trains to enable them to operate outside the electrified territory.

The mobile power houses were to consist of special diesel-electric locomotives which would have provided the electrical power to the through bus line of the train, enabling the train equipments to continue to operate without a track power supply. They would have had only sufficient traction power of their own to enable shunting to and from the trains to be accomplished. The disadvantage of this proposal was that it was in operating terms little different from the existing arrangement of locomotive change from steam to electric and would have provided few savings in manpower in return for the additional complication.

The diesel-electric tender proposal was an improvement on this arrangement since the vehicles concerned would be semi-permanently attached to the through train, but built low enough for the driver to operate from his normal controls. The diesel engine would have been started up at the end of the electrified territory and the generator would have fed power into the train bus line, giving the advantage that no additional crewing was necessary. There was however the technical difficulty of providing these tenders at either the front or rear of the train, or both, and exercising control from the leading driver's position. These plans were abandoned in favour of the extension of electrification.

One of the other features much discussed at the time concerned the need to retain the highest possible ratio of seats to total capacity for stock with a 40-mile working range (Aldgate to Aylesbury). Compartment stock with swing doors and a large number of seats had to be replaced by saloon cars with air doors, fewer seats and more standing accommodation. The difficulty of operating swing door stock on the 'in town' section of the railway, in addition to the need to provide a through gangway in emergency from car to car for safety reasons in tunnel working, precluded the continuation of the traditional compartment type of rolling stock. The main problem in providing air doors to a compartment type seating accommodation is in the need to accommodate the door itself in the open position without obstructing the passenger access. The stability of the door requires the provision of a 'tail' and this, together with the door engine, can occupy more space than the door itself.

Much thought was given to how sliding doors could be combined with compartment style seating and a number of sliding-door compartment coach mock-ups were built at Acton just before the war. Preoccupation with problems on the newly-introduced 1938 tube stock then pushed into the background these experiments and when, in 1944, the next Met electrification mock-up was built at Acton, the idea of sliding-door compartment coaches had been dropped.

A mock-up built in 1939 in the wood shop at Acton Works using a compartment type configuration for the seating, but with air doors. The doors would have doubled as windows and would have opened for only half their length. Adjacent doors, such as those either side of the London Transport name on this mock-up, would have overlapped in the door pocket. Door-closing as well as door-opening buttons are provided for passenger use.

A mock-up of another, less fussy, design of air-door compartment-type stock built about the same time as the one above. Again, the doors would have opened for only half their length.

Interior of the mock-up produced at Acton Works during the war, on which the design of experimental car 17000 was based.

Interior of car 17000 as originally built. The side corridor and island seating proved unpopular with passengers and the layout of the car was subsequently changed. Door closing buttons were provided in addition to door-opening buttons and horizontal handgrips were placed above the windows for standing passengers. Although arm rests were not provided, the seats were shaped to define the seating division.

Car 17000 after its seating layout had been changed and its renumbering to 17001.

Several designs were considered after the war, and two experimental bodies of the saloon type were built at Acton Works on the underframes of two T stock motor cars which had been withdrawn from service. The first of these two vehicles was numbered 17000, and incorporated a novel seating arrangement which provided a total of 57 seats against the normal 40 for an open saloon car. The layout of the car provided for a through corridor yet divided the car into three sections, each almost self contained except for the corridor provided down one side. Although this corridor was placed down one side, the end doors were fitted in the conventional position on the centre line of the car on top of the central buffers. One serious disadvantage of this layout, causing its unpopularity, was the fact that it provided hardly any 'window' seats, as most of the seats were installed on 'islands' in the middle of the sections, not against the carbody sides.

The three pairs of double doors fitted down each side of the car were air-operated and incorporated a novel feature associated with the passenger open control. Both leaves of all doors could be opened and closed by the guard, but each pair of doors was provided with passenger buttons for opening and closing. The opening button only opened one leaf of the pair, while the passenger after entry could reclose this door by pressing a close button. This feature was aimed at reducing the heat loss on air-door stock at exposed terminal stations.

Car 17000 went into passenger service for an experimental period on 26th January 1946. Its unpopularity with passengers caused a reconsideration of the seating layout and three years later it was withdrawn for this to be changed. The side corridor was replaced by a middle gangway with three-passenger seats on one side and two-passenger seats on the other, a layout that was eventually used on the A stock. The modified car re-entered service on 2nd November 1949, renumbered 17001.

Interior of car 17001 with an off-centre gangway giving space for three seats on one side and two on the other, a layout finally adopted for the A stock. Some of the seats in 17001 were provided with high backs and some with low backs.

Above Car 20000 and car 17000 in train formation outside Acton Works, together with the T stock car which provided the guard's position and door controls. *Below* Interior of car 20000. In common with car 17000, as originally built, the seating was fitted with semi-loose cushions.

A second car, numbered 20000, entered service in June 1947 and was coupled with 17000 to T stock control trailer 6727, which had been modified to contain door operating gear and lighting switches in the control compartment. Car 20000 seated 56 passengers, all in pairs, with a centre gangway. The seats had recessed armrests and moulded back squabs. Although this car also was said to be divided into three sections, it was virtually an open saloon car with two large vestibules placed away from the car ends. The air-door equipment was similar to that provided in car 17000.

In order to test another matter about which there was, and still is, some controversy, one vestibule was provided with doors having a centre pillar dividing the doorway into two sections. This vestibule was also fitted with a vertical handpole in the centre of the floor area. In the other vestibule no centre door pillar was installed, nor was there a centre grab pole in the middle of the circulating area, but handgrips were suspended from the car roof.

The two cars were equipped with fluorescent lighting which had at this time not yet been adopted as a standard arrangement for rolling stock. The motor-alternator providing a.c. power at a frequency of 1200 cycles for both cars was placed on car 17000. Both cars were carried on 'K2' bogies which were fitted with the standard 36-inch diameter trailer wheels: consideration was given to using British Railways 43-inch diameter wheels to provide a better riding characteristic, but this idea was never developed.

These cars were finally withdrawn from service in 1953 because the T stock train in which they operated required a second guard to manipulate the door controls, and this was expensive in manpower. The cars were scrapped in 1955, having served their purpose in connection with design work on the replacement Met rolling stock.

Another mock-up for Met electrification stock was built at Acton Works about 1952, but the electrification was again postponed and the design was not proceeded with. The circular windows in the door-pocket positions were copied from a modified 1938 tube stock car given these in 1949. An off-centre gangway with three-plus-two seating was again employed, a layout to which the designers seem by this time to have become firmly committed to provide the maximum seating.

A for Amersham Stock

One of the first A stock trains to enter service, seen at Harrow when new.
The first six units had black-painted roofs as seen here, while the rest had grey ones.
The cars with black roofs subsequently had them painted grey to reduce the absorption of heat from the sun.

When the programme for replacement of the Metropolitan rolling stock was finally formulated there were five types of rolling stock operating the services from Baker Street, each incompatible with the others. Although one type could sometimes be substituted for another on some services, this was not always an easy procedure. The P and F stocks operated the Uxbridge services with a few P stock journeys occasionally to Watford. The Circle service was operated by CP stock, which was P stock converted to PCM control, and these trains worked some of the early morning main line duties out of Neasden Depot before taking up Circle workings, because at this time CP stock was maintained from this depot. These trains were of five-car formation at the time. The T stock made up into six- and eight-car formations worked the Watford and Rickmansworth services, while the locomotive-hauled steam stock worked the Aylesbury, and Chesham through trains.

In 1959 an order was placed with Cravens of Sheffield for 248 cars. These were to replace the T stock and the locomotive-hauled steam stock following the extension of the electrified territory from Rickmansworth to Amersham, including the branch to Chesham. The letter 'A' was chosen as the alphabet had nearly been exhausted, and 'A' was appropriate for the destination Amersham. Subsequently a further order was placed for 216 similar cars to enable the services to Uxbridge to be provided by the same stock, allowing the F stock to be scrapped and the OP stock to replace Q stock on the District Line after conversion to PCM control.

The first batch of stock making up 31 eight-car trains was known as A60, while the second batch making up a further 27 eight-car trains was designated A62. The two batches of stock were virtually identical and interchangeable, being formed into four-car units — two being coupled together to make an eight-car train. Each unit consisted of two trailer cars between two driving motor cars. The units were not 'handed' and the Wedglock automatic couplers fitted to the outer ends of driving motor cars were equipped for 'reversibility'. This avoided the problem which arises with 'non-reversible' stock when a unit turned end for end is unable to couple to a unit which has not been similarly turned.

There were in fact two ways of turning trains in service on the Metropolitan Line, either by reversing while on the Circle service or by operating to Watford and back via Rickmansworth or vice versa. It was normal operating practice for some trains to work to Watford and then to Rickmansworth on the same journey without retracing the return journey to London. The provision of 'reversibility' is obtained by the duplication of train wires through the automatic coupler. Each side of the centre line of the coupler requires to have an identical circuit to the other, and this provision now required 64 connecting studs against 28 on the P stock. Where the units are non-reversible, the provision of duplicate studs does, of course, improve the circuit reliability, but is only worth doing for this reason where circuit resistance is particularly critical.

Top An A stock train at Neasden Works alongside two of the types it replaced on the Metropolitan main line; F stock and P stock. *Above* Interior view of an A stock car. High-backed seating was provided to cater for the long-distance nature of many of the journeys made on the line. *Below* The guard's end of an A stock motor car.

The driving motor cars were fitted with 54 seats and the trailer cars with 58. The motor cars had four tip-up seats attached to the bulkhead of the guard's gangway, which was provided in the traditional position at the trailing end of these cars. There was also a seat for the use of the guard placed in the end draughtscreen. All fixed seats were arranged across the cars for three passengers on one side of the gangway and for two on the other side. The rows of seats were arranged to face each other. At the trailer car ends there were two pairs of seats, one each side of the communicating door.

The bodies were constructed mainly of light alloy, but the headstock and bolster underframes were of welded steel fabrication. Light alloy castings were used for doorway and corner pillars, which also formed part of the exterior finish of the cars. Except where these constructional members formed part of the external appearance, the external panelling was of alloy sheet unpainted. The driving cab was fitted with hinged doors, and the guard's gangway had a single air-operated sliding door on each side which could be used by passengers when not required by the guard. Two pairs of sliding doors were provided down each side, while the trailer cars had no end doors but three pairs of air-operated doors down each side.

Glass fibre windscreens glazed above the seat backs were installed at all door openings. These screens virtually formed a partition, which carried at roof level across the car a plastic route diagram.

The saloon was illuminated by 4ft fluorescent tubes, with 17 in each motor car and one more in trailer cars. These tubes were powered by a.c. supplied from a motor-alternator-rectifier set, the output from the alternator being at 220 volts, 850 cycles. The fluorescent lighting supply was obtained by means of a transformer to bring the voltage down to 115, the frequency remaining at 850. The transformer also fed a germanium full-wave bridge rectifier to provide 50 volts d.c. for the battery supplying the various control circuits. This

d.c. voltage was controlled by a magnetic amplifier-type regulator which had no moving parts. The use of this equipment reduced the maintenance liability of the vibrating carbon-type equipment previously installed in earlier types of stock.

The emergency lighting was originally provided by three of the fluorescent lamps fed from the 50-volt d.c. battery supply by individual transistor invertors. This equipment did not prove reliable in service and the cars were later fitted with tungsten emergency lamps fed directly from the battery.

Because of the longer travelling time for passengers on the Metropolitan services the heating installed in the cars was increased from 4kw per saloon to 7kw and this was provided by new-type pyro-bar heaters. All axles of the motor cars were motored so that each motor bogie carried two traction motors of type LT114, manufactured by the General Electric Company. These axle-hung motors were of 300 volts, two in permanent series across the line. One PCM traction control unit controlled four motors. Each motor was bolted to a roller suspension sleeve fitted to the axle.

The four-motor traction control equipment was basically similar to the two-motor equipment but designed to withstand a higher current rating. One additional piece of equipment not previously installed was a wheel spin relay to safeguard against one motor of a pair in permanent series spinning.

The differential voltage relay provided had two coils, one across each motor. When the voltage balance between the two becomes disturbed, the line breakers trip out, causing the PCM equipment to return automatically to the off position, and the accelerating sequence to restart.

The required train performance necessitated the provision of two accelerating rates and two balancing speeds. The flag switch indicator installed controlled not only the motor field strength but also the accelerating rate. With the flag switch down, for operating in the inner section, the master controller would give both accelerating rates, but only full-field strength on the motors would be provided, and consequently a low balancing speed. With the flag switch raised only the low accelerating rate could be used, but the balancing speed would be increased by the selection of 60% field strength for the motors. This field strength provided a maximum speed of 60mph for the outer suburban sections.

The car bodies of the A stock were built to the maximum width and length permitted by the Metropolitan loading gauge in order to allow the five seats, plus a gangway, across the car. The width of the cars was 9ft 8in and the length 53ft. Considerable criticism of the design of the stock arose because even these dimensions would only provide an eight-car train seating capacity of 464 against 600 with five a side on T stock having the old-fashioned compartments with swing doors. The 'A' stock train, however, had reasonable standing accommodation for 1,380 passengers; only 900 could be carried on a T stock with five standing in every compartment in great discomfort. The wide vestibules with the air-operated doors gave standing accommodation for the short-distance passengers, while the transverse seating provided good seating for the long-distance passengers. The design, therefore, gave as much as possible to each of the

Driving cab on the A stock.

An A stock motor bogie.

An A stock train on the East London Line at Shadwell.

conflicting requirements of the two types of service the trains had to provide.

The civil engineering works, including the four-tracking to Watford South Junction, were completed at the same time as the A stock was introduced, and enabled timetable improvements to be arranged on the Metropolitan Line which, together with the improved reliability of the rolling stock, provided a service never previously achieved.

The electric train service to Chesham with some trains to Amersham began on 12th September 1960, but the 'Steam' stock workings did not cease until almost exactly a year later, when the locomotive change at Rickmansworth was discontinued and London Transport trains ceased to operate beyond Amersham. Soon afterwards most of the Metropolitan services north of Harrow were being provided by A stock trains.

Until the advent of the A stock the open saloon stock requirements on the Metropolitan Line necessitated the operation of 15 eight-car trains and 9 six-car trains in the peak period. Eight of the eight-car trains were provided by the F stock while the remainder were supplied from the O/P stock pool composed of two and three car units. The six-car sets ran all day but the eight-car trains were only required at the peak times, which produced an unbalanced mileage for some cars. The F stock were operated in block eight-car sets and the two-car O/P stock were only required to form eight-car trains on the Metropolitan main line service. This imbalance was eliminated by the changeover to A stock, formed into eight-car trains with two interchangeable four-car units either of which could be operated independently when uncoupled. Later it was found that the provision of rolling stock for the Metropolitan Line had been generous as the services did not develop as anticipated, so that there were a number of spare units. Advantage was taken of this to provide a number of the A stock for experimental work and, when some cars were damaged in collision, these were scrapped and not replaced. Car Nos. 5170 and 7160 are now missing from the fleet list.

Car No. 5218 was used as a test bed for air metacone suspension in 1966, the prototype of the C stock arrangement. Ten years later this car was modified to take bogies with a new form of air suspension (as a proposal for the D78 stock). This work was undertaken at the Metro-Cammell Works in Birmingham. In the event, however, this arrangement was not specified for the D78 stock and the car was further modified to take the rubber suspension which did become the prototype for the D78 stock. All this work resulted in this unit being out of passenger service for very long periods. The unit was also provided with an experimental parking brake.

After minor civil engineering work had been undertaken on the East London Line A stock units began working this service from 12th June 1977. The alterations were to overcome the running restrictions imposed on the stock because its dimensions exceeded the surface line standard loading gauge. Civil engineering alterations would have been expensive on St Mary's Curve (joining the East London Line to the District) so special signalling controls have been installed to prevent two units passing each other at this point.

The Amersham, Watford and Chesham lines are more vulnerable to winter conditions than most other lines of London's Underground system. Some A stock units were, therefore, chosen for the fitting of de-icing equipment to trailer cars of passenger trains for test purposes. These tests proved reasonably successful and 18 A60 stock trailer cars have been equipped with de-icing equipment. The cars chosen were the even numbered trailer cars from 6088 to 6122. These cars have a letter 'D' added underneath the number to denote that de-icing equipment is carried.

One unit, formed by cars 5060-6060-6061-5061, has been fitted with experimental Davies and Metcalfe braking equipment. Exhaustive tests were conducted on this equipment and eventually, on 20th November 1977, the unit was released for passenger service. The modifications involved in fitting this brake gear had made it incompatible with the other A stock units which were equipped with basic Westinghouse equipment. When the unit was selected for the tests it was intended that it would be confined to operating the Chesham shuttle service (which requires a four-car train) but the introduction of A stock on the East London improves its availability for operating passenger mileage.

Five A stock four-car trains are allocated to the East London Line depot at New Cross and the main Metropolitan service is operated from Neasden depot with eight-car trains.

C for Circle Stock

The C69 stock was delivered for use on the Circle and Hammersmith & City Lines.
It was followed by similar C77 stock for the District Line Edgware Road to Wimbledon service.

In May 1968 an order was placed with Metropolitan-Cammell Ltd of Birmingham for a total of 212 cars to make up 35 six-car trains plus one spare two-car unit. Arising out of the integration of the Circle and Hammersmith & City stock, which was achieved when the O/P stock was all converted to PCM equipment and the Circle service raised from five-car to six-car formation, it had now become possible to order one set of new stock to continue this integrated policy with economical provision of spare rolling stock. The 35 six-car trains are required to meet a daily service of 31 trains, 17 for the Hammersmith & City service and 14 for the Circle. This reduction of spares provision was made possible by the train formation adopted which had to meet two requirements: the operation of six-car trains in the immediate future and the possibility of an eight-car formation subsequently. After considerable examination of the problems involved, both technical and financial, a two-car unit was adopted with a driving cab at one end only, each unit being fully reversible and identical, without specific 'A' or 'D' ends. The six-car formations are formed either:

M-T+T-M+T-M
or M-T+M-T+T-M

The motor car is a driving car with the cab at the outer end only, and the trailer car has no driving position provided. In normal circumstances an equal number of units will face each way, but in order to equate wheel wear, which in practice has been found to be uneven due to the stock on these lines always working the same way, arrangements are made in the timetables to reverse the trains. This can be done easily by working certain Circle train duty cycles to and from the depot by way of Whitechapel.

Subsequently a problem arose with the two-car unit formation because of a change of policy on 'No Smoking' accommodation. As originally built, motor cars were 'No Smoking' and trailer cars 'Smoking' which gave a 50 per cent mix. When it was agreed that only two cars in every train would be provided for smokers, it was necessary to arrange for the trailer car in the middle unit to be a 'non-smoker'. It was essential for availability purposes that this was not a permanent arrangement because the reduction in spare units had been made on the basis that any two-car unit unit could substitute for any other. For this reason a removable sign had to replace the more permanent labels fixed to the windows indicating the 'No Smoking' accommodation.

This stock had been designated C69 stock in the hope that its year of birth would be 1969. In the event this proved to be optimistic and the first trial run of a four-car train of this stock took place in the summer of 1970.

The letter C was chosen in preference to B because of the association of the stock with the Circle Line.

While the view of the driving end of C stock is somewhat similar to the A stock, the side elevation appearance and dimensions are different.

Some difference in dimensions is produced by the fact that the general arrangement drawings of this stock were set out in metric units for the first time. The A stock cars, both motor and trailer, were 53ft 0in over body ends: the driving motor car of C69 stock is 52ft 7in (16,030mm) and the trailer car 49ft (14,970mm). The differences between the two types of car has been brought about by arranging for the passenger accommodation in both cars to be the same and adding to the driving motor car one driving cab. In order to reduce the body overhang by this arrangement the bogie centres of the two cars are different. The driving motor car has bogie centres 35ft 6in (10,820mm), which is the same as A stock, but the trailer car has bogie centres of 31ft 6in (9,600mm).

Each car is provided with four pairs of double doors down each side to give the maximum passenger flow on the Circle service, where passengers travel only for short distances and there is a constant interchange. Between each pair of double doors, pairs of facing seats are fitted, while at the body ends including the cab-end of the motor car, longitudinal seats for two on each side are provided. These arrangements reduced the number of seats available in each car to 32. The A stock had 54 seats in the motor cars and 58 in the trailer cars. A great deal of additional circulating and standing space was provided which, together with the setting back of the windscreens so that doorways are not obstructed by standing passengers, reduces delays at critical stations.

A six-car train has a length of 93 metres (309ft 8ins over buffers), which is controlled at present by the limitation imposed by Circle Line stations between High Street Kensington and Paddington, and the stations on the Hammersmith & City Line. The length was also influenced by the fact that provision was made for this stock to be operated by one man in the future, when it will be essential that the leading driving cab should not be in tunnel when the train is at a station.

The ventilation of the car body is provided by fixed openings above cantrail level, similar to the arrangement installed on the 1967 tube stock on the Victoria Line and not by hinged ventilators of the design incorporated in A stock. In addition roof-mounted heater/blower equipment was used for the first time in general service on Underground rolling stock. However this arrangement did not prove adequate in hot weather and after collision damage repairs Car No. 5567 was returned to service with additional ventilators in the door pockets at the transverse seats. The C77 batch of stock, ordered for the Edgware Road to Wimbledon service of the District Line, had these additional vents incorporated in the cars when they were constructed.

The air-operated sliding doors are top-hung with an open-type sill plate to reduce the problems associated with door obstruction interfering with the proper closing of the doors. With one-man operation it will be necessary to ensure that the train cannot be started until all the doors are closed.

The door-control equipment is fitted in the driving cab and not in the conventional position at the trailing-end gangway. This arrangement was to facilitate one-man operation, although the equipment is so arranged that the door control can be worked from any cab on the train. An additional facility was arranged to avoid the necessity for all the doors to remain open at terminal stations. A 'selective close' button is fitted which will close three of the four pairs of double doors.

One of the more novel features of this stock is the introduction of an air-operated sliding door to the driver's cab, with draughtproofing provided by inflatable air seals. This air seal is fed by an air valve operated by the movement of the door engine arm. Provision has also been made for this door to be opened by a key from the outside or by staff from the inside in depots when air is not available. The cab doors can be interlocked at the driver's end with the traction control circuit to ensure that the train does not move off with these doors open when the train is operating in one-man mode. Such a provision is not essential when two men control the train.

The auxiliary power supply is obtained from a motor-alternator-rectifier unit carried on the motor car of the AEI MG 3007 AY type, which produces a.c. at 230 volts, 850 cycles a second. The output from this machine is then treated in several ways for auxiliary purposes. A transformer converts the 230-volt supply to 115 volts without alteration of the frequency for the main fluorescent lighting circuits. A rectifier unit converts the a.c. supply to 50 volt d.c. for charging the auxiliary battery and providing control current. This 50-volt d.c. supply is re-inverted to produce 230 volts, 50 cycles a second a.c. for the provision of power to the blower heater fans and for the emergency lights.

The main lighting is supplied chiefly by 4ft (there are some 2ft) fluorescent tubes powered from the 850-cycle supply. Emergency lighting if the motor alternator fails is obtained by supplying two tubes in each car from the 50-volt d.c. battery through an inverter.

The four blower heater units are fitted in the ceiling of each car, each capable of providing 1.8kw of heat.

The inverter carried on the trailer car supplies the four fans on the driving motor car as well as those on the trailer car. The fans can deliver hot or cold air according to whether heating or ventilation is required. A thermostat is provided to control the heating. A fan heater is also provided in the driver's cab.

Also carried on the trailer car is a compressor, either a Reavell Mawdsley two-cylinder type TBC38Z or a Westinghouse three-cylinder type 3HC43 machine; an equal number of each has been provided. Compressor synchronisation, which ensures that all compressors normally operate on a train when replenishing the air supply, is provided by a new method. Each compressor contactor has two operating coils, one fed from each end of the train, which provides greater reliability by duplicating the control feeds.

The entry into service of C stock replaced the last of the clerestory-roofed trains on the Underground; the Q stock dating back to 1923. A C69 stock train and a COP stock train are seen with Q stock car 4248 at Hammersmith on a special Q stock farewell tour on 26th September 1971.

Interior view of a C69 stock car. All seating is transverse, increased standing accommodation being provided by the four sets of double doors.

The two-car units have automatic couplers at the outer ends, and because of the reversibility feature and the provision of additional equipment controls, a total of 76 studs had to be provided. The A stock units, also reversible, had 64. Space for the additional studs was found by reducing their diameter in all but the centre row, which has been arranged to carry those circuits with the heavier currents.

Various features introduced in the 1967 tube stock were incorporated in the C69 stock. The control feature, which enables the driver to isolate from his leading cab part of the train, is provided. However, because the train formation is six cars composed of three two-car units the train cannot be conveniently halved as, for example, in the 1967 tube stock. On the C69 stock this has necessitated the provision of some of the additional control wires across the automatic couplers.

Provision has also been made for similar communication systems to those provided on the 1967 tube stock, but initially the inter-train radio and the carrier wave system was not provided, as this equipment cannot be used until all trains using the tracks are similarly equipped. Only a public address system, to enable the driver to address the passengers, and a cab-to-cab telephone, enabling speech between all driving cabs, were fitted when new.

The driving motor cars have four traction motors of type LT117, manufactured by Brush of Loughborough, mounted on Timken roller suspension sleeves in a similar manner to A stock. The motors, however, have a lower gear ratio and run at a higher speed than those on the A stock. Although capable of 60mph, this speed is not achieved on Circle or Hammersmith & City workings, where the relatively short distances between stations dictate a maximum speed of about 45mph. The speed capability is useful however on the odd occasions when C stock is used on the 'main' line. The small pinion size required for this gear ratio necessitated the provision of a 'plug-in' pinion for the first time. This means that the pinion is made integral with a small shaft which is pressed into the end of the armature shaft. All pinions on previous stocks have been shrunk on to the armature shaft. The motor, too, has a circular frame instead of the 'octagonal' traditional type traction motor frame.

The motors for C69 stock are of the 300-volt type, two being arranged in permanent series. The control is provided by PCM-type equipment manufactured by AEI Ltd, but arranged to give rheostatic braking by the system first introduced on the Victoria Line on the 1967 tube stock. On the C69 cars, however, being heavier and with higher speeds having to be catered for, the equipment is modified accordingly. In addition there are two new features of this equipment; the provision of virtually constant acceleration irrespective of train loading conditions and the external excitation of the motors to ensure the build up of rheostatic braking.

The bogies are provided with chevron rubber type axle-boxes, but the secondary suspension between the body and the bogies incorporates the use of air-metacone suspension. This rubber/air springing unit is so arranged that as the weight of the body increases by the acceptance of passengers, air is admitted to the metacone unit carried on either side of the bogie, which automatically maintains the car height. This feature of the car springing is used to control both the acceleration and the braking since it is equivalent to weighing the passenger load on the car. The air suspension pressure, therefore, has a control effect on the rate coil setting of the notching relay of the PCM control equipment, and thereby ensures sensibly constant acceleration irrespective of load. A variable load valve controlled by the air pressure setting from this suspension arrangement also controls the maximum brake pressure applied to the car. Braking forces up to the point of wheel pick-up for each car can, therefore, be arranged, and are not limited by the braking rate which may pick up the wheels on the least loaded car. Higher accelerating and braking rates can safely be arranged on trains having this equipment. The resetting of the air-metacone suspension is arranged to take place each time the doors are opened.

The braking arrangement for this stock provides for the minimum rate to be achieved on the driving motor cars by application of rheostatic braking, which will then be supplemented as required by air-brakes on the trailers, followed by air-brakes on the driving motor cars. The effective overall braking rate required at any time, and whichever combination of air and dynamic braking is needed to effect it, is controlled by a series of mercury retardation controllers

A handbrake or parking brake is provided in each driver's cab which is hydraulically actuated. To assist the driver and reduce the physical effort needed in applying this brake a motor-driven pump is fitted to provide the hydraulic pressure, but it is possible to apply the brake without the assistance of this device by means of an emergency hand-pump.

The trains are not equipped for conversion to Automatic Train Operation but were designed to be capable of operation by both one or two men without any circuit alterations. Television cameras and monitors were installed at Circle and Hammersmith & City stations to enable the introduction of One Man Operation, but failure to reach an agreement with the unions about the rates of pay for such operation has delayed its introduction.

Top Driving cab of a C stock train. Provision is made for eventual one-man operation and door-control buttons are installed each side of the cab. *Above* C69 stock bogie.

Units of C69 and C77 stock are fully interchangeable and are often seen together in one train. A complete train of C77 stock is seen here when new, Lillie Bridge service stock depot providing the background.

Fourteen C69 stock trailers (numbered between 6543 and 6556 inclusive) were equipped at the carbuilders with de-icing equipment. This equipment can be controlled from any leading cab so that it is operative in either direction of travel and does not depend on the motor car with which it is paired being at the leading position.

The delivery of C69 stock allowed the transfer of the remaining CO/CP stock to the District Line, enabling all the Q stock to be scrapped. Operation of the District services has always been inhibited by the need to run only six-car trains on the Edgware Road services while services on other parts of the line could be worked by longer trains. An opportunity was taken to eliminate this problem from consideration of the design for new District Line rolling stock by purchasing 11 further C stock cars for working the Edgware Road services. This decision provided the opportunity to concentrate the maintenance of all C stock at Hammersmith Depot, but presented the problem that such action mixed District and Metropolitan train workings (if the advantage of a common pool of spare rolling stock was to be gained).

As nearly 10 years had gone by since the original stock was designed some minor changes were made to the new cars (designated C77 stock). The most important of these were to the heating and the provision of additional ventilators in the door pockets, but the two car units were interchangeable, being intended to be mixed indiscriminately with the earlier stock and not kept in train formations. The first C77 cars were delivered on 30th July 1977 and entered service on the Hammersmith & City Line on 12th December 1977. The operation of C stock on the Edgware Road service began on 17th April 1978.

Unfortunately at East Ham, on 15th March 1976, while in service as part of a Hammersmith-bound train, motor car 5585 was damaged beyond repair by a bomb. The driver of the train lost his life in the incident, although not directly from the explosion. An additional C77 car was constructed, utilising as much as possible material salvaged from the damaged car. The new car was given the original number. There is one car within the C69 group of numbers, therefore, which is virtually a C77 stock car.

D for District Stock

A D stock train at Olympia on the special exhibition service between that point and High Street Kensington.

Seventy-five new trains for the District Line (designated D78 stock) have now been built by Metro-Cammell Ltd in Birmingham to replace the CO/CP stock and the R stock. For the first time since electrification the District Line main service is now worked by a single train formation made up of one stock type.

Train lengths have always been a problem on the District. Although almost all the platforms were made capable of handling eight-car trains, achieved by providing narrow cat-walk platform extensions, passenger control was difficult. In addition, the services to Edgware Road had to be operated by six-car trains because the platforms between there and High Street Kensington could only accommodate these. Even when uniform train formations had been established, eight-car sets were worked in the peak periods until 1970, with uncoupling to six cars at other times. When it was decided to accept the unsymmetrical seven-car formation for main line working, some six-car units were retained to operate the Edgware Road services.

With the C stock provided for Edgware Road services, the new District Line stock design was completed without any external constraints. On the District Line there are very few severe curves involving station platforms, so that it was possible to utilise a car of 18 metres in length compared with the conventional 50ft (16 metre) car, so that a train length of 110 metres could be made up with six cars (rather than seven cars of the old conventional size of stock).

There were two immediate advantages, a reduction in total cost because six larger cars were less expensive than seven shorter cars, and a reduction in total weight because there were fewer bogies and auxiliary equipments to be transported. The stock has been designed with one-man operation (OMO) in mind so that door controls and the guard's operating position are located in the driving cab. When a guard is carried he will work from the rear cab, but when OMO is achieved all these controls can be worked from the leading cab.

Each six-car train is made up by coupling two three-car units together. There are, however, three types of three-car unit. There are 65 'A' and 65 'D' units, which normally couple together to form a six-car train. These units have driving cabs at one end only. In addition there are 20 'C' units which have driving cabs at both ends, so that these units can substitute for either 'A' or 'D' units, giving flexibility.

All the units comprise two motor cars with a trailer between, which has been designated for 'smoking' passengers. The cars of a unit are connected together by a semi-permanent bar coupling. The inner motor cars of the 'A' and 'D' units are classified as non-driving motor cars, but have simplified cabinet-mounted driving controls to enable depot shunting to be undertaken with maximum safety.

The non-driving motor cars however have fully automatic Wedglock couplers at the outer end. The driving motor cars carry only mechanical automatic couplers except those placed on the ends of the double-ended 'C' type units which must couple to non-driving motors when making up six-car trains.

The 'A' units are numbered from 7000-17000 -8000 (all even numbers), while 'D' units are numbered beginning with 8001-17001-7001 (all odd numbers). The 7xxx cars are driving motor cars while the 8xxx cars are the non-driving motor cars.

The twenty 'C' units are numbered beginning 7500-17500-7501, the 75xx even numbers being 'A' ends and the odd numbers the 'D' ends. The trailer cars of the first 25 'A' end units have been fitted with de-icing equipment.

The dimensions of these cars are based on metric measurements but they are about 60 feet long compared with earlier District stock which had a maxiumum length of 52 feet. The driving motor car cabs are the longest at 18·37 metres, while the trailers and non-driving motor cars are 18·12 metres over body ends. As with the C stock, the cars were designed with the same passenger area in both motor cars and trailers. This gives a train made up of 'A' and 'D' units having a length of 363 feet, almost the same as a seven-car train of 'R' stock with conventional 50ft cars. The trailers and non-driving motor cars, have been provided with 48 seats while the driving motor cars lose 4 seats. This gives a 272 seat train.

The internal layout consists mainly of longitudinal seats but a centre bay has four transverse seats. The allowable height of the car body from rail level is 3·75 metres, almost a metre more than allowed for tube rolling stock. This height allows the car floor to be flat so that any layout for seating and door positioning is possible.

The cars have four passenger doorways on each side, and a single-leaf door instead of pair of doors. This single leaf provides an opening of 1,067mm (3ft 6ins) compared to the double doorway at 4ft 6ins of the R stock. However, these single-leaf doors are spread down the train giving a better distribution of door openings. In order to assist disabled persons at stations where it is necessary to step up into the cars, one doorway on each side of each car has been fitted with a grab-handle. This was not a feature of the original design and motor car 7082 was the first to be delivered with it, earlier cars being modified at Ealing Common depot. The adjacent draught screens to the doorways are set back eight inches so that passengers standing near the doorway do not obstruct it at stations.

Driver's console on D stock, showing the joystick controller with forward movement for drive and backward movement for braking. Door control buttons on the console are provided for one-man operation.

The new feature associated with these doors is a passenger-actuated door arrangement. Such a system is not new, it was introduced in 1938 before the second world war and was intended to be used throughout the Underground. However when black-out conditions were imposed to reduce identification of cities by aircraft the passenger-controlled door operation was withdrawn. Subsequently after the war the difficulty of maintaining complicated equipment coupled with the unsatisfactory operating arrangements caused the system to be abandoned in spite of its advantages as a contribution to passenger amenities.

In the new system adopted for the D stock the passengers were normally required to open the doors at all times and the guard was required only to close them. The passengers either inside or outside the trains press an illuminated button which opens an adjacent door. On reaching the station the guard energises the operating circuit which also lights up the selector buttons. The position of the selector button has been arranged to be low enough for children capable of travelling unaccompanied, yet high enough to be suitable for adults. In addition, the passenger open circuit is inoperative at speeds over 6mph so that should the button be pre-selected, the doors will not open unless the train is almost stationary.

The guard or train operator has an overriding close button but if the doors do not fully shut because of an obstruction, the guard is provided with a selective re-open button which enables him to re-open the obstructed doors only. In addition a selective close button has been provided which closes three of the four doors on each side of each car. This is of use mainly at terminal stations so that in cold weather all the doors are not kept open while the train is standing for long periods in the station.

The train operator has a special key-operated switch which is provided to enable all the doors to be opened in an emergency. This switch was modified subsequently to enable the guard to override the door-opening arrangements during hot weather. Ventilation problems were encountered during summer months because not all the doors were opened at each station. To accommodate the motors required for the D stock's wider doors a new type of door engine was developed, in which the cylinders on either side are similar in size and each is charged in turn to open or close the doors.

The body structure itself is unpainted riveted aluminium fixed on an aluminium underframe. In order that the longer car fits into the structure gauge, it must be narrower to negotiate curves. The bodies have been built as wide as possible at the floor level, but taper to the roof so that although the sides of the cars are flat they slope at a slight angle. The doors are made of lightweight 'honeycomb' material because, being larger than the car doors previously fitted to surface stock cars, they would otherwise require a higher force for operation. The differential door engine which had become standard on all Underground air-operated door stock has now been replaced by a double-acting door operator in which air is applied to either side of the piston as required to open or close the door. Hydraulic dampers are fitted in the closing direction to prevent excessive slamming. Although the door is virtually mechanically locked in the fully closed position by the rotary motion of the arm, a spring is provided which allows a small movement to be achieved against the door mechanism. This allows coat-ends and small obstructions to be dragged free without the necessity of re-opening the door.

Both the service and emergency braking applications are controlled electrically. During braking, the traction motors provide the appropriate retarding force on the motor cars and normally air is only applied below 10mph should this rheostatic electric braking, which is load controlled, fail. The trailer cars at the same time have their appropriate retarding force applied by friction brakes, air actuated and also load controlled. The brake cylinders apply only one block on each wheel. The use of dynamic braking and the reduction in the total train weight has reduced very materially the brake block and wheel tread wear, so that both tyre life and brake block mileage has been increased.

The service brake works on the principle of 'energise to apply' by four electrically-controlled braking steps and is adjusted by a 'load weighing' device so that the braking effect is increased in proportion to the increase in the weight of the car.

During a normal service brake, the motor car attempts to achieve the whole braking requirements by the traction motors, but when the current is below the required value to achieve this, air is supplied to the brake cylinders to supplement the braking force. The rheostatic braking is normally adequate from 55mph down to 12mph.

The emergency brake, however, works on the principle 'energise to release' and, with no graduation, it is either on or off. It is maintained 'off' by the security of an electrical circuit passed round the train. Any break in this circuit causes the emergency brake to be applied. The passenger emergency alarm can be arranged to break this circuit or can be modified to alert the train crew so that the train may be driven forward to the next station. This electrical circuit replaces the Westinghouse train line which, when exhausted of air, caused an emergency brake application. An additional safety feature on this stock is the provision of a spring-applied parking brake. This brake is held in the release position as long as there is main line air pressure available. When a train is stabled the emergency air brake is applied and, as the air leaks off, the spring applied brake is actuated on each wheel of the motor cars. This brake removes the need for a hand brake. Another arrangement allows the spring brake to be latched up for safe brake block changing and to allow emergency propulsion, as a dead car.

These latches retract automatically as soon as main line air pressure is applied, avoiding danger of the brake being left inoperative after blocking.

One compressor is provided on each unit but 'C' units (which are double ended and which may be required to operate as a train on a future shuttle service) are fitted with two. This has been achieved by fitting the Westinghouse type 3HC43 to each driving motor car, but not to the non-driving motor cars, so that the double ended unit has two compressors. The D stock, in fact, requires less compressed air, since most of the braking is electrical.

The main line air pipes which connect all the compressors' output together have some special features because it has been found that burst air hose pipes connecting the cars together have been the main causes of breakdowns causing very long delays.

The inter-car hoses have been duplicated, but are combined together at the end of each car by means of a special cut-off valve. If one of the hoses should fail then the increased unbalanced flow of air causes this cut off valve to restrict the flow and prevents loss of control of the train. The small amount of air which continues to flow gives an audible indication of trouble when the train is inspected.

Each motor car carries a motor alternator rectifier set which provides a.c. at 850 cycles at 115 volts for the main fluorescent car lighting and 4kw of d.c. at 52 volts to charge a 48 volt battery from which all control and emergency circuits are energised. These sets are of GEC manufacture (type MG3007AV).

A 50-cycle 250 volt a.c. supply is obtained from 6kv-a motor alternator sets provided by Mawdsley and known as MG7CA units. One of these sets is fitted to each trailer car to provide a feed for auxiliary equipment on all three cars of the unit.

The D stock has headlights located at floor level, on the underframe, one on each side of the coupler together with stabling lights and calling on lights. The calling-on lights are for eventual one-man operation, since in the event of a train requiring assistance from the following train some visual form of communication is required to ensure that the trains are brought together.

Melamine finishes are used throughout the interior of the cars. The seating is covered in an all wool moquette over a fire-retardant high-resilient foam. The floor continues to be the traditional grooved, flameproof, Canadian Maple. No floor material except metal has been found that is totally fireproof, but the London Transport experience has been that no better material for this purpose than the hard-wearing Canadian Maple has yet been found. It has non-slip properties, can be easily replaced, and after flameproof treatment requires to be attacked by a very high temperature flame before any fire danger arises. If by chance it should smoulder in an emergency, noxious fumes do not generate, an additional problem with most types of plastic tiles.

As originally constructed, recirculating fans were provided along the ceilings of each car. Recirculation of air was arranged to take place at temperatures above 70°F. Additional ventilation was provided by fans mounted in the roofs at the car ends to blow fresh air into the cars. These arrangements proved unsatisfactory in hot weather and complaints about the extreme stuffiness of the cars caused modifications to be made. The recirculating fans were abandoned and the cars were provided instead with side ventilators in those sections of the car body which did not require door pockets. Units of D stock were returned to the car builders, Metro-Cammell, for this work to be done.

The car heating is provided by low temperature heater pads placed on the seat risers. These provide a wide heat distribution with the surface temperature maintained at 49°C above the ambient. The operation of both the

Left D stock bogie, showing the absence of headstocks and the use of small diameter wheels (31 inches) which are interchangeable with 1973 tube stock. *Right* Rubber cushions provide the suspension on D stock. This photograph shows the underside of a D stock car without the bogie in place.

Interior view of D stock showing the use of longitudinal floor grooving throughout and the return of vertical grab poles in the standing areas.

heating and the ventilation fan is thermostatically controlled so that as long as the circuit is switched on no action is required by the train crew.

The bogie of the D78 stock is of a new design formed from an 'H' frame without headstocks. The frame itself is of a welded steel-box section in place of welded and riveted plate frames. The secondary suspension between bogie and body is of rubber.

Each motor bogie carries two 300 volt traction motors (designated LT118B) almost identical to those provided for the 1973 tube stock. In fact the motors will be interchangeable in use. The motors are nose-suspended and axle hung from a suspension tube mounted on the axle.

The motors are fitted with pinions, having 17 teeth which mesh with gear wheels mounted on the axles with 75 teeth. The road wheels on the axles are small for surface stock, being 790mm (31 inches) in diameter when new, the same as provided for the 1973 tube stock, so that wheel sets as well as traction motors are interchangeable with this stock.

This is the first time that both pairs of wheels and traction motors have been interchangeable between surface stock and tube stock. Surface stock motor wheels, when new, have never been smaller than 36 inches in diameter in the past.

The traction control equipment is based on the well tried and reliable PCM equipment with the rheostatic braking system incorporated. This type of equipment was first introduced on the Victoria Line. Experiments are being made with chopper control systems which, when problems of interference and reliability have been overcome, may provide a new generation of traction control equipment. Meanwhile the basic PCM equipment continues to serve London since it first appeared in 1936, because the reliability has been of a very high order.

The driver's cab and controls have been improved and for the first time the driver has been provided with a swivelling seat mounted on a pedestal bolted to the floor. In all previous cab designs the driver's seat has retracted into the bulkhead. This new type of seat provides a greater range of adjustment both in height and in its distance from the driving controls.

Another new feature is the provision of a missile-proof glass in front of the driver and because this type of glass cannot be produced with a curve the front cab windows are flat. But for this requirement, the cab windows would probably have been of the wrap-round type as first used on 1967 tube stock.

The principal innovation found in the driver's cabs of these trains is the 'fore-and-aft' control handle provided in the driver's console instead of the traditional rotary handle. A short lever is pushed forward to provide motoring and pulled back for braking. The lever is gripped at the top by means of a horizontal handle which has to be twisted slightly to obtain movement. This twisting operation incorporates the dead man's control, since it has to be held against a spring which the motorman has to continually overcome. This replaces the button used on the conventional rotary controller which has to be kept depressed to overcome the deadman's feature. This arrangement is considered to be equally effective and may prove less tiring in continuous operation. It has the added advantage that it can be operated equally well with the right or left hand. Although this 'fore-and-aft' controller is ambidextrous, it is placed in a position relative to the seat more suitable for the usual right-hand operation.

A weak-field flag switch, manually selected, provides the high-speed characteristics when the yellow-and-black flag is exposed, by weakening the traction motor fields. It has, however, been desirable to reduce energy consumption as much as possible and this is achieved by ensuring that some coasting between stations is arranged at the expense of a slightly longer run time. An additional flag switch has been provided (coloured white and green) which, when selected, cuts out a predetermined coasting speed. On the inner section of the District Line between Turnham Green, Putney Bridge and Bow Road, a low coasting speed at 31mph (with re-motoring taking place when the speed has dropped to 28mph) has been arranged but in the outer sections, coasting occurs at 40mph with re-motoring when the speed has dropped to 36mph. When both flag switches are exposed the maximum speed possible is attainable.

D stock motor car 7537 at Acton Works after its visit to Metro-Cammell's factory for additional ventilation to be fitted, including opening windows.

A train equipment panel has been provided on the offside console which is fully visible from the driving position. The TEP on 1973 tube stock shows both normal and abnormal indication but the D78 equipment has been simplified so that it illuminates only when equipment is not functioning normally. One particular feature which is very helpful during heavy loading conditions is that if the passenger emergency alarm is activated in any car, the TEP immediately informs the driver on which car the alarm has been pulled. Until the advent of the D stock it has always been the practice for the emergency brake to be applied immediately a passenger emergency alarm is operated. Consideration has now been given on a world wide basis to the fact that this does not necessarily ensure the safety of the passengers. The D stock arrangement is capable of modification to enable the train to proceed to the next station under the driver's control should an alarm be activated between stations, if considered desirable.

Delivery of D stock was completed from the manufacturers in April 1983. None of the surface rolling stock now in use on the Underground entered service earlier than 1961 and so further new stock will not be needed until the end of this century, when the A stock will be due for replacement. Surface rolling stock should therefore now commence a period of stability unprecedented in the 120-year history of the lines dealt with in this book.

Diagram of six-car train formations, D stock and C stock.

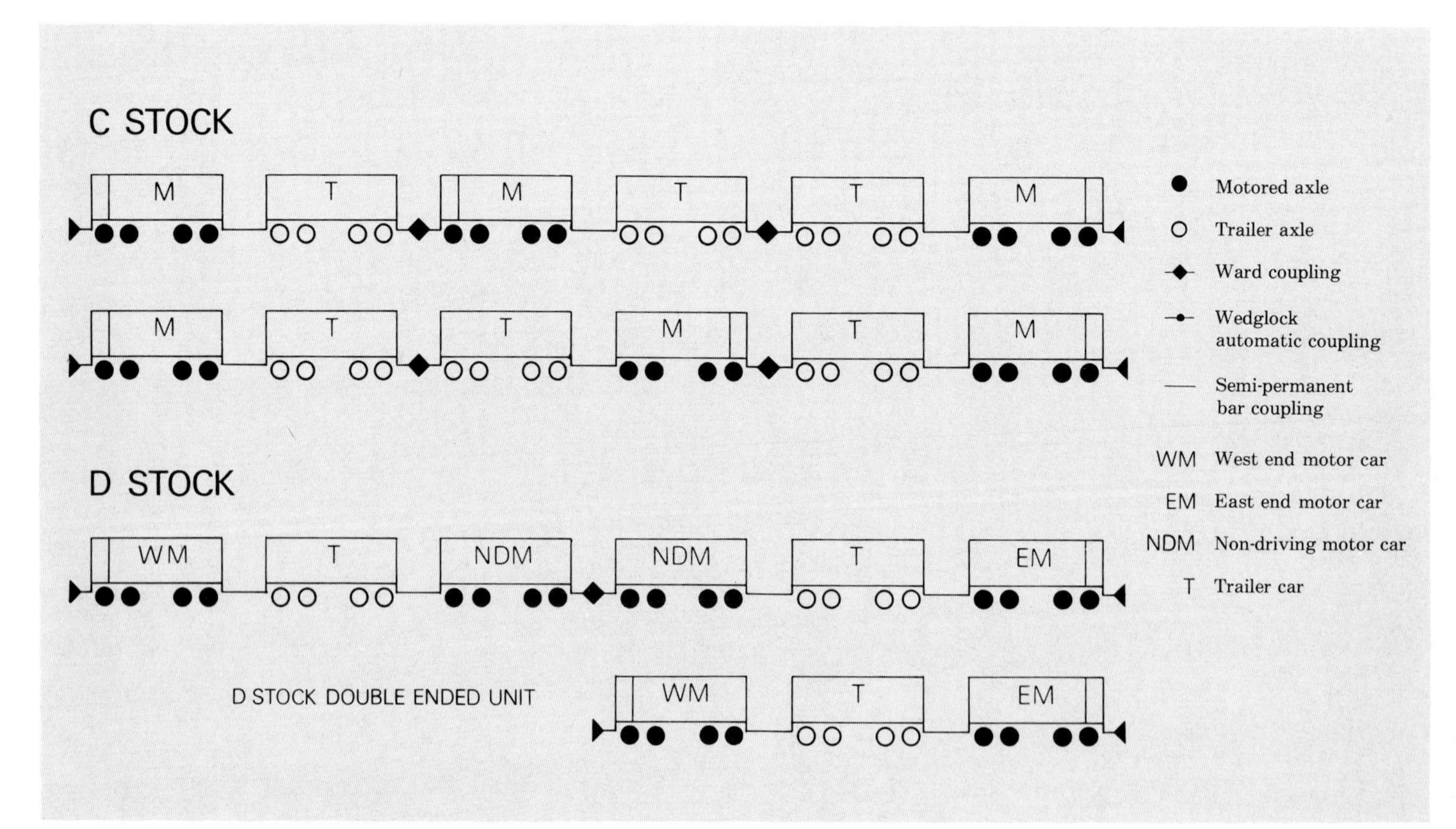

Note on Carbuilders and Principal Equipment Contractors

Throughout these pages many firms that have been associated with the building of the Metropolitan and District Line rolling stock have been mentioned. Some of these names have now disappeared, having been absorbed, amalgamated, or ceased to trade, but they are linked with the development of London's Underground and a brief historical review is not out of place.

The largest portion of the rolling stock of London's Underground has been built by Metro-Cammell Ltd of Birmingham or its predecessors. This company originated from the railway rolling stock manufacturing business set up at Saltley in 1835, then a village on the outskirts of Birmingham, by Joseph Wright, a London coachbuilder. This business was conducted under the title of Joseph Wright & Sons until 1862, when it became the Metropolitan Railway Carriage & Wagon Co. Ltd.

In 1902 the Metropolitan Amalgamated Railway Carriage & Wagon Co. Ltd was formed by the combination of this concern with four other carbuilders:

(1) The Ashbury Railway Carriage & Iron Co. Ltd with works at Openshaw, Manchester;
(2) Brown Marshalls & Co. Ltd with works at Adderley Park, Birmingham;
(3) The Lancaster Railway Carriage & Wagon Co. Ltd with works in Lancaster;
(4) The Oldbury Railway Carriage & Wagon Co. Ltd, Oldbury, Birmingham.

Following a number of other financial exchanges, including the acquisition of a substantial interest in Docker Bros, the paint manufacturers, the name of the concern was changed in 1912 to the Metropolitan Carriage, Wagon & Finance Co. Ltd.

In 1917 this company, in conjunction with Vickers Ltd, the steel and shipbuilding concern, acquired a controlling interest in the British Westinghouse Electric & Manufacturing Co. Ltd which in 1919 changed its name to Metropolitan Vickers Electrical Co. Ltd. At this time, too, an exchange of shares was arranged so that the Metropolitan Carriage, Wagon & Finance Company became a wholly-owned subsidiary of Vickers Ltd.

Ten years later in 1929, Vickers and Cammell Laird (both in the steel and shipbuilding industries) decided to amalgamate their carbuilding interests, forming the Metropolitan-Cammell Carriage, Wagon & Finance Co. Ltd to control these interests. This reorganisation gave the carbuilding concern a controlling interest in the Midland Railway Carriage & Wagon Co. Ltd, with further premises in the Birmingham area, and in the Leeds Forge Co. Ltd. As a result, the Metropolitan-Cammell railway rolling stock manufacturing became concentrated in three large factories, located at Saltley and Washwood Heath in Birmingham and at Old Park in Wednesbury. All these works shared in the manufacture of rolling stock for London Transport or its predecessors.

In 1934 the 'Finance' part of the name of the company was dropped and in a further reorganisation in 1965 the company became Metropolitan-Cammell Ltd. The carbuilding activities were then confined to Washwood Heath. The C and D stocks are products of these works.

Cravens of Sheffield were also carbuilders of long standing but, apart from some steam stock for the Metropolitan Railway, had never built electric multiple unit stock until the order for the A stock was placed with the Company in 1958. In 1965 Cravens transferred their carbuilding business to Metropolitan-Cammell.

The Brush Electrical Engineering Co. Ltd, of Loughborough, has built few cars for the Underground since the original District Railway electric rolling stock. It is now concerned with the manufacture of the traction motors by the merging of its traction interests with Crompton Parkinson Ltd of Chelmsford.

This latter firm has slightly deeper roots, being registered in 1888 as Crompton & Co. Ltd, and being concerned with the early electric traction equipment for the City & South London Railway. The name was changed in 1927 to Crompton Parkinson Ltd after amalgamation with E. & A. Parkinson Ltd. In 1966 the business was acquired by the Hawker Siddeley Group, which had already obtained control of Brush, and the traction interests have now been merged.

Another carbuilding firm which has built a number of cars for London Transport in the past is the Gloucester Railway Carriage & Wagon Co. Ltd, originally registered in 1860 as the Gloucester Wagon Co. Ltd. This concern is now a member of the Babcock & Wilcox Group and specialises in bogie manufacture, but has not participated in London Transport requirements since the R stock.

So far, no personal names of the many people involved in these companies' activities have been mentioned. Although they are legion, just the industrial essentials are necessary to these notes, but one name must be mentioned; that of George Westinghouse—a veritable giant of a man in the industrial field. George Westinghouse was born as long ago as 1846, and not only invented the air-brake which will forever carry his name, but also developed a vast electrical industry. In 1889 the Westinghouse Electric Company of London was formed, which, after the acquisition of land at Trafford Park, Manchester, became in 1899 the British Westinghouse Electric & Manufacturing Co. Ltd. The main purpose behind the establishment of this concern on the scale which it was initially planned was to provide a means of electrifying the railways of Great Britain! All the technical 'know how' was initially to be provided by the parent American firm, the Westinghouse Electric Company of Pittsburgh. An American financial crisis and the First World War did not help the finances of the British Westinghouse concern, and in 1919 (as has already been mentioned) the name was changed to Metropolitan-Vickers Electrical Co. Ltd following its acquisition by the Vickers group from the American Westinghouse interests.

In 1928 the Vickers Group sold its interest in Metropolitan-Vickers to the International General Electric Company of the United States, which already controlled the British Thomson-Houston Co. Ltd, and this set the stage for the formation of Associated Electrical Industries Ltd as the holding company for both concerns which continued to trade as separate organisations until 1967. The International General Electric Company in 1952 relinquished management control, but the interchange of technical information and patent rights was maintained for many years, and this enabled the PCM type of traction control equipment to be developed by the BTH company for service on London's Underground from basic designs provided by the American General Electric Company.

The British-Thomson-Houston Co. Ltd was, in fact, formed in 1896 to exploit in the United Kingdom and Europe the patents of the American Thomson Houston Company which, following amalgamations in America, became the General Electric Company of America. The name of the English associate could not be changed to General Electric Company because such a concern, purely of English origin, had already existed since 1889.

In recent times the AEI, GEC and English Electric traction interests have been brought together under a new GEC which has been responsible for manufacturing the more recent equipments.

The traction motors originally manufactured by BTH always bore the prefix letters GE, following the American designs of this associated concern. The (British) General Electric Company when it began manufacturing traction motors, therefore, used the letters WT (after Witton, where the works were situated).

The Westinghouse-designed motors were not officially distinguished by the use of a letter but a W was often used for convenience. Later, when the name was changed, MV was used. In 1938 a motor was designed by Crompton Parkinson to London Transport requirements to be constructed by any traction motor builder, and the LT100 came into being which was, in fact, manufactured both by the General Electric (British) and Crompton Parkinson.

The LT111 for the R stock was manufactured by three motor manufacturers—Cromptons, Metro-Vickers, and BTH—and all motors since have been specially designed to London Transport requirements and have, therefore, borne the letters LT instead of those of the manufacturer.

The Underground group of companies tried carbuilding on its own account by bringing into activity the Union Construction Company in 1925 to reconstruct the Central London Railway tube cars from hand-manipulated gates to air-operated doors. Having set up the organisation for this purpose including premises at Feltham, Middlesex, it was a short step to the building of new rolling stock. Large numbers of tube cars were built, and tramcars known as 'Felthams' or UCC cars, but the only surface stock built there was a batch for the District completed in 1932.

The Union Construction Co. originated in 1901 in the fashion of contemporary American traction business to construct the property of the parent operating concern. If the parent concern was financially unstable the 'Construction' company would lease or lend the operating equipment which it had built until the financial situation improved. In the event, the Metropolitan District with which it was associated did not need this support, although it was far from being financially robust, so the Union Construction Co. was not required to function at this time. The opportunity came, however, in 1925, with the heavy programme of modernisation of tube rolling stock (subsequently extended to the modernisation of the associated tramcar fleets).

To accord with the principle of leasing and lending of equipment the name of the company was changed on 4th February 1929 to the Union Construction & Finance Co. Ltd.

Under Section 21 of the London Passenger Transport Act of 1933, which created London Transport, the new Board formed at the time was expressly forbidden to manufacture rolling stock except of an experimental nature. The Union Construction & Finance Co. Ltd, therefore, ceased to exist on 1st July 1933.

Another carbuilding name which has ceased to manufacture rolling stock for the Underground is Hurst Nelson & Co. Ltd of Motherwell, Scotland, which became a public company in 1909 and was very active in the building of tramcars over the golden years of electric tramway construction. After the C stock of 1911, the company did not maintain its interest in the supply of vehicles to London's Underground.

The Westinghouse Brake & Signal Co. Ltd, together with its predecessors, has been responsible for providing the air-brake equipment, when fitted, for practically all the rolling stock of London's Underground. This concern originated in England in 1881 as the Westinghouse Brake Co. Ltd to exploit George Westinghouse's brake patents. Subsequently, interest in signalling equipment was acquired, and the combination of these two interests has played no small part in enabling equipment to be manufactured which made the automatic train control system used on the Victoria Line possible.

Note on Electric Braking

Because a direct current motor and a direct current generator are basically the same machine, it follows that any d.c. motor, if driven by an external power source, will generate electricity. This fundamental fact means that electric braking of a train using direct current traction motors is possible. During motoring, electrical energy is taken from the supply system and converted into movement or kinetic energy as the train accelerates. During electric braking this kinetic energy is converted back into electrical energy as the train slows down.

There are two fundamental but related systems of electric braking, sometimes called dynamic braking, using ordinary direct current traction motors: (a) rheostatic braking and (b) regenerative braking. In rheostatic braking the electrical energy developed by the motors is fed or loaded on to resistances carried on the train itself, and the energy generated is dissipated in heating up these resistances. In regenerative braking, the energy developed is returned to the supply system for other customers to use, so reducing the load on the power plant and actually saving electrical energy. Since the introduction of electric traction, engineers have tried to find solutions to the problems involved. Unfortunately, as with many other things which are basically simple, there proved to be many complications and difficulties in actual practice.

The first two problems which have to be overcome in electric braking are to absorb the maximum kinetic energy at the start of braking, smoothing it off as this energy is absorbed or lost when the speed comes down; and secondly to bring the train to rest at the correct point when little kinetic energy is left at the low speed.

As the kinetic energy is proportional to the square of the speed most of the generation of electricity occurs at the beginning of the braking cycle. For example, if a train is being braked electrically from a speed of 40mph there is only one-sixteenth of the total energy left below a speed of 10mph. Provision, therefore, is made in most systems for a friction brake to take over to stop the train. The transition from electric brake to friction brake has to be smooth and although the solution to this problem is not simple it can be achieved.

When a rheostatic system is employed it has the advantage of being independent of the power supply and track conditions, and the controls applied are consistent for each and every braking stop.

The spreading of the electricity load throughout the braking cycle with a rheostatic system is relatively simple in that it is the opposite of acceleration and can be obtained by limiting the current generated to a predetermined amount and when this begins to fall off, arrangements are made for the friction brake to take over.

Having realised that it is relatively simple to make motors generate electricity under braking conditions, it follows that this electricity could be available for useful work elsewhere, and such a system would be described as regenerative. However, under a regenerative braking system, it is the voltage which has to be limited because this is controlled by that of the supply system into which the regenerated current must be pumped without a severe limitation on the current being regenerated. Therefore, the size of the motors, power cables and switch gear must be robust enough to withstand overloads under excessive braking conditions. Unfortunately, because electricity can be stored in only relatively small amounts, it must be used immediately it is produced. If electric braking is to be of value, then the energy changed into electricity must be used elsewhere at once. The greatest problem in this connection, however, is that most of the energy produced from braking occurs in the first phase of the braking.

In simple terms, this means that while a train is braking, three others must be starting up at the same time to use the electricity being produced. This of course very rarely occurs, so arrangements must be made for the system to be receptive whether other trains are starting up or not, by having some artificial load available either at substations or on the trains to absorb the excess energy which cannot be used as it is produced.

The Metropolitan Railway carried out some experiments at Neasden with two electric locomotives obtained from the Central London Railway in 1905 when these were offered for sale following the introduction of multiple unit trains. The system employed for these experiments was one that had been successfully applied to tramcars. While it could be said that there was no difficulty in getting generation, there was considerable trouble in controlling it to do just what was required in stopping a train at a fixed point. Making an electric train accelerate from rest is a simple matter and variations in performance from one vehicle to another in the train are not critical. But to stop a train at an accurate final point of rest, taking into account variations in performance between vehicles on the train, becomes difficult.

It is one thing to achieve regeneration on a locomotive in which all the controls and switchings are related to one set of equipment, but with a multiple unit system where several equipments have to work in unison, further complications arise.

The metadyne system introduced to London Transport in 1936 on the O stock was the first multiple unit control system in the world which incorporated a practical regenerative braking system. The metadyne was a rotating machine interposed between the supply line and the traction motors which, putting it very simply, converted a constant voltage supply to a constant current output.

This is basically what a series-parallel resistance control system tries to do in a very crude way. The constant voltage from the 600-volt supply is reduced by inserting resistance so that the current supplied to the motors is limited to a maximum value. As this current falls with the rotation of the motors so resistance is cut out in a series of notches restoring the current to the maximum value, until full speed is reached. The metadyne did this without using resistances, maintaining a smooth accelerating current without any notching. The main advantage of the system, however, was that whatever the voltage of the current produced when the motors became generators under braking conditions, this was converted to a higher voltage compatible with returning the power produced back to the traction supply to do useful work elsewhere.

When receptive line conditions existed an excellent rate of regeneration was achieved, but conditions were not always right and because the substations were not receptive the selection swiches carried on the trains more often than not cut out the regenerative system, substituting rheostatic braking. This was not unsatisfactory since electric braking was still available, saving brake blocks and giving a smooth stop. The metadyne system was a technical achievement of considerable merit but unfortunately did not gain the success it deserved, mainly for two reasons; the power supply system was not designed to accept a regenerative system and the equipment was complicated and less reliable in general operation than contemporary series-parallel equipments. The equipment was also very heavy.

With the lack of complete success of the metadyne system, which would not have been suitable in any case for tube rolling stock because of the limited clearances for the housing of the additional equipment, the development of electric braking on the London Underground was allowed to lapse. The feeling persisted, however, that a potential source of energy was being wasted and that some savings could be achieved if some form of electric braking were produced. Beginning in 1957, experiments were conducted on a further regenerative system. This system was very complex and required the provision of a bus line to tie the multiple unit equipments together to avoid the effect of current rail gaps. The provision of a bus line was considered to be a retrograde step for safety from fusing incidents and the scheme was abandoned.

It was thought, however, that some advantage could be obtained by utilising the experience gained to develop a rheostatic braking scheme which would not require bus lines and which could be applied to a multiple unit train. Rheostatic braking had already been applied on many systems throughout the world where all the train axles were motored. This is an expensive practice both in capital and maintenance when the acceleration required does not warrant this provision. However, where only 50% of the axles are motored the problem of apportioning train braking between the motors and the friction brakes can only be solved by complicated equipment which increases the cost.

An equipment for providing rheostatic braking with only 50% of the axles motored was developed for the Victoria Line stock and has been applied to all stocks subsequently constructed. This type of equipment has proved to be a technical success. The advantages are a reduction in brake block and wheel wear with a consequent reduction in the accumulation of dust in the tunnels.

The scheme adopted has been built round the well-used PCM traction control system and, therefore, utilises the control units which have already proved reliable in service. The rheostatic scheme, however, requires virtually two equipments, where only one was needed for accelerating the train, and in addition it requires complicated equipment to transfer from electric braking to the friction brake.

With a multiple unit train operating a rapid transit type of service, an infinite variety of braking rates is not required because a predictable service pattern can be established. Only three rates of braking are provided: (a) rheostatic on the motored axles only, (b) rheostatic on the motored axles together with friction brake on the trailer axles, and (c) friction brake on all axles.The selection of the rate of braking on the Victoria Line is outside the control of the driver because of the automatic train control and the variation between the three rates of braking is automatically adjusted.

Unfortunately a rheostatic braking system does nothing towards conserving energy or keeping down the tunnel temperatures, which is the advantage of a full regenerative braking scheme. So engineers must continue to search for a solution to the problems involved in providing a fully regenerative scheme.